IMMIGRATION AND THE CONSTRAINTS OF JUSTICE

This book explores the constraints which justice imposes on immigration policy. Like liberal nationalists, Ryan Pevnick argues that citizens have special claims to the institutions of their states. However, the source of these special claims is located in the citizenry's ownership of state institutions rather than in a shared national identity. Citizens contribute to the construction and maintenance of institutions (by paying taxes and obeying the law), and as a result they have special claims to these institutions and a limited right to exclude outsiders. Pevnick shows that the resulting view justifies a set of policies – including support for certain types of guest-worker programs – which is distinct from those supported by either liberal nationalists or advocates of open borders. His book provides a framework for considering a number of connected topics including issues related to self-determination, the scope of distributive justice, and the significance of shared national identity.

RYAN PEVNICK is Assistant Professor in the Department of Politics at New York University. He has published articles in numerous journals of political science and philosophy.

IMMIGRATION AND THE CONSTRAINTS OF JUSTICE

Between Open Borders and Absolute Sovereignty

RYAN PEVNICK

New York University

CAMBRIDGE
UNIVERSITY PRESS

CAMBRIDGE UNIVERSITY PRESS
Cambridge, New York, Melbourne, Madrid, Cape Town,
Singapore, São Paulo, Delhi, Tokyo, Mexico City

Cambridge University Press
The Edinburgh Building, Cambridge CB2 8RU, UK

Published in the United States of America by Cambridge University Press, New York

www.cambridge.org
Information on this title: www.cambridge.org/9780521768986

First published 2011

A catalogue record for this publication is available from the British Library

Library of Congress Cataloguing in Publication Data
Pevnick, Ryan, 1980–
Immigration and the constraints of justice: between open borders and absolute sovereignty / Ryan Pevnick.
p. cm.
Includes bibliographical references.
ISBN 978-0-521-76898-6
1. Emigration and immigration – Government policy. 2. Distributive justice. I. Title.
JV6038.P48 2011
325'.1–dc22
2010037295

ISBN 978-0-521-76898-6 Hardback

To my family

Contents

Illustrations

Acknowledgments

I have had a lot of help in the course of writing this book. A number of friends and colleagues have provided helpful comments on drafts of one or more of the chapters. This includes Michael Blake, Allen Buchanan, Mat Coakley, Sarah Fine, John Echeverri-Gent, Daniel Kofman, Dimitri Landa, Jennifer Rubenstein, Herman Schwartz, Annie Stilz, and the late Perez Zagorin. Several times I learned from spirited arguments with Loren Lomasky. Bernard Manin provided helpful advice and reassurance on important problems. Hilary Gaskin has been an ideal editor. Amongst other things, she solicited the comments of very helpful anonymous reviewers. Their conscientious feedback, for which I am very grateful, led to significant improvements.

Additionally, several others contributed enormously. Ingrid Creppell and Melissa Schwartzberg read drafts of chapters at very early stages, and treated them with a seriousness that they surely did not merit. Much more importantly, both have been enormously supportive and encouraging.

In addition to the general influence that he has had on my thinking, the comments John Simmons provided led to substantial improvements. Stephen White was a trustworthy source of advice, consistently nudging me in the right direction with thoughtful questions. George Klosko supported me in every way possible throughout the writing of this manuscript. Most importantly: the unbounded (and surely undeserved) confidence that he showed in me was supremely important as I went through the trials of writing. Likewise, Colin Bird has been an enormously caring, dedicated, and generous friend. He has many times helped me sort through and clarify the project's arguments. Having said all of this, I can only note that where my work falls short, it is neither for lack of models nor for lack of help.

Finally, I wish to acknowledge, albeit much too briefly, several important personal debts. A number of close friends contributed enormously, albeit rather indirectly. My parents and grandparents insisted on the importance of education, supporting me wholeheartedly even when my interests turned now and again to what must have seemed like quite arcane topics. I am endlessly grateful for their support. Likewise, my brothers – each in their own way – have been provocative and inspiring. Finally, Kathleen embraced all of the anxieties that – at least for me – accompany the writing process. I shudder to think of how lonely and frustrating it would have been without her. She has been unfailingly loving through the hardest moments; and I have relied on this tremendously.

CHAPTER I

Introduction

Modern states claim enormous power over the lives of individuals within their territories. In order to bring into view the extent of these powers, I begin by recounting the story of an immigrant to the United States:

> Mezei, a long-time resident of the United States who had journeyed abroad to visit his mother, was excluded on undisclosed security grounds when he returned. After some sixteen months in custody, the government announced that it had abandoned its futile efforts to find a country to which he could be deported. Thereafter, Mezei remained on Ellis Island in what Justice Black in dissent described as an "island prison" in which Mezei must "stay indefinitely, maybe for life." The Supreme Court summarily rejected Mezei's challenge to his exclusion.
>
> Having never seen the government's evidence, there was of course little for the Court to say. Mezei, it noted, was actually the beneficiary of "legislative grace"; as an excludable alien, the authorities could have kept him aboard the vessel that brought him here rather than extending "temporary haborage" at Ellis Island. Mezei's complaint was with the countries that would not accept him, not with the American government. "An alien in [Mezei's] position," the Court concluded, "is no more ours than theirs."[1] (Schuck 1998, 36)

Mezei's story is at least a bit frightening because it vividly illustrates the power that others, through state institutions, regularly claim over us. With no charges presented to him (much less established before a jury of peers), Mezei was prevented from going about his regular life, from traveling, visiting family, and – more generally – building his life as he chose. Although the story is unusual and legal precedent in regard to it has shifted, the powers that allowed it are routine in the modern world and are at the core of the claims to sovereignty made by states.

Because quotidian and widely accepted claims of sovereignty can impinge so severely on the lives and dignity of potential immigrants, it is not surprising that many citizens feel genuinely torn about how to respond to the claims of would-be immigrants:

[1] See *Shaughnessy v. United States ex rel. Mezei* 345 US 206 (1953).

> Many Americans feel hostile toward faceless newcomers – less so toward immigrants, more so toward refugees, insisting, when asked, that the United States admits too many foreigners, too many refugees. But when these same Americans are presented with a prototypical immigrant or refugee, most will say they favor his admission. Americans, thus, may be hostile to a foreign group, but accepting of the individual stranger. We fear the hordes, while we welcome the family. (Zucker and Zucker 1987, xvii)

Thus, even if it is easy, generally speaking, to capitulate to the legitimacy of the state's claims to sovereignty, the issue is made more difficult when such claims are in tension – as they so often are – with important interests of foreigners.

Immigration thus raises difficult questions about the moral significance of shared citizenship, the types of claims that may be legitimately pressed by foreigners, the justifiability of a militarized border, limits on the obligations of the welfare state, and the proper scope of sovereignty and self-determination. It should not be surprising, then, that disagreements about the proper, fair, or just course for immigration policy are significant and contentious throughout today's major receiving countries. As Stephen Castles and Mark Miller note:

> Immigration may lead to strong reactions from some sections of the population. Immigration often takes place at the same time as economic restructuring and far-reaching social change. People whose conditions of life are already changing in an unpredictable way often see the newcomers as the cause of insecurity. One of the dominant images in the highly developed countries today is that of masses of people flowing in from the poor south and the turbulent east, taking away jobs, pushing up housing prices and overloading social services. (Castles and Miller 1998, 13)

Indeed, immigration policy is now a major and divisive issue in US politics. Hundreds of thousands of people have turned out to rally against stricter immigration regulations. Similar protests, and even hunger strikes, have occurred in European states. US presidential candidates have built sizable followings by criticizing the government for failing to control movement across territorial borders. And, in other countries, nationalist political parties have gained substantial power by criticizing government – sometimes in racially charged manners – for their leniency toward immigrants.

Meanwhile, the United States has turned to the National Guard to aid in controlling the border (despite already budgeting nearly $2 billion for border control in 2008). This further militarization of the border carries with it serious humanitarian risks. Indeed, since the US government increased forces devoted to border control in the early 1990s, the rate of deaths by those attempting to cross the border has tripled. It is estimated, for example, that in 1998 approximately 350 people lost their lives – primarily as a result of suffocation, heat exhaustion, or drowning – attempting to cross the border (Massey *et al.* 2002, 114).

However, while there is widespread agreement that changes to existing policy must be made, there is little agreement regarding the *direction* reform efforts ought to take. Anti-immigration groups are furious about immigration of all kinds. One such group, the Federation for American Immigration Reform, declared in 2008 on its website:

> Both legal and illegal immigration are grave and serious threats to the United States. The number of immigrants reaching our shores each year is staggering. The problems resulting from our ever-increasing numbers of people are myriad and they affect all aspects of our lives including the environment, our public schools, our political institutions, and the freedoms that we are losing every day.

A prominent like-minded commentator insists that "this is an invasion, the greatest invasion in history . . . We are witnessing how nations perish. We are entered upon the final act of our civilization" (Buchanan 2006, 5–6).

While immigrants present – according to this view – "grave and serious threats" to the country, pro-immigration groups regularly present such individuals as the country's lifeblood – the very source of economic and cultural dynamism. In their view, generous admissions policies are an integral part of America's historical promise. They cling to Emma Lazarus's famous words, according to which part of the American project is to provide refuge for the world's poor and oppressed:

> Give me your tired, your poor,
> Your huddled masses yearning to breathe free,
> The wretched refuse of your teeming shore.
> Send these, the homeless, tempest-tost to me,
> I lift my lamp beside the golden door!

It is no doubt part of the self-image of the American state, part of its public conception of justice, that it is a country of immigrants. Moreover, advocates of this view regard restrictions on immigration as "the modern equivalent of feudal privilege" – a practice that coercively and illegitimately restricts the life chances of those who happen to be born to the "wrong" group (Carens 1987, 252). Behind these diametrically opposed attitudes toward immigrants lie very different conceptions of justice and objectives for public policy.

I SOCIAL SCIENCE AND POLITICAL THEORY

There is, of course, a vast social scientific literature addressing immigration policy. Such work importantly contributes to our understanding of the types of effects different policies will produce, and I will draw on it in what follows. However, such work is of little help in determining the types of *ends* at which countries may justifiably aim. Instead, the arguments of those who seek to advocate particular policies based on empirical research rely on implicit or submerged commitments to normative positions.[2]

For example, Otis Graham argues for a restrictive immigration policy by insisting that "mass immigration of low-skill, low-wage labor harms American workers and adds to poverty" (Graham 2004, 112). Adding labor to the US market indeed increases the supply of workers and thus decreases the wages of those who are forced to compete for jobs with immigrants. Without questioning this empirical claim,[3] it is important to see that it hides a normative assumption.

While Graham rightly insists that low-skill immigration harms American workers and contributes to poverty (in the United States), the same phenomenon can be – still truthfully – *re*described as follows: mass immigration of low-skill, low-wage labor increases wages and decreases existing poverty. Indeed, the economist Lant Pritchett argues for open borders (that is, the *elimination* of immigration restrictions) in just such terms: "Because unskilled labor is the primary asset of the poor world, it is hard to even imagine a policy more directly inimical to a poverty reduction agenda or to 'pro-poor growth' than one limiting the demand for unskilled labor (and inducing labor-saving innovations)" (Pritchett 2006, 1). Pritchett portrays increased immigration as a way to decrease poverty and make opportunities available to workers by allowing the impoverished access to productive economies.

It is important to recognize that the dispute between Graham and Pritchett is not an empirical one, and thus is not likely to be settled by further social scientific research.[4] They already agree – at least on the major points – about the likely effects of various immigration policies. Instead, Graham and Pritchett are at odds because they disagree about how to *interpret* the empirical information. Pritchett judges policy by how it affects poverty worldwide, while Graham assesses policy by how it affects the least

2 Of course, many social scientists – concurring with this line of argument – already avoid making policy proposals as a result of empirical analysis.

3 Some do question this claim. Because economic activity is not zero-sum, it is possible that all could be gainers from immigration (Fix and Passel 1994). Partially the dispute depends on differing time horizons.

4 In principle, it is possible that it could be so settled *if* it turned out that some policy X is best for both the domestic and global worst-off. However, because the two groups are likely to compete for the same types of jobs, it is unlikely that such a policy exists. In any case, the criteria subscribed to by Graham and Pritchett for judging policy are just two possibilities of many. It could be that all plausible criteria would recommend the same policy, but such a scenario seems extremely unlikely.

well-off Americans. Thus, the disagreement regards the appropriate *ends* of policy, and therefore the normative criteria by which we ought to assess legislation. Because they agree about the relevant empirical data but disagree about how these data should be weighed, the only way to settle the dispute is to make clear and assess the normative assumptions underlying their views.

It is worth noting that the same problems will arise for an approach that aims to sidestep the difficulties of normative argument and instead push ahead with a cost–benefit analysis. Should we count the costs and benefits that apply only to citizens? Should the way policy affects foreigners count? The point is just that there is no empirical or value-neutral way of defending a given policy proposal. As a result, it is not fruitful to continue debate *solely* at an empirical level. Instead, proponents of different positions are stuck talking past one another because they are committed to disparate normative criteria. So, in order for opposing sides to present reasons that can be appreciated by others, the argument will have to be joined at the normative level. Understanding the effect various policies will have is insufficient (though still integral) if there is disagreement over how to assess those effects.

I should note that many empirical scholars of immigration accept the importance of normative debate to policy conflicts surrounding immigration. For example, in an article regarding the availability of welfare benefits to immigrants, two influential social scientists remark that the underlying issues "are more philosophical than legal . . . rais[ing] questions about the meaning of membership in US society" (Huber and Espenshade 1997, 1046). Likewise, a number of empirical scholars explicitly recognize that their public policy proposals grow from normative commitments (see, for example, Borjas 1999, 187; Cornelius 1981, 12; and Massey *et al.* 2002, 154–156).

Roughly, these types of normative disagreement might be settled in either of two ways. First, those with the power to do so might simply insist on the relevance of the normative assumptions they wish to privilege. This may be accomplished by presenting such assumptions as natural or beneficial to all. In *The German Ideology* Karl Marx insists that "the ideas of the ruling class are in every epoch the ruling ideas," that "the class which has the means of material production at its disposal, has control at the same time over the means of mental production," and that "the ruling ideas are nothing more than the ideal expression of the dominant material relationships" (Marx 1978, 172). In this extreme version of the view, there is relatively little point to (or even the possibility of) sorting out the conflicting normative criteria because it is material power that will ultimately determine which set of ideas wins out.[5]

Second, we might embark on a discussion regarding the justifications underlying the various normative positions. Rather than submerging the operative normative assumptions, we bring them into the light and attempt to defend the plausibility of one set of assumptions rather than another. This approach depends on sorting out the legitimacy of various criteria or underlying frameworks. It involves examining to what extent and in what type of circumstances frameworks for thinking about immigration are consistent with considered moral convictions.[6] While, and indeed because, I do not doubt the importance of the material power behind a certain set of ideas, I regard it as worthwhile to pursue the second tack. One reason to do this is to help strip advocates of the first tack of the false legitimacy of having "the facts" on their side.

It is important to deny the putative naturalness of positions and instead assess the assumptions on which they rely. Justifying an immigration policy depends on making explicit and defending the normative assumptions underlying the position. The major task of this book, then, is to introduce and defend a novel approach for thinking about justice and immigration, which I call the associative ownership view. Throughout I will try to show that this approach provides a better framework for thinking about the issues than can existing alternatives.

It is worth pointing out that disagreements about the ethics of immigration policy are sometimes a reflection not of substantive disagreement but of a difference in the goals of commentators. It is thus useful to distinguish between and be cognizant of two different approaches to the problem. On the one hand, one might describe the ideal immigration policy. This approach picks out that policy that is preferable all things considered. Alternatively, one might set about trying to describe the *set* of acceptable policies by explicating the constraints imposed by considerations of justice. According to this view, although justice excludes from consideration some set of policies, its requirements do not specify a unique solution.

[5] Even if one does not accept this vigilant subjugation of ideas to interests, one can still accept that ideas gain an important advantage by being promulgated by powerful and influential individuals. So much, at least, seems relatively uncontroversial. The fact that Marx spent his life trying to expose the ideas of the ruling class suggests that even he did not accept an extreme version of the materialist conception of history. Further evidence for this interpretation of Marx is provided by Engels's "Letters on Historical Materialism" (Marx 1978, 760–765).

[6] I proceed via a process of reflective equilibrium (for more detailed considerations of this approach see Daniels 1979; Rawls 1951; and Scanlon 2003).

The former approach aims to describe the policy that is ideal, while the latter aims to describe the range of policies that do not violate the constraints of justice.[7] I will focus on describing the constraints imposed by justice and, thus, on the acceptable range of possibilities. I proceed in this way because, just as I doubt whether the demands of ethics can be properly seen as prescribing a uniquely acceptable line of action for individual agents, I doubt whether most interesting policy questions admit of only one acceptably just solution.

II STATISM, OPEN BORDERS, AND SOCIAL TRUST

As I noted above, our view of political controversies depends on the paradigm used to conceptualize them. Citizens of the United States are likely to think very differently, for example, of a president declaring that his first-born son will take office at the time of his death than would subjects of a seventeenth-century monarch. Part of the difference between these two scenarios is the paradigm that underlies the political thinking of the audience. It means something different to be a political executive in a seventeenth-century monarchy than a twenty-first century democracy. Different expectations are built into these descriptions regarding the proper way to pass on power. Thus, the way we respond to political events depends on the paradigm employed to think about or conceptualize them.

In the same way, we will respond very differently to developments regarding immigration depending on the paradigm, framework, or set of expectations that we use to conceptualize the issue. For example, our opinions on how to treat illegal immigrants or whether to militarize the border depend on underlying views about the nature of state sovereignty and the legitimacy of state control over territory. Thus, skipping over these deeper philosophical conflicts in order to get directly to policy issues promises to leave us begging the question against those with whom we disagree.[8] Accordingly, once again, in order to adequately understand policy conflicts regarding immigration it is imperative to assess the various paradigms people use to conceptualize controversies surrounding immigration. It is in the arguments for these various paradigms that the crucial, if somewhat buried, disputes about public policy issues reside.

[7] A similar distinction is urged by Carens (Carens 2005, 30).

[8] This is why Rawls insists that ideal theory provides "the only basis for the systematic grasp" of "more pressing problems" (Rawls 1999b, 8).

Although there is a wide array of positions in the literature addressing the ethics of immigration policy,[9] three basic paradigms dominate debate: statism; open borders; and shared identity. In the remainder of this chapter, I introduce these positions and briefly indicate the key points I wish to make in criticizing them. First, however, it is worth noting that advocates of these views are not homogeneous. There are different types of open-border views just as there are different types of statist and shared-identity views. In the chapters that follow, we will have the opportunity to investigate such differences, but for now it will suffice to give a general sense of the main existing paradigms and the difficulties they face. This will help set the stage for arguments in favor of the associative ownership view.

A Statism

Advocates of *statism* hold that considerations of justice are inapplicable beyond state borders and, accordingly, that citizens should select that immigration policy which is best for current citizens. According to this view, little or no weight ought to be given to the interests of foreigners. For example, George Borjas insists that "immigration policy should be set in ways that further the national interest, and the nation's interest may simply not coincide with giving any particular person or any particular ethnic group the opportunity to partake in the unrivaled opportunities that the United States has to offer" (Borjas 1999, xxii).

Consistent with this view, Borjas then outlines a set of policies, focused on recruiting potential migrants with specially needed skills (such as highly trained IT workers). This approach is meant to maximally benefit current citizens.

Indeed, advocates of this view often suggest that selecting a policy that fails to advance the national interest – however that interest is understood – is foolish, utopian, or even dangerous. For instance, an editorial in *The Washington Post* called current limits on recruiting skilled immigrants a "self-inflicted wound," and argued:

> The lunacy of the current state of affairs is exposed by the fact that from 2001 to 2003, Congress raised the number of visas for skilled workers to 195,000 annually, in recognition of marketplace realities, then allowed it to revert back to 65,000 through what amounted to inattention ... But there's no excuse for the current logjams ... America's knowledge-based economy is increasingly dependent on the best and brightest immigrants. (*The Washington Post* 2007)

[9] For a recent survey of the literature see Seglow 2005.

According to advocates of this view, immigration policy should seek out, and give preference to, those immigrants who will best promote the national interest (most commonly through their economic contributions).

Of course, the extent to which the recruitment of the most skilled immigrants is in the "national interest" is debatable because the benefits and burdens of immigration policy have effects that vary across the citizen population. Immigration raises distributive issues. As Borjas remarks, "before deciding how many and which immigrants to admit, the country must determine which groups of Americans should be the winners and which should be the losers" (Borjas 1999, xiv). However, before addressing Borjas's question, we must ask whether it is justifiable to simply select that policy that best promotes the national interest.

Immigration policy affects not just citizens, but also potential migrants and those among whom they live. If it is thought that this is reason for allowing these individuals to creep onto the justificatory scene, this would substantially alter the picture. Most obviously, there can be no doubt that – in a comparative sense – access to the United States (and the developed world more generally) carries with it substantial advantages in terms of life expectations. Living in the developed world carries with it significant benefits in income, health, education, and a range of other areas. It is plain, then, that the immigration policies of wealthy countries have important effects on the life expectations of non-citizens. Who gets to pass through the "Golden Door" to the United States is extremely important to potential immigrants.

Recognizing the opportunities that come with admission to the developed world brings forth an obvious question for those, like Borjas, who advocate immigration policies dedicated to recruiting only the most skilled potential immigrants. In particular, because admission to the United States carries with it significant economic opportunities, there may seem to be a certain kind of unfairness in admitting only those who have *already* had the opportunity to receive significant education or training. After all, there are no doubt other individuals seeking admission who have not already had the good fortune of significant training. Do not such individuals have at least as strong a claim to admission as the highly trained? Are governments of developed countries entitled to make decisions that will so dramatically affect the life chances of outsiders in order to secure further economic advantages for their already comparatively well-off citizenry?

Although the access to opportunities seized by would-be potential migrants is perhaps the most obvious sense in which immigration policy affects outsiders, it is far from the only sense in which it does so. Additionally, for example, many development experts worry that policies that encourage the highly trained or most educated individuals to leave developing countries may contribute to the difficulty of economic development by robbing such societies of much-needed human capital (Collier 2007; Kapur and McHale 2005).

Issues regarding the effect of immigration policy on foreigners highlight the normative stance underlying statism. Remember that, in Borjas's view, we must decide "which groups of *Americans* should be the winners and which should be the losers" (Borjas 1999, xiv, emphasis added). This claim, however, masks an important normative assumption: namely, that policy should be determined just by assessing how it will affect *citizens*. Indeed, Borjas is well aware of this issue, remarking that "deep philosophical and moral concerns" are "raised by these questions"; he declines to discuss them, however, instead saying that he "will leave it to others to determine if the immigration policies implied by the country's desire to make its native population better off are morally defensible" (Borjas 1999, 187).

However, as we saw by juxtaposing the views of Graham and Pritchett, leaving these moral issues aside promises to leave the debate stalemated. Because various sides disagree about what counts as appropriate criteria for assessing arguments, leaving the issue to others amounts to withdrawing from debates regarding immigration policy. There is no fruitful way of ignoring normative issues since assessing or applying the empirical evidence requires a normative stance. Thus, Borjas can provide hundreds of reasons why it is in the national interest to admit certain types of workers, but none of these will strike those who disagree that immigration should be set in terms of the national interest (such as Pritchett) as significant. Instead, as we saw, if arguments are to provide reasons to those who disagree, questions regarding the appropriate criteria by which to judge immigration policy must be taken up. In order, then, to adequately substantiate the position, advocates must provide an account of *why* it is legitimate – given that immigration policy has effects that reach far beyond national borders – to focus exclusively on the needs and interests of current citizens.

Most often statism is defended with reference to state sovereignty. The initial difficulty is that we typically recognize a host of limitations on the sovereignty of states. We are perfectly comfortable saying that a state has overstepped the bounds of its sovereign rights if it seeks to violently persecute citizens who are part of a religious minority, if it cancels elections and imposes martial law, or if it invades a neighboring country. Thus, we already recognize a range of limits on the sovereignty of states. Accordingly, it is inadequate to say – when it comes to immigration – that states, because of their sovereign status, may design immigration policy in any manner they like.

Once we recognize that there are limits to the power that sovereignty confers, we must deliberate about the shape of those limits when it comes to setting immigration policy. The only way to come to grips with the limitations of sovereignty in terms of immigration policy will be to come to an understanding of what underlies or justifies the claim of states to act as they see fit. So I will argue that we can make sense of commitments to sovereignty only by giving an account of why it is that citizens – through the state – enjoy a general permission or liberty to design policies of their choice.

It might seem that in addressing the basis of claims of sovereignty, we should start with what John Rawls calls "the most fundamental" premise for developing a "conception of justice" appropriate "for a democratic regime" (Rawls 2001, 5). This is the idea of "society as a fair system of cooperation over time, from one generation to the next" (Rawls 1993, 15). Beginning from this idea, however, immediately raises a question of justification. Namely: what justifies our seeing society in *this* way rather than – for example – as a system of institutions meant to respond to and overcome the otherwise arbitrary distribution of resources or to maximize utility without regard to citizenship? Is seeing society as a fair system of cooperation consistent with treating non-participants as equals? The choice between different conceptions of society is critical because our understanding of the nature of political society determines the path we take with regard to the treatment of foreigners, including potential immigrants.

The associative ownership view aims to help explain *why* it is legitimate to see political "society as a fair system of cooperation over time, from one generation to the next" (Rawls 1993, 15). In short, the associative ownership view insists that the citizenry constitutes an association extending through time that comes to have a claim over state institutions as a result of the efforts – from physical labor and tax payments to obeying the law – that make such institutions possible. In this sense, the citizenry has a special ownership relationship with state institutions that distinguishes their position from that of foreigners. It is, I argue, this relationship that underlies or legitimizes claims of sovereignty. It is this relationship that justifies seeing society as an ongoing system of fair cooperation across generations.

However, seeing the state as in some sense a collective resource of the citizenry implies limits on the extent to which reference to sovereignty can justify an immigration policy focused on the needs and interests of citizens. For example, it is relatively uncontroversial to say that those with access to an abundance of resources have an obligation to share those resources with the less fortunate, especially when this can be done at little or no cost to themselves. Variations of this principle are widely accepted. One example comes from John Locke, who argues that "*justice* gives every Man a Title to so much out of another's Plenty, as will keep him from extream want, where he has no means to subsist otherwise" (Locke 1988, 170). Similarly, albeit from a different perspective, Peter Singer famously argues for a duty of rescue: "If I am walking past a shallow pond and see a child drowning in it, I ought to wade in and pull the child out. This will mean getting my clothes muddy, but this is insignificant, while the death of the child would presumably be a very bad thing" (Singer 1972, 231). Singer argues that if one agrees that there is a duty to save the child, then one must also accept (at the very least) a principle that says that "if it is in our power to prevent something very bad from happening, without thereby sacrificing anything morally significant, we ought, morally to do it" (Singer 1972, 231). Following Locke and Singer, I will assume that rejecting entirely some such principle of rescue or charity is inconsistent with seeing others as equals.

If this is correct and sovereignty represents a kind of collective ownership, there is reason to think that it comes with limits, including responsibilities toward non-owners. To instead insist that immigration policy ought to be formulated in a way that furthers only the needs and interests of citizens because of the sovereign nature of the state is to misunderstand the grounds and responsibilities of that sovereignty, or so I shall argue.

B Open borders

The second major position in the literature on the ethics of immigration policy is *open borders*. Although less prominent in the popular debate than statism, this position is advocated by *The Wall Street Journal*, which supports a constitutional amendment reading: "there shall be open borders" (*Wall Street Journal* 1984, 24). The most well-worked-out defense of open borders is developed in an impressive and provocative series of essays by Joseph Carens. He argues:

> Borders should generally be open and . . . people should normally be free to leave their country of origin and settle in another, subject only to the sorts of constraints that bind current citizens in their new country. (Carens 1987, 252)

Carens explains this commitment by saying that it "is *not* readily compatible with the idea of equal moral worth" to exclude those who want to join and, thus, "if people want to sign the social contract, they should be permitted to do so" (Carens 1987, 270). Elsewhere he insists:

> The presumption is for free migration and anyone who would defend restriction faces a heavy burden of proof . . . The right to go where you want to go is itself an important freedom. It is [also] essential for equality of opportunity. You have to be able to move to where the opportunities are in order to take advantage of them . . . [And] freedom of movement would contribute to a reduction of political, social, and economic inequalities. (Carens 1992, 25–26)

Thus, the argument for open borders rests, in two ways, on a commitment to the basic equality of all individuals.

First, if individuals are fundamentally equal in a sense that requires that differences in treatment be justified on impartial and non-arbitrary grounds, then there is no obvious reason why one individual may legitimately employ political institutions to restrict the movement of another. If individuals are to be restricted, a reason must be given for why this is – despite appearances – consistent with their equal status. Second, if individuals are equal in a more robust sense requiring equality of opportunity, then – whatever the preferred metric or strictness of the commitment – there is at least *prima facie* reason to allow individuals to move to opportunities. This is especially true in a world, such as ours, in which available opportunities are distributed very unequally across geographical and political space. As Carens notes, these arguments are meant to establish a "presumption" in favor of free movement. They demand that those who would restrict movement provide reasons for so doing. I attempt to meet this challenge by, in chapters 4–5, criticizing arguments for open borders and explaining how the associative ownership position takes seriously the equal status of foreigners and so meets the challenge posed by advocates of open borders.

In particular, I argue that the attractiveness of the open borders position depends on ignoring the historical contributions to institutions made by political communities. When a group of individuals construct programs of mutual benefit, from pension programs to schemes for public health insurance, they gain *prima facie* control or ownership over the benefits and resources that result. It is only through their efforts and contributions that the resources at stake in disputes about immigration exist in the first place. Another way of putting this point is to say that advocates of open borders fail to appreciate the sense in which political communities are ongoing schemes of cooperation among members. Although the arguments of advocates of open borders provide strong reason to loosen restrictions on some foreigners (particularly the severely impoverished), I argue that they are not sufficient to establish the illegitimacy of all restrictions on immigration.

C Shared identity

The third major set of views in the literature on the ethics of immigration is based on the putative normative significance of *shared identity*. Proponents of such views are more heterogeneous than advocates of open borders or statism and, thus, more difficult to accurately introduce in brief. While in chapter 6 we will have occasion to investigate a variety of connected views, I here focus on one of the most important types of shared identity arguments: those based on the importance of social trust.

The social trust view hinges on two assumptions. First, its advocates insist that justice requires public redistributive institutions along the lines of the modern welfare state.[10] Second, advocates of this view insist that the efficacy of such redistributive institutions, and thus the possibility of a just society, depends on citizens sharing a common public culture or national identity. This claim, like the previous one, though controversial, is nevertheless widely held:

> [The] presence of fellow-feeling obviously facilitates co-operation on common projects and makes redistribution within the polity more acceptable. (Barry 1983, 141)

> Communal solidarity creates a feeling, or an illusion, of closeness and shared fate, which is a precondition of distributive justice . . . Consequently, the community-like nature of the nation-state is particularly well suited, and perhaps even necessary, to the notion of the liberal welfare state. (Tamir 1993, 121)

These theorists hold that some kind of solidarity is a necessary condition of a just society and an efficacious welfare state.

The idea, then, is that justice requires a commitment to certain egalitarian policies and institutions (such as those embodied by the welfare state) and the efficacious functioning of such policies hinges, in turn, on the existence of a relatively unified group of citizens.[11] Individuals, according to this view, will only be willing to support the required policies if they are *already* linked by a measure of trust-inspiring shared identity. From this juncture, it is a relatively short jump to an argument for immigration restrictions. For instance, one commentator argues that

> liberal egalitarian principles can only be realized in communities where relations among citizens are characterized by solidarity and trust, relations that are often

[10] For prominent defenses of this position, see Dworkin 2000; Goodin 1988; and Rawls 1999b. Nevertheless, this is a controversial claim, and as a result these arguments will not appear persuasive to all interlocutors.

[11] The precise sense in which it is claimed that citizens must be united varies depending on the theorist in question, but this detail need not detain us here.

sustained by a shared culture and can be jeopardized by large, short-term changes in membership. (Gibney 1999, 174)

If immigration threatens to undermine the social unity that is a prerequisite for an efficacious set of policies required by justice, then there is reason to restrict it. Immigration, by this account, threatens justice by endangering its enabling machinery. Indeed, much of the vehemence of the public debate on immigration policy seems to be a reflection of the threat immigrants putatively pose to the continued viability of the welfare state.

The social trust view is similar to the associative ownership view in that both hold that citizens have a special claim and connection to the institutions of their states. However, this connection is understood in a very different way, and this difference has important ramifications both for the legitimacy of the view and the implications of accepting it. Chapter 6 will delve into these differences in some detail, and explicate a number of objections to views based on shared identity. Here, I want to briefly preview one important difficulty with such views.

In particular, I will argue that shared identity views misdescribe the relationship between citizens and state institutions as one based upon shared cultural commitments rather than claims of entitlement. Imagine that country X says to outsiders: we cannot accept you because doing so will jeopardize our common culture and, as a result, put our redistributive institutions at risk. Such an argument is incapable of providing reason to reject those from some country Y who speak the same language, practice the same religion, and already live under a similar type of government. If the whole world shared these practices, would country X be obliged to maintain open borders? This example brings out an oddity of views that attempt to describe the relationship between a state and its citizens solely in terms of cultural similarities. It fails to recognize the *particularity* of the relationship between citizens and their state, for it sees all those with similar cultural values as equivalent.

Moreover, the thought experiment raises an issue which is more than purely hypothetical. Imagine that the United States offers the social trust argument as a public justification for the exclusion of foreigners. Even if one thinks that those hailing from Mozambique or Laos are sufficiently different to undermine some shared national identity, does the same hold for foreigners from Canada or Great Britain? The social trust view seems to lead us back toward the discriminatory era of country-by-country quotas favoring Western Europeans, for it provides most reason to exclude those who are culturally different from current citizens, and no reason to exclude those with significant cultural similarities.

Table 1 *Overview of central positions regarding justice and immigration*

	Open Borders	Statism	Liberal Nationalism	Associative Ownership
Immigration restrictions?	No	Yes	Yes	Yes
Who can be denied admission?	Not applicable	Anybody	Non-nationals	Those whose claims to entry do not outweigh the ownership claims of the political community
Justification for denying admission?	Not applicable	Considerations of justice are inapplicable beyond state borders	Shared national culture is a prerequisite for a just society	The political community has an ownership claim over the goods at stake
Policy proposals?	Eliminate all restrictions on immigration	Select that policy which will be best for citizens (typically, emphasizing highly skilled immigrants)	Sharply limit immigration of non-nationals and work toward the assimilation of immigrants	Loosen restrictions on asylum/refugee policy, implement guest-worker program, and increase recruitment of highly skilled workers when it can be done without harming developing economies

This is a mistake, because it fails to recognize that the connection citizens have to their states depends not just on some cultural affinity, but on the contributions citizens make to their *particular* states. Like advocates of open borders, proponents of shared identity views ignore the contributions citizens make to their states and the way in which such contributions can ground legitimate entitlements to state institutions. Thus, I will argue that while advocates of shared identity views correctly insist that citizens are entitled to special claims over their state's institutions, much better sense of these claims can be made by thinking about them in terms of collective ownership than in terms of cultural commonalities. Importantly, this is not just an issue of theoretical concern. Instead, as I have tried to emphasize, the way in which we conceptualize the relationship between citizens and states will have important ramifications for the kinds of immigration policies we are willing to support.

I offer table 1 as a brief guide to thinking about the different positions and their implications.

III OUTLINE

Having sketched my intentions, I now want to describe how I intend to proceed:

- chapter 2 rejects statism and offers a preliminary justification of the associative ownership account;
- chapter 3 further clarifies and defends the associative ownership position;
- chapters 4–5 argue against open borders;
- chapter 6 highlights the limits of shared identity views; and
- chapter 7 explains the implications of the associative ownership view for a range of controversial policy questions.

Before beginning the argument in earnest, I would like to make a brief note about the status of the claims I am putting forward. I make two major types of claims.

First, I offer the associative ownership view as a way of understanding the special relationship between citizens and their institutions that does not depend (at least not in any direct way) on claims about national identity. In so doing, I take myself to be offering theoretical support for intuitive convictions that many of us will have regarding immigration that are not well explained, or accounted for, by existing theories. Here, my goal is to keep us alive to intuitively important considerations that I fear are masked by the current shape of the debate. Although there is no doubt that a complete account would require much more than I will offer, my intention is only to emphasize the major features of the terrain. I do this with the best language that I have, fully alive to its various limitations.

Second, I attempt to explain how the argument can be properly integrated with other important considerations and ultimately applied to questions of public policy. As I will emphasize throughout: such applications are inevitably imprecise in a way that will lead reasonable people to disagree about them. Still, I think that the arguments I offer can provide rough guidance for questions of public policy. Accordingly, especially in the later chapters, I apply the position to a number of controversial policy issues (including refugee policy, border control, and guest-worker programs). Despite the imprecision of this approach, I think it is vastly preferable to the available alternatives (namely, either applying with precision a theory that we know to be too simple to do justice to the complexity of our convictions or proceeding via appeal to intuitions without pausing to consider the justifiability of, or connection between, them). It is worth noting that one may accept my theoretical claims about the importance of the associative ownership account without also accepting my application of that position to current policy disputes.

Moreover, although the associative ownership framework is general enough for the first kind of claims to be relevant across countries, particular applications of it and judgments about its overall weight or significance differ from country to country. The historical experiences of countries affect the types of policies they may legitimately pursue. The considerations relevant to the United States are insufficient for considering the legitimacy, for example, of Israeli immigration policy. The Israeli political project is different in important and obvious ways that are relevant to the type of immigration policy Israelis ought to support. Altogether, I hope to show that a position built around the associative ownership argument (a) better reflects the terrain of considered convictions than existing alternatives; and (b) provides guidance in disputes regarding the shape of a justifiable immigration policy for the United States.

CHAPTER 2

Statism, self-determination, and associative ownership

Although there may be discord about the scope and limits of self-determination, it is widely accepted – in everyday political discourse, international law, and political theory – that some principle of self-determination is justified.[1] This chapter argues for a particular justification and account of the right of states to govern themselves. Appreciating the justification for self-determination will allow us to better understand how the principle bears on arguments regarding immigration.

I begin by considering and rejecting a position according to which sovereignty is unlimited, such that the needs and interests of foreigners impose no constraints on self-determination and the formulation of immigration policy (section I). Having seen that an unlimited principle of self-determination cannot pass muster, it becomes important to understand the justification or basis for accepting a principle of self-determination. This is because it is only by understanding the justification for such a principle that we will be in a position to understand its limits.

After explaining the difficulty of justifying self-determination (section II), I introduce the "associative ownership" account (section III). Although I believe that this is a natural and intuitive basis from which to defend a principle of self-determination, it is important to provide an explicit defense. Moreover, explicating the associative ownership view demonstrates that it – unlike other justifications of collective self-determination – can be extended to states (section IV). I then show that this view coheres with, and can account for, intuitive judgments regarding the appropriate bounds of self-determination (section V). Having shown that the associative ownership account can justify a principle of self-determination, I then argue that

[1] More controversial is the separate idea that all *nations* (or groups sharing some broad cultural identity) have a right to self-determination. A variety of defenses of this principle have been offered (see, for example, Margalit and Raz 1990 and Miller 1995, chap. 4). I will discuss this line of argument in chapter 6.

this defense of the associative ownership account provides grounds from which to dismiss the otherwise tempting idea that democrats are obliged to enfranchise all those whose interests are affected by a decision (section VI).

Thus, I pursue three main goals in this chapter. First, I reject the view that claims of sovereignty or self-determination justify the unrestricted pursuit of the interests of citizens. Second, I argue that the associative ownership account can explain and justify the claim that states enjoy a right of self-determination. Third, I use this account to argue that – despite its popularity among democratic theorists – the idea that governments are obliged to enfranchise all those whom their policies affect is mistaken. In sum, this chapter sets the stage for our more direct consideration of immigration by providing a justification of self-determination that can help guide our thinking regarding its appropriate limits and applications.

I STATISM

Often implicit in public discussion of immigration policy is the *statist* idea that, as a result of claims to self-determination, citizens ought to be free to construct such policy in any way they wish. The distinguishing feature of this view is that the demands of justice are inapplicable beyond state borders and, as a result, the interests of foreigners do not impose constraints on justifiable immigration policy.

Such a view is often taken as obvious or in no need of defense in public debate regarding immigration reform. We are told, for example, that the question of who may immigrate is "the exclusive, sovereign, unilateral right of the recipient nation to determine" (James 1991, 29). If correct, this suggests – as noted in the introduction – that

> immigration policy should be set in ways that further the national interest, and the nation's interest may simply not coincide with giving any particular person or any particular ethnic group the opportunity to partake in the unrivaled opportunities that the United States has to offer. (Borjas 1999, xxii)

The claim here is that immigration policy ought to be formulated so as to best advance the interests of the citizenry regardless of the needs and interests of foreigners. According to statists, because citizens constitute a sovereign group, the interests of foreigners can impose no constraints on their collective will or power of self-rule. Thus, we should accept that immigration policy which is best for the citizenry.

My overall goal in this section is to persuade the reader to set statism aside and accept the view that the needs and interests of foreigners are neither beyond the scope of justice nor trumped by considerations of sovereignty. It is important to note that this means neither that the interests of foreigners must always be given equal weight to those of citizens nor that citizens do not share a special moral relationship which involves some permission to design their collective political life in accordance with their wishes. Instead, my claim is only (a) that justice demands that all are treated as possessing an equal moral status;[2] and (b) that recognizing this places bounds on the sovereignty of states. Thus, I argue that one should accept that claims of foreigners may impose significant limits on a citizenry's right of self-determination.

John Mearsheimer argues that "the overriding goal of each state is to maximize its share of world power, which means gaining power at the expense of other states" (Mearsheimer 2001, 2). He describes the situation thereby generated as "genuinely tragic" because even "great powers that have no reason to fight each other – they are merely concerned with their own survival – nevertheless they have little choice but to pursue power and to seek to dominate the other states in the system" (Mearsheimer 2001, 3). The explanation for this is straightforwardly Hobbesian:[3]

> The structure of the international system forces states which seek only to be secure nonetheless to act aggressively toward each other. Three features of the international system combine to cause states to fear one another: 1) the absence of a central authority that sits above states and can protect them from each other, 2) the fact that states always have some offensive military capability, and 3) the fact that states can never be certain about other states' intentions. (Mearsheimer 2001, 3)

Like Hobbes, Mearsheimer claims that the anarchic structure of the international system prohibits actors from respecting the needs and interests of those with whom one does not share citizenship.

Note first that the inquiry in which we are engaged is not empirical social science and I do not offer arguments that are designed to predict or even explain state behavior. Thus, if it turns out that Mearsheimer's realist paradigm yields very powerful predictive models, I have no objection to its being employed by social scientists for descriptive or predictive purposes.[4]

Mearsheimer alleges, however, that the model is more than just explanatory. He argues that "it is also a prescriptive theory. States *should* behave

[2] It is important to note, and I will have much more to say about this as we move forward, that this will not mean that they need to be always *treated* equally, for differences in circumstances permit differences in treatment.

[3] For an explanation of the connection between Hobbes and contemporary realists as well as a classic criticism of the normative legitimacy of the realist perspective, see Beitz 1979.

[4] I am grateful to Colin Bird for helping with this formulation.

according to the dictates of offensive realism, because it outlines the best way to survive in a dangerous world" (Mearsheimer 2001, 11). According to this view, policy that does not seek survival above all else amounts to "foolish behavior" which "invariably has negative consequences" (Mearsheimer 2001, 12). If this view is correct, we *ought* to adopt that immigration policy which best promotes our place in the balance of power and, thus, does as much as is possible to ensure our survival.

In this view, in an anarchic system (e.g. one without a sovereign) justice does not apply and, thus, cannot put any constraints on the policies the sovereign ought to pursue. Again, this basic argumentative framework was classically expressed by Thomas Hobbes, who argued that:

> In all times, Kings, and Persons of Soveraigne authority, because of their Independency, and in continuall jealousies, are in the state and posture of Gladiators; having their weapon pointing, and their eyes fixed on one another; that is, their Forts, Garrisons, and Guns upon the Frontiers of their Kingdomes; and continuall Spyes upon their neighbours; which is a posture of War . . . To this warre of every man against every man, this also is consequent; that *nothing can be Unjust. The notions of Right and Wrong, Justice and Injustice have there no place.* Where is no common Power, there is no Law: where no Law, no Injustice. (Hobbes 1985 [1651], 187–188, emphasis added)

Again, the claim being advanced here is that given our anarchic world system, the concept of justice is inapplicable. States are not constrained by its guidelines. Instead, they both should and must – at the risk of elimination – select those policies that do as much as possible to ensure their survival. Because this claim purports to tell us how we ought to interact with other states and so, by extension, how we ought to design immigration policy, it is important to consider the arguments that putatively justify it.

In this section, I argue against this position by explaining how at odds it is with intuitions about morality and acceptable state policy that we can take as provisionary fixed points as we attempt to address more controversial issues. Before doing so, however, it is worth allowing that realism draws on some plausible and, indeed, unobjectionable basic commitments. Foremost among these is the idea that states have a legitimate interest in their survival and quite often ought to act to ensure the accomplishment of this goal. This much, it is important to emphasize, is not in dispute. Instead, the argument is about whether or not justice imposes constraints on states' right to pursue survival.

While, as we have seen, Mearsheimer and Hobbes dispute this claim, it is deeply at odds with ordinary intuitions and conflicts with the commitment to the equal moral value of all individual lives (a commitment few are willing to explicitly cast off).[5] To see that this is true, consider the following example:

> You are the leader of a country and have ultimate and unconstrained legal control over its foreign policy. Currently, you are peacefully coexisting with all other countries. Nevertheless, no overarching sovereign exists and you cannot be sure of the future intentions of others. Your chief advisor comes to you and explains that government scientists have (at last!) succeeded in developing *The Vaporizer*. This weapon is capable, at the push of a button, of eliminating all humans who are not citizens of your country. Perhaps best of all, it can do this without imposing any damage on the environment or fellow nationals living abroad. The choice is yours: *Should* we detonate the weapon?

I believe, and believe most of us believe, that the choice is clear. To use the weapon would be to kill – and, because unprovoked and deliberate, to murder – billions of people. The actions of Hitler, Stalin, and history's other antagonists would pale in comparison. This is true regardless of calculations about how use of the Vaporizer would affect national survival.

Once this is allowed, however, we are forced to set aside the claim that justice is entirely inapplicable in world affairs or somehow trumped by the sovereignty of states. Instead, the example demonstrates that – at least sometimes – justice constrains the actions of states, even beyond their borders. Moreover, fanciful examples are not needed to make the point. Although people might disagree empirically over whether the firebombing of German cities or the use of the atomic bomb during World War II served military purposes, there is little doubt that *if* it is true that such acts had no tactical purpose, their use constituted a deep injustice. Moreover, to the extent that those affected were entirely innocent (as many no doubt were), the injustice is deepened. That we can understand and make sense of these claims shows that the concept of justice is not simply trumped by appeals to self-determination. There is thus a range of policies that states *ought not* to pursue because of the interests of non-citizens, and this is true even if such acts might increase their relative power and/or overall odds of survival. One cannot deny this and insist that there are other-regarding reasons to refrain from using the weapon in our example.

[5] Throughout I work from the premise that all individuals – regardless of citizenship – are to be seen as, on some level, moral equals. Like Rawls (Rawls 1993), I resist giving an argument for that claim and instead focus on trying to explain its implications (Dreben 2003).

Mearsheimer is not oblivious to this disconnect between realist policy prescriptions and the core moral intuitions of normal citizens. He allows that realism's "central message . . . does not have broad appeal" and that, as a result, "realism is a hard sell" (Mearsheimer 2001, 22–23). However, he goes on to explain that

> Americans tend to be hostile to realism because it clashes with their basic values. Realism stands opposed to Americans' views of both themselves and the wider world. In particular, realism is at odds with the deep-seated sense of optimism and moralism that pervades much of American society. (Mearsheimer 2001, 23)

Although this assessment mirrors much of what I have just argued, Mearsheimer suggests that there are two reasons to discount Americans' "moralism" and follow the dictates of realism.

First, he suggests that the disconnect between public opinion and public policy is a result of the fact that "Americans are basically optimists" while "realism, by contrast, offers a pessimistic perspective on international politics" (Mearsheimer 2001, 24). Suggesting, however, that realism lacks prescriptive popularity among the public because citizens are "optimistic" while realism is "pessimistic" is a red herring; it distracts us from the important point. Citizens do not object to the policy prescriptions of realists simply because they see the glass as half full while realists insist that it be seen as half empty. The difference in views is not simply a result of disagreements regarding the dispositions of elites and citizens.

Rather, as I argued above, citizens object to the realist perspective because it is deeply at odds with their basic moral commitments and, thus, with their understanding of themselves as people willing to pursue their interests only within certain constraints. This is not just a difference in disposition, but instead a disagreement about the kinds of lives people want to live and the actions they are willing to authorize. Moreover, in labeling these preferences "optimistic" and discarding them accordingly, Mearsheimer provides no reasons to those with whom he disagrees; instead, he simply insists upon his own preferences without argument.

Second, Mearsheimer informs us that "behind closed doors . . . the elites who make national security policy speak mostly the language of power, not that of principle, and the United States acts in the international system according to the dictates of realist logic" (Mearsheimer 2001, 25). This argument relates to the first because it purports to explain why Mearsheimer's preferences ought to be taken more seriously than that of the giddily optimistic citizenry. However, it is important in assessing this attempt at mitigating the disconnect between justice and realist dictates to keep in mind our previous distinction between prescriptive and descriptive accounts.

That policymakers deceive the citizenry by, behind closed doors, pursuing policies that citizens refuse to countenance may be correct as a descriptive claim. Prescriptively, however, it provides no reason to *accept* such policies. Instead, it only provides reasons to attempt to improve the accountability of public officials. Officials act in the citizenry's name and these actions are not somehow beyond the claims of justice; it is this conviction – and not just differences in disposition – that render the prescriptions of statism unacceptable. Nor is the idea that citizens can force their officials to adopt policies that more closely approximate the citizenry's desire to advance the interests of non-citizens simply utopian.

One example concerns the epic earthquake that occurred off the coast of Indonesia in 2004. The ensuing waves struck the eastern coast of Sri Lanka and immediately derailed a train, drowning nearly 1,500 people. The tsunami affected several Southeast Asian countries and the count of known deaths rose mercilessly: 12,000 on December 26, 27,000 the next day, 50,000 on the 28th, 77,000 on the 29th, 124,000 by the end of the month, and ultimately between 225,000 and 300,000. This was a horrific natural disaster.

In response, the US government initially pledged $35 million in relief aid. In the statist view, even this much is just money down a hole; there is no clear sense, after all, in which such money can be expected to advance the relative power of the United States. US citizens, however, excoriated their representatives. After a public outcry about the inadequacy of the initial aid pledge, the US government increased its commitment to $350 million on December 31. This was later again increased to nearly $900 million. Whether or not this much larger figure was apt is a separate question.

The point is simply that citizens have it within their power to hold public officials to the ideals to which they are committed. They need not accept the claim that ideals of justice are excluded by the need to pursue survival. While the fact that state officials pursue policies that clash with the basic moral values and self-perception of those they putatively represent provides reason to reject such officials, it fails to cast doubt on the commitments at stake. Thus, Mearsheimer fails to produce reason to discount the typical commitments of citizens.

It might seem that although it is wrong to detonate the Vaporizer, the reason for this is not – as I have been suggesting – that claims of justice extend beyond state borders.[6] Instead, one might suggest that there are important

[6] I thank an anonymous reviewer for helpful thoughts along these lines.

gains to be had via cooperation and, so, even a purely self-interested state should countenance the existence of foreigners if this can be done without too much threat to survival. According to this view, Mearsheimer goes wrong by assuming that survival is the only important interest that the state must advance, and not by insisting upon an overly narrow scope for justice.

In fact, I believe that Mearsheimer goes wrong in both of these ways. So, it is true that while Mearsheimer represents agents as *exclusively* interested in survival, people generally care quite a bit about the method by which such survival is achieved as well as the shape that it takes. I hasten to add, rather obviously, that this is *not* to say that survival ought not to be an important goal; instead, it is just to say that valuing survival to the exclusion of *all* other goods is deeply at odds with the way people typically think about how one ought to live. Indeed, if we took survival that seriously, we would hunker down in bunkers – never emerging for fear of an auto accident or the like. Survival is a goal, and an obviously important one, but to act as though it were the *only* objective misrepresents what most value and, indeed, substitutes a means for an end.

We can modify Mearsheimer's position in order to account for this criticism. We can, for example, recognize that (a) people's interests extend beyond survival (to wealth, income, opportunities, etc.); and (b) foreigners are sources not just of potential threat, but also potential cooperation. On this modified account, even a purely self-interested state would not necessarily have reason to detonate our hypothetical weapon. Instead, it would have to make some judgment about how to weigh the costs and benefits of countenancing the survival of other states. On this view, while it is wrong to detonate the weapon, it is wrong for prudential reasons (because it amounts to forgoing potential gains) and not for the kinds of justice-based reasons I previously suggested.

Although it is true that other ends need to be accounted for and that foreigners are valuable as partners in cooperation, it is important to recognize that these prudential reasons supplement rather than replace the reasons of justice discussed previously. This is just to say that even if it is a mistake to detonate the weapon for prudential reasons, there remain purely other-regarding reasons to oppose the policy as well. Showing that there are self-interested reasons not to use the weapon does not also show that we are without reasons of justice to oppose its use. And, indeed, that there are reasons of justice not to use the weapon seems beyond doubt.

My overall goal is to describe the constraints justice imposes on the construction of immigration policy. Advocates of statism purport to greatly simplify this task by showing that because nations are sovereign units stuck in a structure that forces them to pursue survival, the claims of foreigners can impose no constraints on the construction of such policy. My hope is that the arguments developed above successfully rebut this position by showing it to depend on a misguided commitment to unbounded sovereignty. Against the statists, then, we should accept that foreigners, because of their equal moral status, can lodge claims of justice, and that these claims of justice may rightfully constrain the citizenry's formulation of immigration policy.

Having established this point, the relevant question becomes: to what *extent* do the interests of foreigners constrain the range of acceptable approaches to immigration? In the sections that follow, I attempt to present a framework for addressing this question by explaining the justification for a principle of self-determination. Once we understand the justification that underlies self-determination, it will be easier to understand the scope and limits of such a principle.

II INDIVIDUAL AUTONOMY AND COLLECTIVE SELF-DETERMINATION

Although I have rejected views that insist that self-determination justifies unlimited sovereignty, I do not reject the principle of self-determination. Instead, in the remainder of this chapter I propose an account that is consistent with the claim that political communities have a right to self-determination. By this, it is simply meant that the members of a state – whether or not they share a *national* identity – have a *prima facie* right to make their own decisions about the policies under which they live (including policies regarding membership). Citizens are to be their own rulers.

A group's right to self-determination is frequently taken as unobjectionable. For instance, a congregation that together builds a temple, and institutes a youth education program and a support group for widows, would generally be seen as well within its rights to exercise a certain degree of control over future policies (including those related to membership). While the congregation may not act so as to violate the basic rights of non-members and may – in extraordinary circumstances – be expected to yield its building space to victims of emergencies, it is entitled to invite only certain individuals to benefit from, and participate in, its historic accomplishments. Likewise, it is entitled to determine for itself – within certain constraints – the shape and direction of future policies. We would typically say the same of business partners, student groups, and universities. Surely these groups may exclude at least some individuals from their joint pursuits.

Perhaps the most obvious way of explaining or justifying this pre-theoretical intuition is to insist that a group's right to self-determination is a consequence of each individual member's right to self-determination. In this view, each member of the congregation has a right to be a self-determining agent. When one joins the congregation, she gives up some freedom in exchange for the benefits of membership, and does so with an understanding of how future decisions of the congregation will be made. If we *force* the congregation to make membership available to all, we thereby undermine the autonomy of individual members. Perhaps there will be ample reasons to do so, but there is a clear sense in which violating the self-determination of the congregation also violates the autonomy of individual members.

On this account, we are obliged to respect the self-determination of groups as *part* of our commitment to individual autonomy. This view is a familiar one in the history of political thought, for it underlies the social contract tradition. For example, Jean-Jacques Rousseau insists that the fact that man "is everywhere . . . in chains" can be made legitimate by ensuring that those chains are the result of individual choices; that is, that they are a manifestation of the autonomy of individual agents (Rousseau 1987, 17). This is why he insists that "the law of majority rule . . . presupposes unanimity on at least one occasion" (Rousseau 1987, 23). This instance of unanimity is meant to ensure that group autonomy promotes individual autonomy. Rousseau's basic idea, that individuals have a natural right to freedom that – after its transfer to the political community – justifies the community's right to pursue a range of policies for the purposes of mutual benefit, is central to the social contract tradition.

Despite the prominence of this line of reasoning (by which the autonomy of states is justified as a consequence of the autonomy of its individual members), the argument from individual autonomy cannot in fact be extended so as to justify the claim that *states* have a parallel right to self-determination. The reason that such arguments cannot be used to justify the self-determination of states is that most citizens stand in a non-voluntary relationship vis-à-vis their state.[7] Because individuals are typically born into states that impose laws upon them regardless of their decisions or consent, we cannot trust that providing for the autonomy of the state will

[7] John Locke attempts to avoid this difficulty via appeal to "tacit consent," but this tack faces now familiar difficulties (Simmons 1979, chap. 4).

advance the autonomy of individual citizens.[8] Because majority rule does not, in the case of modern states, lie on a bed of unanimity there is no reason to trust that respecting the autonomy of states amounts to respecting the autonomy of individual members.

To see why this matters, imagine that I am kidnapped by the aforementioned congregation:

> It forces me to attend its services, pay its dues, and recite its doctrines. When I make a plea to putatively benevolent outsiders to save me from this imprisonment, they – citing the congregation's recent decision to hold all kidnapped individuals indefinitely (reached by a majority in an election in which I was given a vote) – refuse. The benevolent outsiders say that, while they sympathize, to interfere with the congregation would be to fail to respect the group's right to self-determination and, by extension, *my* autonomy. They have, they say, no choice but to force me to be free.

Clearly, the benevolent outsiders are wrong to equate my autonomy with that of the group. Because I am an unwilling participant in the practices of the congregation, there is no guarantee that respecting the group's self-determination will in any sense further my own autonomy.

Because (a) this follows from the non-voluntary nature of my membership in the congregation; and (b) the vast majority of citizens hold this status non-voluntarily, the idea that states have rights of self-determination that grow straightforwardly from a commitment to the autonomy of individual citizens cannot be correct.[9] For similar reasons, it is a mistake to argue that the state's right to self-determination can be rightly defended as a consequence of a commitment to the right of individuals to freely associate.[10] Because citizens do not associate with one another freely, it is a

[8] This important point has been made, in various ways, many times before. For two influential examples see Beitz 1979, 77–83 and Simmons 1979, chaps. 3–4.

[9] It is possible to argue for an account of self-determination that applies only to *cultural* groups that hinges on individual autonomy. On such a view, one's autonomy is enhanced by being a member of an encompassing group which determines its own future and is generally respected as a self-determining unit. Here, one's non-voluntary membership does not eliminate the sense in which the autonomy of the group contributes to the autonomy of its members. However, such an account – even if successful – can only explain the claims of self-determination of national, cultural, or encompassing groups and not of political communities more generally. For such an account see Margalit and Raz 1990. For important criticisms see Copp 1997.

[10] In an excellent recent article, Christopher Heath Wellman appeals to freedom of association to justify immigration restrictions (Wellman 2008; for a very good criticism see Fine 2010). While the view defended by Wellman is similar in important ways to the one developed here (both, for example, do without appeal to cultural claims), the presumption in favor of the political community's right to control borders can be better explained by reference to the joint contributions of citizens to the existence of goods at stake in arguments regarding immigration than through arguments regarding

mistake to think that the actions of the state might be justified by the right of citizens to associate as they choose.

In response to the conclusion that self-determination cannot be justified via reference to the autonomy of individual members, one prominent view in the literature holds that we should understand self-determination as merely "derivative of more basic principles of justice" (Beitz 1979, 69; similarly see Philpott 1995; and Stilz 2009). For example, Charles Beitz argues that

> what is certain is that members of colonized groups have the right to just institutions; whether they have a right of self-determination depends on the extent to which the granting of independence would, in their particular circumstances, help to minimize injustice. (Beitz 1979, 102)

On this view, the value of self-determination is only instrumental: if it helps us reach the desired end, then it is to be preferred.

The difficulty with this position is that it hinges on the claim that self-determination is merely a potential tool to be used to pursue just institutions. Accordingly, the only reason Beitz can provide to resist rule by philosopher kings or the revolutionary vanguard is the contingent empirical claim that such possibilities promise to be less efficient in the pursuit of justice than would a system of self-determination that instead – through democratic institutions – put governing decisions in the hands of the citizenry. Although I grant that there are important reasons of this (instrumental) type to favor democratic institutions of some kind (Cohen 1986; Przeworski 1999; Sen 1994), I doubt whether such reasons are the *only* kinds of reasons to support self-determination and the democratic institutions that it requires.

I call these instrumental reasons for supporting self-determination contingent because whether they apply depends on the available alternatives. Even if one does not trust philosophers or revolutionaries, the argument suggests that if there are some outsiders who are marginally more efficient in the pursuit of the requirements of justice than are democratic institutions, we should – without regret – outsource governance. A view, such as the

freedom of association. This is for two main reasons. First, there is no obvious sense in which citizens, born into membership, can be said to be *freely* associating with one another. It is a mistake to defend immigration restrictions by reference to the citizenry's claims of freedom of association when the relevant association is not freely entered into. Second, arguments based solely on freedom of association face difficulties in explaining why states, but not other associations (baseball teams, interest groups, or cities), may restrict movement. This suggests that what is needed is an account that explains how the ongoing relationship of citizens provides a kind of ownership claim over territory and institutions that justifies limited immigration restrictions. The associative ownership view can fulfill this role.

one I shall propose, says instead that democratic self-rule is *part* of any attractive ideal of justice and so there is a necessary loss (albeit one that could potentially be outweighed) in terms of justice when self-rule is sacrificed.

In other words: in addition to instrumental reasons, there are reasons of fairness that support democratic self-determination. Only democratic institutions properly respect citizens as part owners of the relevant institutions. That is: only democratic institutions properly respect the individuals in whose name they exercise political power. If this is correct, democratic self-determination is not just a potential instrument for the realization of a just outcome, but is instead itself *part* of a just outcome.

To get a handle on the difference between these views, it is helpful to consider an example provided by Beitz:

> Country A is an imperial country, and area B, a territorially distinct area with generally accepted boundaries, is A's colony. Since A is the most benevolent of all possible imperial countries, there is no reason to think that granting independence to B will decrease the amount of social injustice in B; indeed, the opposite seems more likely because of various political and economic complications inside B which we don't need to explain. Nonetheless, the residents of B, in a fair and free election, overwhelmingly indicate their preference for national independence. (Beitz 1979, 103)

If we accept Beitz's view of self-determination, Country A should resist the results of this election and refuse to grant area B independence. Beitz allows that "intuitively, this seems implausible" (Beitz 1979, 103). He concludes, however, that this line of objection to his position is "weaker than it may seem" because it "simply does not apply to many real world cases" (Beitz 1979, 103).

Although Beitz is surely correct that it will be difficult (indeed, probably impossible) to find "real world cases" with just these features, it is unclear why the unlikelihood of the case should be taken to provide reason to accede to the view; instead, the example brings forth an important oddity in the position. Namely: while we typically think that an important aspect of institutions qualifying as just is that they are – in some relevant sense – responsive to the will of citizens, Beitz's position removes this criterion altogether. This leaves us with a conception of justice that hinges *solely* on the outcome produced by those institutions and not at all attentive to the manner in which such outcomes are produced.

Beitz's view assumes, in other words, that democratic self-rule and justice are independent, whereas the example suggests that attractive conceptions of justice will include within them a commitment to democratic rule. For example, in Rawls's view, the protection of the political liberties is an important element of the overall view of justice (Rawls 1999b, especially §36; also on this point, see Cohen 2003). On such a view, any sacrifice of the political liberties (and so self-determination) *is* a sacrifice of justice (even if it is, all things considered, justified by the results).[11] Although the example is extraordinary in that it brings this issue to the fore, there is nevertheless a real, practical, and important difference between a view that sees democratic self-rule as an element of, rather than simply instrumental to, justice.

Notice that I am not saying that anything willed by the majority is just, or that it will never make sense to override democratic rule in order to promote valuable consequences. Instead, my claim is merely that because democratic rule is *one* important aspect of justice, there are costs to overruling self-determination that are not reducible to the difference in policy outcomes between democratic and non-democratic institutions. This is why we find a view that comes to Beitz's conclusion intuitively odd.

Although intuitive responses to this example support the view that self-determination is an element of justice, we are still not in possession of a *justification* of that intuition that can explain its soundness. One response is to throw up one's hands and abandon the endeavor of locating such a justification. Christopher Wellman takes this tack, saying that although it is unclear what *justifies* self-determination, to forfeit this position would be

> to concede that we do no necessary injustice to groups of people when we colonize them, annex their legitimate states, or dismantle their legitimate democracies . . . Given these awkward implications of denying the deontological reasons to respect group self-determination, clearly we have reasons to posit the basic value of group autonomy even if we know of no straightforward way to square it with value-individualism. (Wellman 2005, 55)

Of course, the problem with this approach is that it merely restates our discomfort with the consequences of Beitz's position.

Without supplementing that discomfort with an understanding of the justification of self-determination, we are without (a) guidance regarding the scope and limits of its applications; and (b) a principled response to those – including Beitz and advocates of the view that all affected by government policies must be enfranchised – who reject the principle altogether. It would be preferable, then, not to skip the question of what justifies self-determination.

Accordingly, in the section that follows, I offer an account of self-determination that does not hinge on the importance of respecting the

[11] Even in Rawls's view, a sacrifice of political liberties could be justified. This, however, would only be the case if it led to a more adequate overall protection of the set of basic liberties (Rawls 1993, lecture VIII). It could not be justly sacrificed, as in Beitz's view, for distributive or efficiency-based reasons.

individual autonomy of citizens and, so, can help justify our response to the example discussed above. I hope that this account can also make sense of the idea of society "as a fair system of cooperation over time, from one generation to the next" (Rawls 1993, 15).

III ASSOCIATIVE OWNERSHIP AND SELF-DETERMINATION

I shall now argue that a principle of self-determination can be justified by reference to the group's *ownership* of goods produced through the labor and contributions of members. In this section, I show only how the argument applies to standard voluntary associations, leaving to the next section the task of applying this argument to states.

The intuition underlying this account is commonplace. Returning to our congregation: the idea is simply that it may claim ownership over its collective accomplishments because without the contributions of members (in time, effort, and money) the support group for widows or the youth education program could not exist. Again, it is only as a result of members' efforts that such programs exist and, as a result, it seems intuitive to say that members can claim an ownership stake in these programs that supplies them a *prima facie* claim to make future decisions regarding the shape of such programs. In other words, members' creation of institutions gives them an ownership claim that grounds their right to make future decisions about the shape and direction of such institutions (in other words, their right to self-determination). This is the intuition that underlies the associative ownership account of self-determination.

This pre-theoretical intuition finds support in arguments that purport to show that labor can ground claims of ownership. As A. John Simmons explains:

> There has been no more widespread or enduring intuition about property rights than that labor in creating or improving a thing gives one special claim to it. We feel that those who innocently work to discover, make, or usefully employ some unowned good ought to be allowed to keep it (if in so doing they harm no others) . . . it would be wrong for others to take it away. (Simmons 1992, 223)

If we can agree that any plausible account of ownership will incorporate the intuition that those who innocently work to make some good come to have a special claim to it, we have enough to say that the congregation is justified in insisting on its ownership over the institutions that it has built. Of course, I hasten to add that this will not be enough to tell us how much weight this claim deserves when it conflicts with other considerations.

I want to briefly explicate the intuition described above. This kind of "labor argument" (familiar from John Locke's work) is – as Simmons remarks – a mainstay of discussions of justice and property rights. Lawrence Becker, in summarizing the core of the view, explains:

> When the labor is (1) beyond what is required, morally, that one do for others; (2) produces something which would not have existed except for it; and (3) its product is something which others lose nothing by being excluded from; then (4) it is not wrong for producers to exclude others from the possession, use, etc. of the fruits of their labors. It is not so much that the producers *deserve* the produce of their labors. It is rather that no one else does, and it is not wrong for the laborer to have them. (Becker 1977, 41)

Despite its Lockean roots, it is crucial to note that the way in which I utilize this line of argument does not depend on the controversial assumptions often associated with Lockean thought (regarding, for example, self-ownership).

Instead, this line of argument is consistent with a wide array of approaches to property rights. John Stuart Mill, for instance, insists that "property, in every defence of it, is supposed to mean the guarantee to individuals of the fruits of their own labour and abstinence" (Mill 1976, book 2, chapter 1, §19). Likewise, it is even consistent with a Humean view according to which property rights are purely conventional because any convention that would advance the utility of all would surely accommodate this intuition. Indeed, Hume insists that successful conventions must "bestow stability on the possession of those external goods" by leaving "every one in the peaceable enjoyment of what he may acquire by his fortune and industry" (Hume 1985, 541 [book 3, section II]). So, rather than hinging on a variety of strongly Lockean claims, this version of the argument merely insists that – in the absence of competing claims – one's working to create a good alters one's relationship with it in a way that gives one a special ownership relationship with the good in question.[12]

So long as the creation of this good does not involve harming others, this much, it seems to me, is quite hard to dispute. Thus, the labor argument explains the intuition that there is reason to allow our congregation to make its own decisions about the future of its education and support programs with reference to the ownership claims of the congregation over

[12] The precise implications of this claim will vary depending on whether one accepts the account of Mill, Locke, or Hume. My point is only that each, despite their very different theoretical frameworks, cannot help but accept the claim around which associative ownership is built. I thank Mat Coakley for discussion on this point.

said programs. The obvious question is whether the intuition underlying this account can be extended to states, given their non-voluntary and intergenerational nature. While I will address these questions in the next section, I first want – by way of qualification – to note three points.

First, it is important that the types of entitlement claims that arise as a result are importantly limited; that is, reason has *not* been provided to claim that laboring on something or bringing it into being gives one *full* entitlement to it. There may well be all kinds of limitations on such ownership claims.[13] For example, we might insist that those excluded are not harmed by this exclusion, that the needs of others impose limits, and perhaps there are other kinds of limitations as well. Thus, the associative ownership argument justifies members' *limited* claim of ownership over the congregation and its institutions.

Second, although, in keeping with Locke's original formulation, I have employed the term "labor," this connotes a kind of strain, struggle, or drudgery. We envision the laborer bent over an anvil, sweating and plodding through heavy work. However, we should not be misled into thinking that it is the *difficulty* of the endeavor that lies behind the intuition that laboring can give one a claim to a good. Exertion is neither a necessary nor a sufficient condition for claims of ownership; instead, labor is important for its creative and directive qualities, rather than the pain or exertion that sometimes comes along with it (Russell 2004).[14] Thus, we need not be concerned that few of us have the experience of sweating over an anvil, forging new political institutions. The more ordinary experience that most of us do have – paying taxes and contributing to collective political decisions – suffices, regardless of the exertion or lack thereof involved. These activities bring forth and direct political institutions. It is only as a result of these activities that political institutions come into being.

[13] Locke himself insisted upon two important kinds of limitations. First, that those who do not have enough to survive despite the plenty of others have a "title" to the excesses of others (Locke 1988, 170). Second, that property claims are only legitimate in cases "where there is enough, and as good left" for others (Locke 1988, 288). Incidentally, these limitations are sufficient to demonstrate that Jeremy Waldron is wrong to claim that those who accept a view centered around a principle of just acquisition also accept the view that "there are actions which individuals can perform whose moral effect is to place millions of others under obligations whose discharge may require them to place their own survival in jeopardy" (Waldron 1988, 267). Although this is true of Nozick's *particular* conception of historical entitlement, the duty of charity and Lockean proviso interpret the idea of just acquisition in a way that ensures that it is not also true of Locke's conception of historical entitlement and, so, demonstrates that it is not true of the category of views as a whole.

[14] This is a point about which more would ideally be said, but I trust that the general point or intuition is clear enough.

Third, it is important to notice that the congregation does not deny the *personhood* (or equal status) of outsiders by refusing to grant them a say in decisions about future policy or membership. Even if, as Peter Singer suggests, outsiders would be – and would have been – happy to contribute to the provision of such goods (Singer 2002, 168–170), the fact remains that they did not. Likewise, I may have been happy to contribute to the founding of Google, but this is insignificant in the face of the fact that I did not. The founders of Google do not fail to treat me as an equal when they, in the process of refusing my claim to their bounty, point this out. These are goods established only through the joint labor of members as coordinated by the association. Such exclusions need not deny the humanity of outsiders; rather, they reflect the fact that outsiders did not play a fundamental role in the creation of the relevant institutions.

I have thus argued that the right of groups to self-determination can, at least in some circumstances, be explained in terms of their ownership claims over the relevant institutions or practices. It remains to be shown, however, that this argument can be extended to states.

IV ASSOCIATIVE OWNERSHIP, SELF-DETERMINATION, AND STATES

In this section, I extend the associative ownership account to show that it is capable of justifying the claims of self-determination not just of voluntary associations such as congregations, but also of states. To do this, I argue that the associative ownership account applies even to associations that are non-voluntary and intergenerational. As we noted above, states are non-voluntary: most of us are conscripted into citizenship and have laws enforced upon us. Indeed, it was this characteristic of states that prevented us from saying that states' rights to self-determination follow straightforwardly from the interest individual members have in autonomy.

We were able to see this by considering the case of a kidnapped member of the congregation. It was clear that this individual's autonomy was not enhanced by respecting the self-determination of the congregation and, as a result, we concluded that collective self-determination could not be grounded in individual autonomy when membership in the relevant association is (as in states) non-voluntary. I believe, however, that the associative ownership account – unlike views grounded in individual autonomy – applies even to participants in non-voluntary groups. We can see this by considering two examples.

The first case that I would like to consider is that of the *Kidnapped Lecturers.*

> Unhappy with the high price of higher education and the low quality of publicly available political theory lectures, Mary kidnaps several promising young political theorists. Holding them in captivity and under threat, she forces them to work together recording a series of bold and captivating lectures. Just as the lectures are completed, the police are tipped off, Mary is arrested, and the political theorists are freed. In the wake of this story, the lectures become a kind of public curiosity and sell widely (at least by political theory's modest standards).

Although the political theorists were forced into this joint work, one cannot reasonably doubt the claim that their labor gives them a right to the profits that result from the sale of the lectures as well as future rights to, and control over, the material therein. This suggests that lasting claims of ownership can originate in non-voluntary associations.[15]

One could insist that although the lecturers have a right to profit from the material, their claims of ownership should also eventually expire, with the material at that point becoming owned by all. Even if true, the question of fading entitlements does not arise in terms of ownership over state institutions because this is a story that is constantly being rewritten, with new participants engaging in the project in ways that renew claims of ownership (through their own contributions, the remaking of political institutions, and the ongoing commitment to society as an intergenerational scheme of social cooperation).

The second case I would like to consider is that of the *Family Farm.*

> John is born to a family that earns its living through a long-established family farming business. At his birth, his family makes him a full and equal member of the business (although some of the privileges that go along with that status are delayed until he reaches an appropriate age).

In my view, John's family has a claim of ownership over the farm, one element of which is a right to make decisions regarding its future (including decisions about who will make such decisions in the future).[16] This justifies their passing down the farm through the family despite its intergenerational nature.

[15] This suggests that even non-democratic states may have the right to control immigration.

[16] Of course, the rights of others impose limits on how this self-determination may be rightfully exercised. So, for example, it is clearly outside of their rights to turn the farm into a death camp that seeks the elimination of members of a nearby religious sect. Any plausible justification of a principle of self-determination will come with limits.

If outsiders show up after control of the farm has shifted to John and demand that he adopt a new system of irrigation on grounds that it will render the operation more profitable, we would hardly hesitate to say that the choice should be left to him. If the outsiders protest that John was simply born into the family and so not entitled to any special right to govern it, this fact would have no bearing on our judgment. Instead, it would be quite strange to say that John has no more of a right to shape the future of the business than do these outsiders. Unlike the outsiders, John was passed control of the farm by its previous owners. If we accept this commonplace judgment, we have enough to also explain the right to self-determination of states – which is, in important regards, analogous to this example.

Like the family farm, the construction of state institutions is a historical project that extends across generations and into which individuals are born. Just as the value of a farm very largely comes from the improvements made on it, so too the value of membership in a state is very largely a result of the labor and investment of the community. The citizenry raises resources through taxation and invests those resources in valuable public goods: basic infrastructure, defense, the establishment and maintenance of an effective market, a system of education, and the like. As with the system of irrigation on John's farm, these are goods that only exist as a result of the labor and investment of community members.

Although it might seem that the examples from which I have generalized (regarding farms, lecturers, and congregations) are too distant from our ordinary experience of political institutions to support conclusions about the latter, I am convinced instead that they help bring out and explain a feature of our ordinary thinking about political communities that has been too often missed in discussions within political theory. We have too often fallen into the trap of assuming *either* that any special obligations that accompany shared citizenship must be justified via similarities in national (or cultural) identity *or* that the relationship between compatriots is not importantly different from the relationship among those not sharing a political community. Instead, the associative ownership view helps explain the connection between citizens and the institutions of their state in a way that does not depend on similarities in national identity.

The intergenerational nature of the political community is classically expressed by Abraham Lincoln in the Gettysburg Address:

> It is for us the living, rather, to be dedicated here to the unfinished work which they who fought here have thus far so nobly advanced. It is ... for us to be here dedicated to the great task remaining before us – that from these honored dead we take increased devotion to that cause for which they gave the last full measure of

devotion – that we here highly resolve that these dead shall not have died in vain – that this nation, under God, shall have a new birth of freedom – and that government of the people, by the people, for the people, shall not perish from the earth. (Lincoln 1863)

By insisting that the living take over the "unfinished work" of the dead and recommit themselves to their joint cause – the endeavor of democratic government – Lincoln insists that the political community is a project that exists across generations. According to this view, perished members have passed on its institutions to current generations as part of a trust to be taken forward to future generations. This, I think, explains what Rawls means when he suggests that the fundamental organizing idea of democratic theory is that of "society as a fair system of cooperation over time, from one generation to the next" (Rawls 1993, 15).

Thus, the associative ownership view is one that we recognize both in everyday discussions (as in the congregation example) and political discourse (as in Lincoln's Gettysburg Address). It is this intergenerational nature of the political community – by which members build, contribute to, and pass on a legacy of political institutions to future members – that can be captured and illuminated by the associative ownership framework. The above examples help show that the intuition underlying the congregation's claim of ownership over its institutions can be extended to states by showing that the admitted disanalogies between states and congregations (the non-voluntary and intergenerational nature of state membership) do not undermine the argument.

It is crucially important that I am *not* saying that ownership claims justify an unlimited discretionary power such that citizens may pass down the benefits of membership in *any* way they choose. In rejecting statism, we have set aside that possibility. Instead, my claim is only that positions that hinge on ignoring the historical process by which state institutions came about and the connection between such institutions and the political community that constructed them (such as open borders views) are necessarily *incomplete*. They unhelpfully abstract from the relationship between state institutions and the concerted collective effort that brought them into existence. In this way, they deny the importance of self-determination.

None of this, however, is meant to suggest that citizens have unlimited prerogative in making decisions regarding future membership. Instead, granting membership to non-owners is sometimes the only way to treat them as equals. Asylum-seekers require membership in order to avoid a dangerous life. Children of illegal immigrants are, through no fault of their own, born into the country, and their life chances depend on the status and treatment granted to them. In both of these cases, the ownership claims of the citizenry pale in comparison to the needs of those petitioning for citizenship. There are clear reasons of justice – reasons that *outweigh* considerations of ownership – to grant such individuals full citizenship (both of these cases will be considered at some length in the chapters that follow).

Similar considerations, albeit even stronger here, explain why – even if a state purported to have been constructed through the contributions of a certain minority group (say, white male property owners) – advocates of the associative ownership position should conclude that the overall balance of reasons weighs strongly in favor of extending citizenship to other groups present in the territory. As in the case of asylum-seekers, it is important that – in our world – the protection of a decent state is a prerequisite (or very nearly so) for a decent life.

Insofar as individuals – through no fault of their own – find themselves living amidst an ongoing scheme of social cooperation, treating them as equals requires that that scheme treat them equally. As we will discuss at more length in chapter 4, the burden of argument for justifying the exclusion of the geographically distant is far lower than it is in the case of those with whom one shares geographical and social space. What is required to treat as an equal an individual who finds herself born into one's scheme of social cooperation that – by and large – distributes all the preconditions for a decent life is different than what is required to treat as an equal an individual who is party to some other scheme of social cooperation that can itself provide the preconditions for a decent life. This is true even if the latter individual would for some reason prefer membership in one's own political community. In the case of the individual born into some other adequate scheme of cooperation, claims of ownership have a strength and relevance that elude them in the other case.

Nevertheless, it is important that although the claims of asylum-seekers or the children of illegal immigrants outweigh the ownership claims of the political community, they do not cast doubt on their existence. Again: to say that the citizenry has an ownership claim over the institutions that it constructs is only to raise *one* relevant consideration. Ownership comes with a range of limits and obligations, and so must be weighed against other considerations. This should come as no surprise. After all, we arrived at the associative ownership view by first recognizing that we needed an account of self-determination that could (in contrast to statism) explain the limited nature of that commitment. Thus, to recognize that there are limits to ownership claims is to reaffirm our rejection of statism; in other words, that our proposed account can be outweighed by other factors is an important virtue of the position.

At this juncture, it is worth addressing two potential objections. First, it might be objected that an account of states' rights to self-determination cannot rest on claims of ownership because the history of states is clouded by injustice in a way that casts doubt on any claims of ownership that they advance. In considering this objection, it is helpful to distinguish between strong and weak versions of it.

The weak version says that all states have been involved in specific injustices that require rectification. The advocate of the associative ownership view is free to accept this claim and simply say: of course, there are particular holdings of states that may be unjust (just as there are particular holdings of individuals that may be unjust), and states may have a responsibility to rectify such injustices. There is significant controversy about which injustices demand rectification and how we should determine the requirements of rectification (Waldron 1992; Simmons 2001a). I want to bracket that dispute here, and simply say that whatever the correct view about how to specify the particular demands of rectification, it should be consistent with the associative ownership approach, for all I have wanted to say is that the associative ownership position suggests that it is possible for a group to have legitimate claims of collective ownership over the institutions they construct. So, the weak version of this objection does not undermine the associative ownership view; rather, it only says – quite rightly – that states do not necessarily have valid entitlement to *everything* they claim. In other words, certain kinds of historical injustices require rectification and, so, impose constraints on the claims that states can legitimately advance.

The strong version of the objection depends on a more sweeping claim, according to which the history of states is *so* ridden with injustice that rectification is hopeless. On this view, *all* claims of states are illegitimate such that any attempt at rectification cannot avoid being hopelessly inadequate. If this sweeping dismissal of historical claims were legitimate, it would – unlike the weak version of the objection – cast doubt on the associative ownership view (by undermining the possibility that states could make legitimate claims). However, I think that – on closer consideration – it is a very difficult position to accept.

This is because our world is without clean slates or immaculate conceptions; as David Schmidtz rightly notes, "we are fated to live in a world of background injustice, all of us descended from both victims and victimizers" (Schmidtz 2006, 209). Although some of these injustices might be particularly vicious or salient in a way that our favored theory of rectification will identify as therefore illegitimate, it is difficult to accept the conclusion that the injustices of the past make it impossible for any person or group to today make legitimate claims of ownership.

This is because discounting all ownership claims advanced by states on account of historical injustice would force us to do away with *all* claims of ownership. Whether advanced by congregations, family farms, lecturers, or states, there are no claims of ownership that are not somehow the result of injustice or stand on the shoulders of injustice. Our history is too unavoidably inundated with injustice for any claim to be purely innocent. However, the rejection of *all* claims of ownership is surely a medicine worse than the symptom. Again, although I do not say that there is never a case for historical rectification of some kind (the specification of which is a separate problem), I do deny that historical injustice somehow delegitimizes (a) all claims of ownership in our world; or (b) all such claims advanced by states.[17] As far as I can see, (a) is unacceptable; and there is no way to justify (b) without also accepting (a). Our task, then, "is to live constructively in a world that we acknowledge is profoundly marred" (Schmidtz 2006, 214). Rather than insisting on the impossible demand that claims have immaculate histories, we can only reasonably judge claims on a continuum: to what extent, we ought to ask, do the particular injustices underlying this claim undermine its legitimacy?[18]

This approach is, I think, consistent with how we normally think about claims of entitlement. Nobody doubts that I have a right to my car, even though there can be no doubt that if we ask enough questions about the history of my money and the corporation's resources, we will uncover some injustice. Did my family, at some stage, make transactions with slaveholders? Did the founder of the car company have resources that were procured as a result of involvement with colonialism? All claims in our world lie on a bed of injustices of this sort.

The worries that arise from these considerations seem quite different than the worries that would arise about my entitlement to the car if it turns out that I had never paid the dealer for it when I drove it off the lot. Again: we need a theory of rectification to explain what it means to have a legitimate

[17] Here, my position is somewhat similar to that of Jeremy Waldron (Waldron 1992). For an opposing view see Simmons 2001b.

[18] Or, as David Copp says in an interesting article, "it is a sad fact that most states were founded in a way that involved wrongful exercises of force and fraud . . . They began by being unjust. Yet unjust or not, they are the ships in which we find ourselves, and we must try to make them just and to make them serve our needs" (Copp 1999, 45).

claim, and I make no effort to present such a theory here. Instead, I just want to insist that although there are surely particular claims made by states that ought to be rejected as a result of identifiable historical injustices, concerns regarding such injustices do not cast doubt on the position as a whole.

Second, it is sometimes thought that any position that attempts to account for the state's right of self-determination via claims of ownership is confused because it is *jurisdiction* rather than property that the state claims over territory and state institutions (Stilz 2009, especially at 189–191).[19] Jurisdiction is the authority to administer a system of property rights; it includes the right to enforce rules, regulate the use of property (as in zoning rules), and adjudicate conflicts. These, and not rights of ownership, are – according to the objection – the kinds of rights that the state claims and that self-determination involves.

Although it is true – as those who object along these lines insist – that the claim of the state that manifests itself in jurisdiction is not an ownership claim that we can understand as a kind of *private* property, it is a mistake to insist that it follows that it is not a kind of ownership claim. Jeremy Waldron explains that

> calling someone the "owner" of a resource conveys no exact information about her rights in relation to that resource: a corporate owner is not the same as an individual owner; the owner of intellectual property has a different array of rights than the owner of an automobile. (Waldron 2004)

Waldron's point here is that to say that one has an ownership claim over a resource is only the beginning of a discussion about the rights one has over it.

We may imagine that if I own a building I may do what I would like with it: I can start a business there, I can invite my friends' children there, or I can tear the building down and replace it with a new one. In fact, though, whether an owner can do these things depends very much on a range of other social and conventional information. I may not be able to start a business there if the area is zoned for residence; I cannot invite my friends' children there if the business I start is a casino in which minors are legally forbidden; and I cannot replace it with a new building if the state has declared the existing building to be an important historical site.

[19] I am grateful to Loren Lomasky for discussion or – more accurately – caustic criticism along these lines.

This is important because it shows that although there are differences between the claims of ownership that underlie private property rights and the jurisdiction of states, this is insufficient reason to conclude that the citizenry's right of self-determination (which manifests in jurisdiction) is not a kind of ownership claim.[20] Incidentally: this is precisely the reason that establishing that the citizenry has a claim of ownership over state institutions is not the end of the discussion in regard to the ethics of immigration policy. We still need to know the shape of that particular ownership claim, and this depends on the strength, shape, and urgency of competing considerations that must also be considered.

Thus, although we cannot rightly understand the state's jurisdiction as a kind of private property (because the bundle of rights included in the claims of ownership that make up private property differs from the bundle of rights that constitute claims of jurisdiction), jurisdiction can nevertheless be seen as a type of *collective* property. In systems of collective property, "the community as a whole determines how important resources are to be used. These determinations are made on the basis of the social interest through mechanisms of collective decision-making" (Waldron 2004). The ownership claim of the citizenry over state institutions justifies an ownership claim in those institutions that is a kind of collective property right and so not equivalent to the claims of ownership that emerge from private property rights – but a claim of ownership nonetheless.

So, the claim is that by jointly constructing state institutions and contributing the resources necessary for their continuing feasibility, the citizenry gains an ownership claim that affords them at least some discretion in making future decisions about how those resources will be used (including specifying to whom the resources will be given in the future). Again: because ownership claims come in an enormous variety of shapes, observing that the state's right of self-determination includes a bundle of rights that is quite different from "ordinary" claims of private property cannot be taken to show that the former are not actually claims of ownership. Instead, the state's right to self-determination is justified by an ownership claim that takes a different shape than the ownership claims that underlie "ordinary" claims of private property.

In sum, the considerations raised in this section – particularly via the *Kidnapped Lecturers* and the *Family Farm* examples – suggest that, unlike accounts based on individual autonomy, the associative ownership

[20] A similar point is made by John Simmons (Simmons 2001b).

justification for self-determination can be extended to states because it is not embarrassed by their non-voluntary and intergenerational nature.

V ASSOCIATIVE OWNERSHIP AND REFLECTIVE EQUILIBRIUM

Grounding self-determination in ownership claims allows us to explain intuitive responses to a wide range of political events. Insofar as "justification is a matter of the mutual support of many considerations, of everything fitting together into one coherent view," this is an advantage of the position (Rawls 1999b, 19). Consider two examples:

1. *Paternalistic invasion*: Country Y announces its intention to invade Country X. Although there is little doubt that the government of Y will better be able to maintain order than X's government (because of a sizable advantage in material resources), we know from polling data that the people of X overwhelmingly prefer their own government. X is also sufficiently just so as to meet minimum conditions of legitimacy. Are there reasons based in self-government to oppose the invasion?
2. *Theft by secession*: Territory A votes to join B, and B subsequently invests substantially in that territory, equipping it with extensive infrastructure from highway systems and educational facilities to airports and environmental cleanup. Having captured the benefits of this union, is A entitled to secede without specific warrant or compensating B for the investments?[21]

Most of us will conclude that (1) there are reasons of self-determination to oppose Y's invasion of X; and (2) A's right to self-determination does not justify their proposed secession (at least not without compensating B). These conclusions, however, are difficult to account for without appealing to some version of the associative ownership view. Notice that rather than arguing for these conclusions in the secession and invasion cases, I simply suggest that *if* one is committed to them, one should also accept the associative ownership view.

Let us begin by considering the case of *paternalistic invasion*. Two prominent analysts explain that

> Claims of self-determination are invariably raised whenever one state invades and occupies another, or a territory belonging to another. Yet it is important to

[21] Similar issues arise in many real-world cases of secession. For example, prior to the US Civil War the North complained that it had just spent considerably upgrading the infrastructure of the South. I use a hypothetical example to focus on the principle at stake and avoid getting distracted by disputed historical claims.

distinguish between the wrongness of military invasion or occupation . . . and the right to self-determination. (Margalit and Raz 1990, 442)

They continue by arguing that the "wrongness of military invasion" is explained by "public-order considerations" which are entirely independent of claims of self-determination (Margalit and Raz 1990, 442). Here, Margalit and Raz claim that the right of non-national groups against invasion has as its primary basis "public-order considerations" rather than claims of self-determination (which, in their view, are the sole right of those groups who share a common cultural identity). The difficulty with such an account is that it cannot explain the intuition that there is something objectionable about paternalistic invasion. Simply put: if the right against military invasion rests solely upon public order considerations, then there can be no objection to invasions that will work to enhance order.

One way of avoiding this conclusion is to suggest that we must account for the precedent set by allowing paternalistic invasion. Along these lines, Allen Buchanan argues that there are public order-based reasons to oppose paternalistic invasions insofar as such opposition "would serve as a deterrent to unjust annexations and would to that extent reinforce the existing international legal restrictions on the aggressive use of force by states" (Buchanan 2004, 356). Although this may be correct, these kinds of pragmatic considerations depend on empirical claims that may or may not obtain and do not explain the full range of our intuitive objection to paternalistic invasion.

Instead, the case of paternalistic invasion offends our commitment to political self-determination (whether or not the invaded territory is controlled by a nationally homogeneous group). As explained by the associative ownership account, one reason that paternalistic invasion is objectionable is that citizens of X, through the contributions they make to the state, become part owners of state institutions and thus have reason to object to attempts to interfere with their control over such institutions.[22] Note that I am not saying that paternalistic invasion could never be all things considered justified; instead, my claim is that even if such an invasion were so justified, there would nevertheless be a loss in terms of self-determination that is not without significance. It is this that is difficult to explain without reference to the associative ownership view.

[22] It is an implication of this claim that failed states cannot resist paternalistic invasion on the grounds of self-determination. I think that this is the correct view, although I will not try to argue for it here.

Second, in regard to *theft by secession*, the associative ownership account offers a principled explanation of the intuition that seceding groups might owe something to the states from which they separate.[23] As we have seen, some argue that claims of self-determination are simply valuable because they promote autonomy. On this view, claims about property are irrelevant; so, for instance, Daniel Philpott insists that "beyond the claim to govern justly a piece of land, groups and governments have no right to call it theirs in any meaningful way" (Philpott 1995, 371n37). This position ignores the investments that a political community makes in a piece of land or accompanying institutions to render it valuable, and the claims of ownership that follow from such investment.

The case of theft by secession makes clear that there are ownership claims at stake in arguments regarding secession, and thus that it is a mistake to follow Philpott in thinking that the only claims a government may have to land follow from justly governing a given territory. Again, neither absolute nor ultimate, such ownership claims obviously do not trump all other considerations. It is a mistake, however, to neglect such claims as one important type of consideration. Thus, the associative ownership account offers a coherent explanation for the intuition that there is something objectionable about the theft by secession case.

By showing that the associative ownership account is capable of explaining intuitive responses to the *paternalistic invasion* and *theft by secession* examples, I hope to have helped affirm its consistency with salient intuitions and, by so doing, increased our confidence in it.

VI AGAINST ENFRANCHISING ALL AFFECTED

By insisting that self-determination is a consequence of ownership and so – within limits – at the discretion of current members, the associative ownership view conflicts with the principle that all those affected by a decision ought to be enfranchised. Because the view that we are obliged to enfranchise all those whose interests are affected by government policy is a prominent alternative to the principle of self-determination, I here attempt to cast doubt on the all-affected view.

[23] David Copp and Allen Buchanan similarly suggest that seceding states may owe compensation to those from whom they separate, but they do not explain why this should be the case (Buchanan 1991; Copp 1997). Something akin to the associative ownership view therefore seems implicit in their positions.

There is a sense in which the idea of enfranchising all affected interests is a natural one. Indeed, it might well seem that this is the principle that lent credence to movements that attempted to ensure that all those taxed would also be represented and movements that extended the franchise to African-Americans and women. This principle also has broad support among democratic theorists. Sometimes the idea that all those whose interests are affected by a policy ought to be enfranchised is taken as uncontroversial. For example, one author complains that even "thoroughly democratic states inevitably exclude currently existing foreigners (and future ones) from domestic decisions, thus ensuring that the interests of these groups will not be given due weight" (Kolers 2009, 77). Such accounts presume the legitimacy of the all-affected view.

Likewise, in considering who ought to be enfranchised, Robert Goodin explains that although political communities are most typically constituted around territoriality, nationality, and history,

> the reason we think that territorial or historical or national groups ought to make decisions together is that, typically if not invariably, the interests of individuals within those groups are affected by the actions and choices of others in that group. Those common reciprocal interests in one another's actions and choices are what makes those groups appropriate units for collective decision making, at least in a rough-and-ready way. (Goodin 2007, 48)

So, according to this view, constituting a demos based on geographical proximity is "only an approximation to constituting it on the basis of what really matters, which is interlinked interests" (Goodin 2007, 49). Thus, according to Goodin, all those whose interests are interlinked such that decisions affect their interests ought to be enfranchised. Here, Goodin's claim is essentially that the principle of self-determination does not have independent grounds of support, but instead serves as a kind of proxy for the claim that all those affected by government ought to be enfranchised by it.

Despite the appeal of the all-affected view, it has long been recognized that it faces important difficulties. In a well-known essay, Frederick Whelan explains that

> before a democratic decision could be made on a particular issue (by those affected), a prior decision would have to be made, in each case, as to *who* is affected and therefore entitled to vote on the substantive issue ... In many cases of political decision-making, moreover, the question of who is affected by a given law or policy depends on *which* law or policy is enacted from among the available alternatives ... Thus to say that those who will be affected by a given decision are the ones who

should participate in making it is . . . to propose what is a logical as well as a procedural impossibility. (Whelan 1983, 19)

In other words: one cannot know who is affected by a decision until the decision is made, but the outcome of the decision depends on who votes on it, which, in turn, is to depend on who is affected. As Robert Goodin notes:

It is incoherent to try to determine who should get to vote by asking whose interests are actually affected by the course of action actually decided upon. It is like the winning lottery ticket being pulled out of the hat by whomever has won that selfsame lottery.[24] (Goodin 2007, 53)

We seem stuck, then, in a vicious circle for, as Whelan notes, this line of criticism establishes the logical – *not just practical* – incoherence of the principle.[25] I would like now to set aside this incoherence and focus on the larger issue: namely, is it in fact the case that we ought to – so far as possible – seek to enfranchise all those affected by a policy?

Despite the prominence of this view in democratic theory, it is quite at odds with ordinary views regarding who ought to have a say in decisions. For instance, if a corporation seeks a new CEO, it has an election among stockholders (or their representatives) to determine who should hold that position. There is not normally thought to be a question of enfranchising all individuals whose interests are affected. We do not, for example, typically think that family members of the various candidates ought to be enfranchised, even though the decision obviously promises to affect them.[26]

[24] In response to the incoherence, Goodin argues that the only way to safely institutionalize the all-affected principle is to "give a say to anyone who might possibly be affected by any possible decision arising out of any possible agenda" (Goodin 2007, 55). This means that "virtually (maybe literally) everyone in the world – and indeed everyone in all possible future worlds – should be entitled to vote on any proposal or any proposal for proposals" (Goodin 2007, 55). His point is that the only way to ensure that everyone affected by a set of policies is enfranchised is to enfranchise everyone, everywhere, present and future. This view does away with self-determination in anything like the typical sense. This is because the expansiveness argument gives all a right to participate. Gone, then, is the idea of a distinct political community stretching across history and collectively making decisions about its own trajectory.

[25] Objections to the all-affected view are often made in terms of the impracticability of the principle (see, for example, Gould 2004, 176). Although such concerns are understandably widespread, I want to focus on whether or not the all-affected view is correct *in principle*. This is important because those who criticize the principle for being impracticable ought to look for the best way of approximating the principle (as Goodin does), whereas I shall argue that, because it is the wrong principle, we ought not to concern ourselves with finding practicable proxies for it.

[26] And this is to say nothing of the expansive nature of the principle. After all, any individual at all *could* be hired. Should everyone be enfranchised?

Instead, being affected by a policy is clearly not sufficient grounds for enfranchisement if the effect is the normal (even if harmful) result of fair interaction. Consider the following case:

> I open a bakery down the street from one that you have been running for years. Because my cakes are much tastier than yours, the presence of my bakery has significant negative effects on your well-being.

We do not want to say that in such a case you are to have a say over whether I can operate a bakery in this neighborhood, or whether I can serve such delicious cakes. Instead, some effects are the simple and unobjectionable result of sharing a social world. There are analogues in public life:

> Imagine that Japanese companies come to dominate the US automobile market, and this is accomplished without unfair practices. Here, increased competition forces American firms to eliminate inefficiencies and, ultimately, lay off American workers.

The advocate of the all-affected view insists that we ought to give citizens of the United States a vote in Japanese elections. After all, US citizens will be affected by the outcome of Japanese elections and subsequent decisions regarding economic policy. But, again: insofar as the effects are simply the result of legitimate competition, they simply follow from sharing a social/economic world with others and demand no recompense (enfranchisement or otherwise). The United States might enact job-training programs for the laid-off workers or assist them via unemployment programs (just as you might search for a way to make a tastier cake), but there is no injustice requiring remedy via enfranchisement.

Moreover, even in cases in which one's actions impose effects on others that *are* unfair, we typically respond by suggesting that the unfairness be stopped and the harmed agents be compensated, and *not* by saying that all affected individuals be enfranchised. Consider the following amended example:

> It is discovered that the success of my bakery is not the result of my superior cakes (as I had thought), but instead an employee of mine spread false rumors about the indecent sanitary conditions of your store. These allegations have a significant negative effect on your sales. When I am made aware of what has occurred, I have an obligation to settle the debt. I should dismiss the employee and compensate you for lost sales and reputation. What I do *not* owe you is an ownership stake (or a vote) in the future decisions of my company.

This shows that although there is a duty to interact respectfully with outsiders, it does not require enfranchising all those affected by one's decisions (even when those effects are substantial in size, negative, or unfair).

Once again, there are public analogues to this case. For instance:

> Many developed countries subsidize their agricultural industries in a way that allegedly dampens the life prospects of competitor farmers in the developing world.

Although advocates of the all-affected view will insist that we enfranchise West African farmers in the elections of the United States and the EU, the typical response is instead that the developed countries simply stop interacting unfairly with the developing world and compensate those harmed for past damages.

I suspect that what explains our intuitions in these public analogues is the commitment to seeing political society as an ongoing scheme of social cooperation among citizens. Understanding political community as this kind of ongoing relationship helps explain why simply being affected by the decisions of a political community is not sufficient to give one standing in that community (even if, as in the case of agricultural subsidies, one may rightfully object to having certain kinds of effects imposed).

These examples suggest that we do not typically think that being affected by a policy is a sufficient condition to have a claim to enfranchisement. Instead, we ordinarily suppose that citizens have a *prima facie*, albeit constrained, right to make their own decisions about policies (including future membership). It is therefore a mistake to think that it is the all-affected principle that is "being implicitly employed in judging all those other methods [territoriality, nationality, history, etc.] of constituting the demos" (Goodin 2007, 49). It is important that the idea that the all-affected principle is implicitly employed is the only justification Goodin gives for it; thus, showing – as the above examples do – that it is not in fact ordinarily used as an implicit measure of the legitimacy of institutions is enough to undermine the position. Throughout I shall try to show why the associative ownership view is both more defensible and more consistent with ordinary intuitions about political morality than is the all-affected view.

VII CONCLUSION

The idea that states enjoy a right to self-determination is a basic organizing principle of contemporary international politics. However, as we saw in investigating defenses of that principle grounded in individual autonomy, it is surprisingly difficult to justify such a principle. Without such a defense it is unclear why, to what extent, or in what circumstances (if any) we ought to accept claims based upon self-determination. In this chapter, I have argued that one way of justifying the right of political communities to self-determination hinges on the claim that they – as a result of their contributions – have an ownership claim over the institutions at stake in the relevant decisions. This position provides an important basis from which to think about debates regarding justice and immigration.

It does this by justifying the claim that citizens stand in a special relationship to the institutions of their state and providing a coherent explication of the idea of "society as a fair system of cooperation over time, from one generation to the next" (Rawls 1993, 15).[27] In what follows, I shall argue that states have claims of ownership over institutions and territory that are an important, though oft neglected, consideration in arguments regarding the ethics of immigration. I will attempt to demonstrate that this account casts doubt on the open borders position and provides us a framework from which we can consider controversial policy questions. For now, though, the important points are that (a) the efforts and contributions of citizens may give them a claim of ownership over state institutions that justifies a limited right of self-determination; and (b) this right of self-determination is an important consideration in arguments regarding the proper shape of immigration policy.

[27] Because Rawls is interested in public reason between citizens, he need not provide an explanation of what justifies our seeing society in these terms. However, once we turn to questions that require providing justification to non-citizens, some basis must be given for understanding society in this way. The associative ownership view is one way of justifying this starting-point. Once we recognize society as an ongoing scheme of cooperation, it does not but make sense to see the benefits of such cooperation as – at least in some sense – owned by those party to that cooperation.

CHAPTER 3

Refining associative ownership

In this chapter, I continue to refine the associative ownership position in order to further explain how it can helpfully frame our thinking about debates regarding immigration by answering a number of potential objections to the position. Recall that according to the associative ownership view, the state is an association stretching through time, whose members – through their contributions – fulfill important needs and provide necessary goods for one another. Goods provided through associational relationships include protection from internal and external threats, risk-protection schemes (such as public healthcare or pension programs), and programs facilitating the achievements of members (such as publicly supported higher education programs).

Such goods only exist through the coordinated decisions, labor, and contributions of members. Given this, members may come, through their efforts, to have an entitlement to the accomplishments and misdeeds of the community.[1] If this is plausible, members of the community are in a position to legitimately deny membership to some outsiders because this entitlement amounts to a *prima facie* privilege to do with it, within boundaries, what they wish. This, as we saw, is one way (perhaps there are others)

[1] In *A Theory of Justice*, John Rawls offers an account of the value of collective political life that is connected to the associative ownership view. Rawls argues that

> because such a society is a social union of social unions, it realizes to a preeminent degree the various forms of human activity; and given the social nature of humankind, the fact that our potentialities and inclinations far surpass what can be expressed in any one life, we depend upon the cooperative endeavors of others not only for the means of well-being but to bring to fruition our latent powers. And with a certain success all around, each enjoys the greater richness and diversity of the collective activity. (Rawls 1999b, 571)

Rawls's view is that the shared contributions of citizens to a framework of publicly provided goods gives each a legitimate stake in the success of their compatriots. In this way, each of us accomplishes more and lives more broadly than any of us could on our own. The idea that "we depend upon the cooperative endeavors of others . . . to bring to fruition our latent powers" is an implicit expression of the associative ownership view, for it holds that contributions to a set of publicly provided goods provide citizens with a kind of claim over the consequent results.

of justifying the quotidian claim to self-determination. On this view, political communities have a rightful claim to selecting their path forward because they have claims of ownership over the goods at stake. Rather than seeing the goods at stake in arguments about immigration – as most of the literature on the ethics of immigration implicitly does – as goods over which nobody has strong claims, we should instead recognize them as goods created and passed down through an intergenerational political community.

Having criticized the statist approach in the previous chapter, I turn here to the further development and defense of this associative ownership position. In particular, I seek to explicate the position by defending it from four important lines of potential objection. According to these objections, even if the associative ownership view can justify the citizenry's claims of ownership over some types of institutions it cannot

- justify the territorial rights claimed by states (section I);
- explain why states rather than political subunits (such as counties and provinces) do not have the right to control immigration (section II);
- explain the intuition that it would be unjust for citizens to exclude from citizenship a minority group that was born in the country, but disliked by the citizenry (section III); and
- distinguish itself from a prominent position according to which the specially coercive nature of state institutions calls forth a special moral relationship between fellow citizens (section IV).

This chapter seeks to defend the associative ownership view from each of these objections.

I ASSOCIATIVE OWNERSHIP AND TERRITORIAL GOODS

It might seem that the line of argument on which the associative ownership argument is based is plausible in regard to membership benefits but not those benefits connected to territorial access. There is, after all, a clear sense in which citizens contribute to and build membership institutions (such as public pension programs, systems of public education, or institutions for the provision of healthcare). The question, though, is whether this line of argument can *also* justify excluding non-members from a state's territory. After all, rather than being constructed through the efforts of citizens, the territory was there long before the political association.

The difficulty is that restrictions on territorial access appear to conflict with Becker's third criterion for claiming ownership: namely, that the "product is something which others lose nothing by being excluded from." When a non-citizen is excluded from Social Security, one may respond by insisting that because the institution would not exist without the contributions of citizens, foreigners are left in exactly the same position they would have otherwise been in.[2] This line of response is not, however, available as a way of justifying territorial exclusions, for prior to the construction of the state individuals had the right to move freely across the lines that now separate political communities. Even, then, if political associations have a right – grounded by entitlement claims – over political institutions, it remains unclear how this line of argument can justify territorial exclusion. So, the question is whether the associative ownership argument can establish the territorial rights claimed by states. In this section, I attempt to explain how the argument presented in chapter 2 can be supplemented in order to justify territorial restrictions.[3]

It is important that, in typical cases, the main value of territorial access results from the labor of the citizenry in providing a set of mutually beneficial goods which render productive life possible. Although this is clearly not true in all cases (think, for example, of the reasons people have for migrating to Israel), in the US case it seems to be broadly (though not without exception) true. Again this set of publicly provided goods includes internal order, defense, basic systems of criminal and property law, transportation and communication infrastructure, and public health measures (such as vaccinations and medical regulations), among others. Without the system of social cooperation instituted by citizens, there can – as Hobbes famously insists – be

> no place for Industry; because the fruit thereof is uncertain: and consequently no Culture of the Earth; no . . . commodious Building . . . no Arts; no Letters; no Society; and which is worst of all, continuall feare, and danger of violent death; And the life of man, solitary, poore, nasty, brutish, and short. (Hobbes 1985, chapter 13)

Here, Hobbes's point is that it is the system of institutions created by the commonwealth that, by making possible productive activity, gives value to

[2] It might be further insisted that while exclusion from state benefits does not harm outsiders in any absolute sense, it does do harm in a relative sense (by placing non-members or members of less successful associations at a relative disadvantage). Such exclusion would then be Pareto superior but not acceptable to all. Candidly, I do not think that there is an entirely satisfactory response to this issue available, at least not one that would not open up quite substantial philosophical questions of its own. One potential line of response that could be explored involves, following Rawls, insisting that allowing principles of justice to foreclose the possibility of gains that bring forth relative disadvantage is "collectively disadvantageous" (Rawls 1999b, 124). It would not, in other words, be accepted from the appropriate *ex ante* vantage point. On this view, one could not reasonably reject principles *just* because they leave one at a relative disadvantage. While I believe that a response along these lines is plausible, I will not attempt to settle the issue.

[3] My position here is structurally similar to that put forth by John Simmons (Simmons 2001b).

territorial access. Although, again, we can recognize that there are exceptions, it is very largely true that the receiving countries are desirable destinations precisely because of the successful system of social cooperation constructed there.

At least in this instance, we can accurately say – with Locke – that it is "*Labour* indeed that *puts the difference of value* on" the goods in question (Locke 1988, 296). It is the system of goods, provided by the citizenry, that has made the economic advances and innovations in the time since Hobbes and Locke lived possible. Indeed, it is largely the publicly provided goods – including a well-functioning market and a well-developed infrastructure – that give land its value in the eyes of foreigners. It is the labor of the political community in developing this system of goods that "pulls" immigrants to it.

In creating this system of publicly provided goods, the citizenry (consistent with Becker's explanation) has produced something that otherwise would not have existed and does not leave those excluded any worse off than they would have been in the absence of their productive efforts. In this way, the basic labor argument that I called upon to demonstrate that the citizenry has legitimate claims of entitlement to publicly provided goods might be thought to show as well that the citizenry has legitimate claims of entitlement to the territory.

This direct extension of the associative ownership argument would, however, be too quick, for it would be vulnerable to an important objection. In particular, it is open to the potential migrant to insist that:

> While it is of course true that the political association provides goods that contribute value to territorial access, this does not show that the state may rightfully block non-citizens from entering the territory. Citizens have a right to the goods they have produced, but not to the territory that long predates such goods. So, in providing such goods, the state may either figure out a way to provide such goods in an excludable fashion[4] or accept that others present in the territory may free-ride on their contributions.[5] In neither case, however, can the citizenry's ownership of a system of publicly provided goods justify the *territorial* exclusion of potential migrants. In other words, it is unclear how contributing to the value of territorial access justifies blocking non-members access to the territory.

[4] Just as wireless internet providers in public places (such as airports) often encrypt access, political associations can figure out ways to limit access to the goods that they provide. Toll roads are one example of states doing this.

[5] We would not say that a preciously cute toddler stumbling across a sidewalk has territorial rights to her surroundings even if observing her brings great value to the location.

The objection demands that the proponent of the associative ownership view more precisely explain the connection between the creation of a valuable system of public goods and the claimed right to control access to territory.

Underlying the criticism is the strong claim that states *cannot* have territorial rights (since they cannot be responsible for the existence of the territory). That this claim cannot be correct is suggested by the following example. Imagine that:

> There is a stateless world, and a group of farmers who share a contiguous territory have worked out an arrangement by which they respect each other's claims to property. This allows them to tend their fields in peace.

Assume for the sake of argument (we can relax the assumptions later) that nobody had any previous claim to the land claimed by the farmers and nobody else lives in the general territory. Now, imagine that a band of pirates from a distant land arrives and begins to pester the farmers, taking some of their hard-earned produce. In response:

> The farmers unanimously decide to form a system to provide for their defense. A few of them sell their farms to the others who, in turn, agree to support these former farmers' full-time efforts at protecting the group from the attacks of the pirates. Over time the efforts at providing collective security grow into a much more expansive network of activities aimed at advancing the interests of the farmers. In addition to defense, the group protects one another from fraudulent activities of other members, they train younger generations, they provide for the health of elderly farmers, and the like.

It seems to me that there can be little doubt that this idyllic group of farmers has a legitimate claim to its land. There is no reason to think, as per the objection, that the farmers are obliged to render territorial access free. Although they certainly have duties of rescue to outsiders (just as they did prior to forming the union), it seems clear that the farmers have a legitimate claim to the land. Not only did they create the benefits that accompany living upon it, but *also* territorial control is a necessary precondition of continuing to provide such benefits (because it is needed in order to make possible their continued efforts at providing security, public health, protection from fraud, discouraging free-riders, and the like).

In the face of this argument, there are, I think, three ways to press the view that states do not have the right to control their territory. The first hinges on the claim that individuals have very strong rights of free movement that render any such restrictions unjust. The second is the claim that considerations of distributive justice require the elimination of restrictions on movement. I will consider (and reject) these two arguments in the chapters that follow. The third way to respond is to suggest that although the farmers in our example have a right to exclude outsiders from their land, such a right does not extend to real states. According to this view, the differences between the farmers and real world situations are significant.

As I see it, there are two important dissimilarities between the state in the example and the states we are familiar with. The first is that existing states are not fully consensual in the way that the state in the example is. Instead, existing states typically claim authority over all present in the territory *regardless* of the consent of those individuals. Second, the history of existing states is – as I noted above – mired in a history of injustices not present in our example. So, the question is whether or not these dissimilarities call into question the territorial rights of existing states. Let us consider each in turn.

Clearly, states are not fully consensual organizations. Typically, citizens are born into a particular state and do not consent to its authority. Instead, they simply find that the state insists that it has legitimate power over them, like it or not. Although this is a clear dissimilarity with our example, I do not think that it casts doubt on the claims of ownership in the case. Instead, as explained in the case of the kidnapped lecturers, this fact might point to an injustice between the state and the individuals over whom it claims authority, but it is hard to see how it could cast doubt on the claims of ownership citizens have vis-à-vis outsiders. In other words, if the question was whether or not a citizen has the right to disobey the government, it is surely a relevant fact that the government imposed its will on the citizen without securing the consent of the citizen. However, it is not at all clear why the non-consensual nature of the citizen–state relationship would be thought to call into question the rights citizens hold against *outsiders*. After all, it remains the case that citizens are responsible for public institutions in a way that is not true of foreigners.

The second dissimilarity – the fact that states come to hold their territory as a result of a series of injustices – is more clearly relevant. After all, if it was the case that the pirates kept coming by because the farmers had previously displaced them from the land in question, we would surely rethink our claim that the farmers could legitimately restrict the access of the pirates to the land. Again, I do not want to deny the importance of considerations of historical injustice. Surely, it is the case that particular historical injustices of this kind must be considered when we consider the legitimacy of restrictions on immigration.

However, as I remarked above, it cannot be the case that *any* injustice in the history of a group's interactions undermines *all* future claims they put forth. Instead:

> Where persons have (relatively) innocently acquired or (relatively) exclusively used land that has been (relatively) freely subjected to state jurisdiction – we tend to be *least* skeptical about states' claims to territorial sovereignty and *most* skeptical about rival claims to that territory. Where territories have been forcibly subjected, where "unimproved" lands have been claimed without use, or where claimed territories have been the subject of rival use or ownership claims, for instance, we tend to be most skeptical about states' claims. (Simmons 2001b, 322)

Claims are – as Simmons insists – *more* illegitimate the more their history is tainted by relevant past injustices. For these reasons, I do not find convincing the view that states *cannot* claim territorial rights. Although the legitimacy of the particular territorial claims lodged by existing states can certainly be doubted, the idea that states may rightfully control territory as a result of the scheme of cooperation that its members have built up around it is difficult to doubt.

Our objector might finally respond by insisting that different plots of territory carry with them different natural resources, and these resources have important value that ought to be shared across humanity instead of being hoarded by the citizens lucky enough to find themselves on such territory. After all, these *natural* resources – once again – existed prior to the state. Although this is true, it is important that there are two plausible ways of sharing the *value* of (mere) territorial access without providing access more broadly.

First, we can maintain access to all those who seek it for reasons fundamentally connected to the territory rather than publicly provided goods. This includes those for whom the territory itself has a sacred importance. It will also include travelers who want to see a feature of the Earth (such as hikers who want to see the Grand Canyon or rock climbers who want to scale the walls of Yosemite).[6] Many such individuals may travel rather than migrate in order to fulfill their interests. Further, even here one sees how little value territorial access has without the associated publicly provided goods. The wonders of nature that people travel to see are accessible largely because of the coordinated labor and contributions of the political community in developing the infrastructure needed to preserve and access parks and wilderness areas.

The issue that arises is that citizens have no good reason to exclude those who seek mere territorial access (such as the hikers eager to see the Grand Canyon or the climbers gearing up to face Yosemite's big walls), but they

[6] As will become clear below, I want to remain neutral on questions related to the ownership of natural resources or how their value is to be shared.

do have reason to block those immigrants (the vast majority) who seek territorial access as a way to gain access to a set of public goods to which they are not entitled.[7] The state, then, is obligated to make a good faith effort to admit those who seek territorial access just for the sake of territorial access, but this obligation ought not to be construed in a way that forces it to admit all those who seek access to the citizenry's package of public goods under the pretense of mere territorial access. To deny political communities this kind of leeway would jeopardize associative ownership.

Second, there are ways to share the *value* of differential access to natural resources without *also* giving territorial access to all who would claim it in order to capture a stake in the publicly provided goods of the political community. For example, Thomas Pogge advocates a tax on the consumption of natural resources that would share the value of territorial access without giving access to non-excludable publicly provided goods to all who could get their hands on them (Pogge 2002). Such possibilities are important because they hold the promise of allowing citizens territorial control (and the control over systems of publicly provided goods that comes along with it) even while sharing the *value* of natural resources.

Whether or not participation in such a scheme is a *necessary* prerequisite for the legitimate restriction of immigration depends upon whether or not it is correct to say that the Earth's resources are collectively owned by all. Because I think there are plausible alternatives to collective ownership (including, for example, the claim that the Earth's resources are owned by nobody until they are claimed either through laboring on them or somehow making them an important element of one's life), I do not commit myself to the claim that sharing the value of natural resources is a necessary prerequisite for legitimate restrictions on immigration. Instead, I want only to say that *even if* it is correct that natural resources are collectively owned, it still would not follow that immigration restrictions would necessarily be illegitimate.

In sum, the general line of argument that I have advocated is that as long as the value of entrance to the territory hinges on the goods that, as a result of the processes of social cooperation, become connected to that territory, it is a mistake to suggest that all have a right to access. Instead, because those goods only exist through the coordinated efforts of the citizenry, the political community has a legitimate claim to controlling the shape of access to them.

[7] Again, this formulation is not meant to exclude those with legitimate claims of asylum, who indeed have a legitimate claim to the system of public goods (though a claim of a different *type* than do citizens).

II ASSOCIATIVE OWNERSHIP AND POLITICAL SUBUNITS

I have now argued that political associations have claims of ownership over political institutions that operate as at least one kind of reason to restrict immigration. This line of argument naturally leads to questions about smaller associations. After all, it is not only at the national level that citizens come together, contribute to, and construct shared political institutions. The same can be said of citizens of Missouri or Los Angeles or the neighborhood in which you reside. As Joseph Carens remarks:

> In the United States as in many federal systems, sub-units bear much of the responsibility for social policy and they differ greatly in the ways they carry out these responsibilities. For example, Wisconsin's welfare policies are much more generous (or much less stingy) than those of the neighboring state of Illinois ... Should Wisconsin have the right to keep out people from Illinois? (Carens 1992, 42; also see Lomasky 2001, 73–74)

If the associative ownership argument provides citizens of the United States with reason to block immigration, does it not also provide members of these subgroups reason to block immigration? Can the citizens of California (or even just Los Angeles) – pointing to the set of goods (from public schools to roads and sewer systems) they provide – likewise legitimately restrict migration?

According to the associative ownership view, the answer is both yes and no. The citizens of California are inextricably linked to the citizens of the rest of the United States because of the contributions those individuals make to the set of public goods enjoyed in California. Citizens of California enjoy the benefits of national spending on defense, social security, the highway system, public education, and the like. So long as California remains integrated into the union via these programs, they cannot legitimately restrict the movement of non-Californian citizens into the state. After all, these other individuals paid their share of the improvement costs; that is, they also helped fund those programs that give California its value. That is the "no" part of the answer.

As I noted, though, the objection is not entirely without merit. If citizens of California want to block movement – and justify their doing so by appeal to the associative ownership argument – they may disassociate themselves from the larger political community. They can reject – and make clear that they are rejecting – the contributions of the larger federated community. They can inform the larger political community that they are no longer interested in shared association and reject contributions to shared goods, from defense to highway funds. In other words, the associative ownership argument does allow California, and even Los Angeles, to block movement – but only at the cost of secession. That this result coheres with, and indeed helps explain, a quotidian element of political morality (that control over migration would only come with secession) is perhaps one more point in its favor.[8]

At this juncture, it might seem that I have circumvented the original objection (the idea that if the associative ownership argument provides reason to restrict immigration, it must do so also at smaller levels of government), but only at the cost of becoming vulnerable to a related objection. In particular, if it is the case that the citizens of Los Angeles would have to reject the goods and contributions of the larger political communities in order for the associative ownership argument for restricting immigration to apply, then does the United States have to disassociate itself entirely with larger political communities and the goods they jointly provide in order for this argument to apply at the national level?

After all, the United States is party to a number of larger political communities that likewise jointly provide a variety of goods. The list includes, but is certainly not limited to, the UN, the WTO, NAFTA, and NATO. Members of these associations jointly contribute to and provide a variety of goods over which members may then rightly make a claim of ownership. Do all members of the UN, then, have a right to migrate to the United States so long as the two remain associated? Does the United States have to disassociate itself from these organizations in order to rightfully exercise control over migration?

I do not think that the associative ownership extends in this way, for two reasons. First, recall that crucial to the associative ownership argument was that the value of migrating to the territory was in very large part the result of the goods provided by the political community. The density of the goods provided by the federal government gives the value to residence in the territory. The same is not true, at least not to nearly the same extent, for goods provided by groups such as the UN, NAFTA, NATO, and the WTO. While the goods provided by the federal government (from national defense and basic public health/sanitation to basic infrastructure and protection of property rights) can be seen as crucial to any decent life, the same does not

[8] This line of argument obviously raises difficult questions related to the ethics of secession. For example, even if Missouri elects to secede it will continue to be provided with many of the benefits of association because of the non-excludable nature of the benefits and its location. Because they would take me too far afield, I cannot take up such issues. For the classic treatment, see Buchanan 2004.

seem to be true of the above associations which – instead – generally provide goods that improve life on the margins (protection against tariffs rising too high, etc.) (Sangiovanni 2007).

Evidence that this is true can be gleaned from the size of these associations. While – once again – the US federal government has an annual budget of nearly $3 trillion, the UN spends just over $4 billion. By way of comparison, this is about 20 percent of NASA's annual budget for space and a tenth of what is spent by the federal government's Department of Veterans Affairs. Thus, comparing the federal government – and the goods that it is able to provide – to associations such as the UN is misleading.

The second reason to resist the extension of the associative ownership argument to international associations is historical. In particular, the agreement that constitutes the union between states delegates the authority over migration to the federal government (Article 1, Section 8 of the US Constitution). Individual states gave up such privileges in order to be a part of the union; again, they may reclaim such privileges, but only by quitting the union. Likewise, if the United States *wished* to forfeit control over migration policy to an institution at an international level it would be free to do so (as members of the EU have partially done). In the absence of such an agreement, however, I see no reason to think that the goods provided through the contributions of international institutions provide dispositive reason for contributors to, say, the UN to have free access to the United States.

The crucial point for now is that it is a mistake to think that the associative ownership argument justifies the restriction of movement by political communities within the United States. While they are – in principle – entitled to restrict immigration, claiming this prerogative would require secession since (a) this is part of what they forfeited in order to join the union; and (b) otherwise they would be taking unfair advantage of the critical contributions their compatriots make in providing goods that are crucial to the value of residing in these smaller territories.

III WHOM CAN OWNERS EXCLUDE?

It is sometimes thought that if we see state institutions as, at least in some sense, the property of those citizens who have contributed to their construction, then it must follow that citizens are entitled to unilaterally exclude those born in the territory whom they dislike. The worry, in other words, is that if claims of ownership sometimes provide sufficient reason to refuse citizenship to those who would like to enter the state, then they must also provide sufficient reason to exclude groups newly born into the territory of the country who – for whatever reason – are disliked by the current citizenry.[9] Like outsiders, newborns cannot have contributed to the association in the relevant way.

In thinking about this question, it may be helpful to consider a couple of examples. First, imagine that:

> The Ku Klux Klan puts forth legislation according to which the benefits of citizenship would not be shared with black children. Advocates reason that state institutions are owned by the citizenry and the citizenry can, as a result, distribute the accompanying benefits as they like. In the associative ownership view, are there grounds for opposing it?

The example suggests that if the associative ownership argument is powerful enough to provide reason to exclude foreigners who would like to join the country, it must also be powerful enough to exclude those born within the territory of the country who are – for whatever reason – disliked by the current citizenry. In other words, the example suggests that embracing the associative ownership view risks making one complicit (albeit perhaps unhappily) in the plans of racists, misogynists, and the like.

There is, I think, one easy response to this line of argument. Although, for reasons that I shall explain, I do not ultimately find this response entirely satisfactory, I do think that it bears some weight and so is worth considering. In particular, such restrictions would fail to respect current black citizens, who are part-owners themselves. Likewise: if I were among a minority of Jewish students at my university and it declared that it would no longer accept Jewish applicants, I could rightly complain that this decision disrespects my status as a full member of the university community. Or, along the same lines, if my congregation elects to no longer admit white members, there is a clear sense in which this decision undermines my status as an equal partner in the association.

For the same reason, I think that it is true that this type of legislation is objectionable because of the sense in which it disrespects current black citizens. Indeed, I think that – on any reasonable judgment – our concern with this disrespect ought to outweigh the reason we have to respect the ownership claims of the citizenry. This kind of argument for limitations on ownership claims is familiar; for instance, we typically judge the disrespect involved in closing one's restaurant to minority groups to outweigh the prerogative one has as a result of owning the restaurant. Although, as I said, I think that this is an important concern, I also think that it is inadequate.

9 I am grateful to Mat Coakley, Loren Lomasky, and Annie Stilz for pointedly raising this issue.

This is because what seems *centrally* objectionable about the legislation is not the way that it disrespects current black citizens (although this is important), but the way in which it disrespects those black children who are born – through no fault of their own – into a political community that rejects them. They innocently find themselves living in a system of social cooperation that both plays a central role in their life chances and refuses to recognize them as members of the political community. We can get at this by slightly amending the example.

> Perhaps as a result of a genetic mutation, it is suddenly the case that a small minority of children is born with bright purple skin. These children, of which there were none in previous generations, are disliked by all (including their parents) and the citizenry votes not to share the benefits of citizenry (which are, after all, the property of the citizenry) with purples. Is the citizenry, on the associative ownership account, entitled to do so?

Obviously, this is quite a bizarre example, and I understand that the use of such examples can sometimes mislead. Here, however, it is useful to have recourse to this type of example in order to block responses – such as the one above – that do not seem to strike at the heart of the matter. The previous response cannot explain objections to this legislation. After all, there are no purples who are already part of the citizenry. Nevertheless, there is – for advocates of the associative ownership position – an available and more basic response that can address even this example.

Again, it is crucial that although I advocate the associative ownership position, it is *not* my position that claims of ownership exhaust the terrain of justice. My point is instead that claims of ownership are one important consideration in disputes about justice and that the citizenry's claim to the institutions it builds, though oft ignored, is at least one relevant consideration in disputes about immigration (and much else in international affairs). However, in the case of the purples, I think that the only reasonable conclusion is that the claims of ownership are dwarfed in importance by the interest these children have in being accepted as full members of the political community.

This is particularly important here because such individuals find themselves – through no choice of their own – enmeshed within a system of social cooperation (and protection) that importantly influences – and to a large extent *determines* – their life chances. Although much the same is at least roughly true of some immigrants (in particular, asylum-seekers and the children of illegal immigrants), the same is *not* true of potential immigrants more generally (who do not find themselves unavoidably enmeshed in an ongoing system of social cooperation in which membership is critical for access to an enormous range of other important goods). Because of the relationship to the system of social cooperation in which purples already stand, there is important reason – reason that (a) outweighs the reasons of ownership that citizens can invoke in trying to reject purples; and (b) distinguishes the case of purples from ordinary potential migrants – to insist that such individuals are only treated as equals if they are given membership in the system of social cooperation.

Unlike in the case of many ordinary potential migrants, it is simply not an option to treat purples as equals by leaving them alone and asking, in turn, to be left alone. Instead, because they find themselves already enmeshed within the scheme of social cooperation, the only available way to treat them as equals is to afford them equal standing in the society (regardless of their lack of an ownership claim to it).

It is very important that in saying this we are not abandoning the associative ownership position. Instead, we are only saying – as we said when we rejected statism – that claims of self-determination come with important limits. To say that citizens have claims of ownership over state institutions is *not* to say that such claims are absolute or that they cannot be outweighed by the claims of outsiders. It is considerations of this kind – and not the disrespect paid to members of minority communities among the citizenry – that best explain the conviction that there is an injustice in excluding disliked minorities from citizenship. Later, I shall argue that similar considerations weigh in favor of granting citizenship to those children of illegal immigrants who are substantially raised in the United States through no choice of their own.

IV COMPATRIOTS AND STATE COERCION

A prominent view in the literature on global justice holds that justice is a relational view that is called forth by the particularly coercive relationship of those who share a state. Because such *coercion-based views* have implications that are in some sense similar to those of the associative ownership view (both of which are, in a broad sense, descendents of the social contract tradition), I would like – in this section – to explain why I reject such views.

According to the coercion-based account, what is important or distinctive about our relationship with compatriots is that we share a particular status vis-à-vis the coercive power of the state. However significantly our personal projects, income, or interests might differ, we are all ultimately subject – without our consent – to the coercive power of the state. The fact that we are in a coercive relationship with compatriots allegedly pushes us into a special moral relationship with them that we do not share with all individuals. Along these lines, Michael Blake contends that the state

> stands in prima facie conflict with the liberal principle of autonomy. Since we cannot eliminate the state . . . A liberal theory that begins with a concern for autonomy may properly develop a concern for relative deprivation as a way of justifying state coercion. (Blake 2001, 282)

On this view, the relationship shared with compatriots – because of its coercive nature – generates a different and more demanding context of justification than does the relationship shared with potential immigrants. The idea that the relationship we share with compatriots vis-à-vis the coercive power of the state justifies a special concern with justice among compatriots is widespread (Blake 2001; Miller 1998; and Nagel 2005).

The coercion-based view thus hinges on traditional liberal anxiety surrounding coercion. In what follows, I argue (1) that this coercion-based view depends on a kind of fetishization of coercion that leads its proponents to mislocate the grounds of justice (section A); and (2) even if we accept state coercion as the relevant grounds of justice, its scope still is not confined to individual states (section B).[10] As a result, I conclude that although this position has implications that are similar in some respects to those that follow from the associative ownership view, it rests on weaker grounds.

A *The relevance of political coercion*

In order to assess the legitimacy of the view, we must understand why coercion is thought to require justification. Coercive acts, as Onora O'Neill explains, necessarily entail "propositional content." That is, "the coercer's aim is specifically to get others to *do* or to *desist.* Coercion, to put it vaguely, operates on the will and not the body . . . Coercers have to communicate with those whom they coerce, and fail if they merely destroy agents whose compliance they seek" (O'Neill 2000, 82).

Accordingly, it is important, and too often missed, that not all violence constitutes coercion. As Robert Nozick says,

> If a drunken group comes upon a stranger and beats him up or even kills him, this need not be coercion. For there need have been no implicit threat of further violence if the person didn't comply with their wishes, and it would indeed be difficult for this to be the case if they just come upon him and kill him. (Nozick 1997, 20)

Worries about coercion stem from two of its typical features.

First, coercion may be objectionable because it restricts the options available to the coerced individual. Second, one might object to the disrespect coercion expresses. Joseph Raz explains that a coerced person

[10] This argument draws – with some changes – on a previous article (Pevnick 2008).

"is being treated as a non-autonomous agent, an animal, a baby, or an imbecile. Often coercion is wrong primarily because it is an affront or an insult" (Raz 1986, 156). So, if I am coerced into attending medical school, the coercion is potentially objectionable on two levels.

First, I might object that I would have preferred that the option to pursue a career in music had been left open. Second, even if I wanted to become a doctor, I might object that the coercion involves a denial of the respect that I deserve as a part author of my life. If this assessment is correct, then coercion may require justification when it reduces available options or expresses disrespect. Additionally, once we accept coercion as worrisome, we have *prima facie* reason to accept all those interactions (coercive or not) that restrict options or express disrespect as worrisome. Those who maintain that coercion is in a class of its own, requiring unique moral attention and justification, must explain why it holds this revered status. It cannot be because of the reduction of option or the expression of disrespect because (a) these features are not unique to coercion (more on which in section B); and (b) coercion does not always entail these features (more on which below).

My core point will be that state coercion that ought to remain in place is importantly different from the examples of coercion that dominate the philosophical literature in that state coercion is necessary to overcome collective action problems, provide benefits, and facilitate peaceful coexistence. The coercion of an effective state thus allows us to live together more profitably and safely than would be possible in the absence of such coercion. This is why it is odd to, with Blake, lament that "we cannot eliminate" the state. The key point of social contract theory is that state coercion is a necessary condition for the provision of a whole set of *benefits* (including public goods) that are extremely valuable and impossible to provide in the absence of such coercion. It is along these lines that I now want to examine state coercion in order to argue that it never requires independent justification via special concern with the needs and interests of compatriots. Instead, state coercion is either justified by the benefits that it is used to bring forth, or not at all.

It will be helpful to disaggregate state coercion into two classes: ideal and non-ideal (as will become clear, I mean for these classes to represent all possible instances of state coercion).[11] Instead, as we shall see, by ideal state coercion I only mean coercion that has a self-enclosed justification – that is, coercion that is justified by its results and rationale.

Importantly, ideal state coercion is not objectionable in either of the available ways. First, ideal state coercion coerces citizens in order to provide

[11] These categories are distinct from, and unrelated to, Rawls's ideal and non-ideal theory.

a framework in which citizens can pursue their respective conceptions of the good life. Thus, I am coerced into driving on the right side of the road because doing so will make all citizens (including me) safer. As Locke argues, law "ill deserves the Name of Confinement" so far as it "hedges us in only from Bogs and Precipices . . . *the end of Law* is not to abolish or restrain, but *to preserve and enlarge Freedom*" (Locke 1988, §57). Unlike the typical objectionable coercion, ideal state coercion increases the value of one's set of options.

Connectedly, ideal state coercion does not disrespect the autonomous capacities of its citizens. Instead, it institutionalizes the respect compatriots have for one another. Properly done, state coercion makes it possible to overcome the threats to individual autonomy that litter the state of nature. The objective is to create a basic structure from which each can fairly pursue her life projects. Hence, respect for citizens' well-being motivates the relevant coercion. *Ideal state coercion, then, is susceptible to neither of the conditions that traditionally render coercion objectionable.* Such coercion stands in need of no independent justification; instead, it is justified by its results (the creation of a just basic structure) and its respectful rationale (the aim of creating a social structure that protects individuals). In this sense, the justification of ideal state coercion is self-enclosed. Thus, it cannot be ideal state coercion that requires justification via special attention to the needs and interests of compatriots. After all: such coercion *already* advances the needs and interests of citizens.

Of course, much government coercion (what I call non-ideal state coercion) fails to live up to this ideal and thus will not be justified by its results and rationale. Nevertheless, it is also a mistake to suggest that this class of coercion may be justified via a special concern with compatriots. To see why, consider the coercion involved in, for example, conscription for an unjust war. It is a mistake to suggest that such coercion might be justified by ensuring that those subject to it did not suffer from unequal means. Instead, prioritizing the welfare of the affected looks more like a bribe than a relevant *justification* of conscription. Indeed, reducing inequality among those subject to conscription seems to miss what could be objectionable about conscription. Rather than seeking independent justification, one ought instead to conclude that such coercion is unjustifiable.[12] If a coercive act cannot be seen to carry a self-enclosed justification, there is no reason to

[12] It has been suggested to me that the question is only whether the system of coercion as a whole is justifiable and not each particular instance of it. I believe that this view is mistaken because it cannot distinguish between the range of potential improvements above the state of nature. Instead, from this perspective, any system that can plausibly claim to have enacted an improvement vis-à-vis the state of nature is legitimate. However, it is clear that properly situated individuals would not be indifferent between all such improvements.

seek independent justification by means of special concern with the needs and interests of compatriots. Such attempts can only amount to a purchasing of acceptance rather than a justification of coercion.

Allow me to briefly summarize what has been argued so far. I have divided state coercion into two groups (jointly covering all possible state coercion) and argued that neither case demands independent justification by way of special concern with the needs and interests of compatriots:

1. *Ideal state coercion*: government coercion that ought to remain in place (such as the coercion used to coordinate drivers on the appropriate side of the road) grows out of a respect for the capacities of the citizenry. Indeed, its results (a more valuable set of options) and its intentions (the expression of respect) *are* its justification.[13]
2. *Non-ideal state coercion*: it is a mistake to seek independent justification for coercive laws whose results and rationale cannot themselves provide the relevant justification. Indeed, seeking an independent justification for such coercion furthers the disrespect involved by attempting to legitimize coercion through outside considerations.[14]

Hence, there is *no* class of state coercion requiring justification via special concern with justice among those subject to it. Again, because neither type of law requires independent justification, there is no suitable place for the justification (by way of prioritization of the needs and interests of citizens in the construction of immigration policy) on which the coercion-based argument hinges.

Having said that, allow me to briefly guard against a potential misinterpretation. In particular, it is not my position that state coercion does not count as coercion. Ultimately, state policy is always backed by the threat of force. Moreover, state coercion can be (and often is) troubling and objectionable, but this will be because of its devaluing of options and/or because of its expression of disrespect. And, such coercion cannot be justified by creating an immigration policy specially responsive to the needs of those subject to the relevant coercion; instead, coercive institutions will either offer a self-enclosed justification (by way of the benefits it brings with it) or will be unjustifiable.

[13] This point is central to traditional liberal political theory. Roughly and briefly, agents contract to leave the state of nature in order to secure the expanded framework for autonomous action provided by the state. *Agents are thus enticed to leave the state of nature in order to secure the benefits of state coercion.* Given that such coercion is something citizens would willingly accept (or hypothetically consent to), a concern for victims of coercion does not provide reason to demand an independent justification of state coercion. Instead, the justification for state coercion is self-enclosed; it is provided by its own results and rationale.

[14] Even if redistribution would give some individuals reason to comply, it would not get at what is objectionable about the coercion.

Thus, it is incorrect to suggest – with advocates of the coercion-based argument – that concern with relative inequality is the due result of the fact that citizens – through the coercive apparatus of the state – stand in an especially coercive relationship with one another. Again, justifiable state coercion is not objectionable in either of the ways available to coercion (and thus requires no independent justification); instead, it seeks to respect individuals as free and equal by providing public goods that act as a basic framework from which to live autonomously. Being subject to the coercive power of an effective state carries tremendous advantages (in terms of the goods such states are able to provide) and requires no further justification.

This is important in the context of the ethics of immigration policy because the claim of advocates of the coercion-based view is that citizens are justified in prioritizing the needs and interests of their compatriots because state laws coerce those individuals. The oddity of this view is that it calls for the prioritization of the needs and interests of citizens as a kind of apology or recompense for state coercion even while immigrants seek to move in droves precisely to capture the *benefits* of the coercion of an effective state (e.g. the protection of individual rights and the facilitation of an effective economy).

Notice, however, that the coercion that citizens are subject to is either justified by its beneficial results and respectful rationale or illegitimate. Thus, there is no reason to suppose that the exercise of coercion in these other areas of governance is of any relevance to the justification of immigration policy. Justifiable state coercion – that coercion that ought to remain in place – carries with it its own justification and, so, cannot also justify the claim that a state's immigration policy must prioritize the needs and interests of citizens as a way of compensating for the coercion citizens impose on one another. Such coercion is either justified on its own merits or unjustifiable.

So, the first part of my argument holds that advocates of the position are mistaken to suggest that claims of distributive justice only arise as a way to make recompense for the coercion they inflict on one another.

B Inequality and interaction

Here I contend (for the sake of argument, setting aside the criticism lodged previously) that even if one accepts that a concern with coercion entails a commitment to a broader conception of justice (including concerns about distributive matters), then one must also accept that this broader conception of justice will extend to at least some non-coercive situations marked by substantial, albeit non-coercive, interaction. This is intended to once again suggest that the special focus on coercion is unjustified.

Recall that the two reasons why one might object to coercion are that it may decrease the value of available options and express a certain kind of disrespect. Remember also that state coercion that ought to remain in place neither reduces the possibility for autonomous life nor expresses disrespect for citizens; it is objectionable in neither of the manners available to coercion. Unlike these acceptable elements of state coercion, at least two common classes of *non*-coercive interaction between citizens of *different* states are sometimes objectionable in *both* these manners. Yet if coercion is thought to require special justification, then non-coercive acts that nonetheless feature the worrisome aspects of coercive interaction must also require such justification. There are (at least) two non-coercive policy categories that may often entail these objectionable aspects of coercion: externalities of state action; and some apparently consensual interactions.

First, the externalities of non-coercive state policy might be objectionable in both manners available to coercive acts. For instance, agricultural subsidies adopted by the EU and United States are non-coercive because they are not undertaken with the specific intent to change the behavior of competitors.[15] Nevertheless (and in contrast to justifiable state coercion), such externalities entail *both* features that typically render coercion worrisome. The subsidies reduce the value of options available for cotton farmers in the developing world by damaging their ability to earn a living. US subsidization, for instance, deflates world cotton prices and prevents

> the poorest people of this planet . . . from doing what they are naturally best equipped to do . . . the low labor costs of peasant producers could (in the right institutional conditions) make agriculture still a profitable activity for them, *and without subsidies*, in a way that it can never, now, be profitable for many Western farmers. (Kitching 2001, 162)

Additionally, because the effects are of considerable magnitude, easily predictable, and pursued within a framework of rules constructed without the input of those affected (and could be reasonably rejected by them), the policy displays a tremendous degree of disrespect or disregard for those individuals.

The externalities of immigration policy adopted by wealthy states may be objectionable on similar grounds. For instance, restrictive immigration laws allow rich countries to select only the "best" would-be immigrants.

[15] Again, a necessary though not sufficient condition of coercion is "propositional content".

Australia, Canada, and New Zealand have point systems that evaluate applicants largely based upon their likely contribution to the domestic economy. Even in the United States (which, since 1965, has based its policy around family reunification), the adoption of a point system (in addition to the already popular H-1B visa program for skilled immigrants) has gained much support.

This is significant because there is concern that immigration from developing to developed countries robs poorer countries of just those skilled individuals that the society needs in order to achieve economic development. Some analysts have suggested that this brain drain is indeed an important obstacle to development. Though development may be largely about having the right institutions in place, the establishment of such institutions depends on the contributions of skilled individuals.

However, "the individuals most likely to be institution builders by talent and temperament are also those most likely to be internationally marketable" (Kapur and McHale 2005, 5). Indeed, for many poor states,

> the share of their skilled nationals residing in rich countries is staggeringly high. The emigration rate among their tertiary-educated populations has been conservatively estimated at 41 percent for the Caribbean region, 27 percent for Western Africa, 18.4 percent for Eastern Africa, and 16 percent for Central America. There is growing concern that such outflows help trap countries in poverty. (Kapur and McHale 2005, 1)

In addition to these regional rates, the rate of skilled emigration from some countries is daunting. Indeed, the emigration rate for the skilled population exceeds 80 percent in Guyana, Jamaica, Haiti, Grenada, St. Vincent, and the Grenadines and 50 percent in five African countries (Docquier and Marfouk 2004). It is important to recognize that these migration rates are not just "natural" rates of migration, but are – at least partially – the predictable response to changes made in immigration policy in the developed world.

It is worth noting that, in response to early literature that saw the "brain drain" as an unmitigated bad for source countries, some recent work has stressed two ways in which migration may benefit source countries: remittances (money sent home from those who have migrated); and incentives for increased education.

First, migrants may benefit their home economy by taking a job in a wealthier country and sending some of the proceeds to family members back home. Remittances may be quite substantial. For instance, remittances reached $80 billion in 2002, compared to only $51 billion in official development assistance; and, further, there is potential for remittances to grow substantially by lowering the fees (averaging 13 percent) typically imposed on such transactions (Martin 2004, 465). Remittances may be an important tool for avoiding poverty and also contribute to increased investment (Adams 2006).

Second, some economists have argued that concerns regarding brain drain miss the larger picture. They argue that the possibility of migration to wealthy countries enhances the incentives for individuals in developing countries to acquire education and other valuable skills. While some of them then migrate, others will not, and it is at least possible that statistics regarding the number of talented abroad miss the point because they fail to ask how many more talented individuals there are as a result of the possibility of migration. However, arguments on this side of the debate are only theoretical, and there is "little evidence suggesting that raising the skill composition of migration has a positive effect on the educational achievements in the home country. On the contrary, the tertiary enrollment ratio in sending countries is negatively associated with the skilled content of migration" (Faini 2005). Thus, empirical evidence seems not to validate the revisionist "brain gain" position (Faini 2006; Schiff 2006, 203). As a result, Faini reports that "by and large the bias toward skilled migration tends to depress growth prospects in sending countries" (Faini 2005).

Thus, despite these challenges, it remains plausible to suggest that by focusing on skilled applicants, immigration policy demonstrates disrespect for citizens of developing countries by (a) showing little regard for potential growth in the developing world; and (b) valuing their citizens only instrumentally (by seeing them as a means to domestic economic growth). Were this to be true, the potentially objectionable aspects of a coercive relationship would obtain between citizens of developed countries and non-migrants in the developing world. Thus, if we take the coercion-based argument seriously, we may (a) be compelled to extend distributive concerns well beyond state borders; and (b) to extend the grounds of justice to many non-coercive interactions.

In addition to the externalities of unilateral action, a concern with coercion secondly entails objections to many apparently mutually agreeable state interactions. For instance, the development of NAFTA suggests that preinstitutional power discrepancies may hinder the likelihood of interactions that treat citizens of vulnerable states as part authors of their lives. Though Mexico's ruling elite was not coerced, the preinstitutional power advantage of the United States allowed its representatives to construct NAFTA without considering the interests or autonomy of Mexican citizens.

Some analysts have suggested that the expected utility of NAFTA was worse for Mexican citizens than the preinstitutional status quo. Notice that this view does *not* depend on denying the general advantages of free trade. On this account, once its northern neighbors decided to proceed with the agreement, Mexico's payoff schedule was negatively affected such that participation became the new preferred option. Lloyd Gruber explains that:

> Once these beneficiaries [in our case, the United States and Canada] resolve to cooperate among themselves – something they would do even if they were destined to be their new cooperative structure's only members – other actors conclude that staying out of that new structure would lead to (even) greater utility losses than they would incur were they to join it . . . The winners do not get the losers to acquiesce by compensating them, via side payments, in some other sphere of interaction. The losers acquiesce because they know that the winners are in a position to proceed without them. (Gruber 2001, 709)

According to this view, the formation of NAFTA exemplifies the ability of powerful states to embed and reinforce their preinstitutional power advantages via subsequent institutions. Thus, consensual cooperative institutions are not necessarily consensual in a *justification-conferring* sense.

Assessing the impact of NAFTA is neither here nor there; perhaps it will ultimately benefit all three countries. The conceptual point does not depend on any particular empirical outcome in the NAFTA case; the important point is just that in cases featuring significant antecedent inequality, we should not assume that all voluntary agreements are justification-conferring. Instead, such apparently mutually agreeable interactions may sometimes be objectionable on the same grounds that render typical coercion objectionable.

These examples show that a concern with coercion may extend to non-coercive externalities of state policy and even consensual agreement between states because of their disrespectful and option-limiting results. Accordingly, if coercive relationships call forth special demands of justice, then so too should policies whose non-coercive effects cross borders. This, as we have seen, is true even when the relevant interactions are not governed by coercive institutions. The critical point here is that the relationships in which citizens of developed countries stand vis-à-vis those in developing countries – though not necessarily coercive – often display those features that may worry us about (typical) coercive relationships.

The point is not that all negative externalities are unacceptable, but that if coercion is thought to create special requirements of justification, there is no clear reason why non-coercive interaction raising equivalent concerns would not. A committed concern for victims of coercion entails a concern for those who are disrespected or face a restricted set of options as the result of non-coercive acts. Because (a) a concern for coercion logically entails a concern both for the reduction of the value of available options and for disrespecting the ability of agents to act as part authors of their lives; and (b) much existing non-coercive international interaction entails these features, the coercion-based view provides reason to extend concern for relative deprivation beyond state borders. In this way, we can see that the concern for coercion accepted by proponents of the view cannot legitimize restricting the domain of justification to state borders. Thus, the position entails a far broader commitment to justification than its proponents claim.

According to advocates of the coercion-based view, considerations of relative inequality need not include the needs and interests of foreigners (beyond their basic human rights). Instead, concerns with relative inequality allegedly only apply within the confines of coercive state institutions. I have objected to this view in two different ways.

First, I have argued that coercion does not require independent justification; instead, it should be assessed by its specific results and rationale. If this is correct, the mere fact that compatriots share in a mutually coercive state does not show that immigration policy must prioritize the needs and interests of citizens. Second, even if one rejects my first claim, I have shown that the coercion-based view does not justify restricting justice claims to state borders. Instead, the objectionable features of coercion can often be found in non-coercive international interaction. Indeed, I suggested that there is no reason to be confident that the worries typically associated with coercive relations will arise within and only within actually coercive interaction.

Accordingly, I conclude that such views depend on a fetishistic concern with the justification of coercion. A preferable view sees state coercion as the institutional outgrowth of social cooperation. It is the gains from social cooperation, the fact that inclusion in such cooperation is non-consensual, and the pattern of close social interaction that comes with it that bring concerns regarding the relative distribution of goods to the fore in political communities in a way that they need not outside of such communities. Thus, although the associative ownership view shares similarities with coercion-based views, it sees the coercion involved as an epiphenomenal outgrowth of the relevant social cooperation rather than itself the grounds for a heightened justificatory relationship.

V CONCLUSION

In this chapter, I have tried to explicate and defend an associative ownership framework for thinking about the ethics of immigration policy. On this view, the contributions of the citizenry to state institutions entitle them to an ownership claim over such institutions. In this way, the associative view provides (against advocates of open borders) a justification of immigration restrictions but (unlike statists and liberal nationalists) it finds the resources for such justification in ownership claims (rather than shared national identity or inherent limits in the concept of justice).

CHAPTER 4

Rights-based arguments for open borders

It is perhaps difficult to imagine, but during the United States' early years a policy of nearly open borders prevailed.[1] Immigrants were an important source of labor for a fast-expanding country busy developing and pushing into frontier territory. In the 1860s:

> Some US consuls hired full-time agents to attract prospective settlers with free land. The federal government was far from alone in this venture. While Western states and territories continued to use immigration agents and publicity campaigns to induce immigration from Europe, railroad companies sent agents to Germany to recruit farmers to develop vast railroad lands. (Tichenor 2002, 66)

The few immigration-related laws passed prior to the Civil War did little to restrict the flow of immigrants, pertaining instead to naturalization and record-keeping. Although almost a century has passed since the United States first developed a comprehensive immigration policy (as opposed to laws meant only to exclude particular racial or national groups), the idea of the United States as opening a golden door for the world's tired and poor retains a foothold in political and popular discourse.

Moreover, in arguments regarding the ethics of immigration policy, many analysts advocate open borders (Ackerman 1980; Carens 1987; Carens 1992; Cole 2000; Dummett 2001; Lomasky 2001; Pritchett 2006; *Wall Street Journal* 1984). For example, Michael Dummett argues that:

> All states ought to recognize the normal principle to be that of open borders, allowing all freely to enter and, if they will, to settle in any country that they wish. (Dummett 2001, 80)

Positions of this sort are defended in three main ways. It is claimed that open borders are (a) required in order to protect individuals' right to free movement; (b) necessary to maximize overall productivity; and (c) a requirement of distributive justice.

[1] Despite virtually no federal restrictions on immigration, state and local government could – in this period – "regulate the admission and legal status of foreigners" (Tichenor 2002, 46).

The open borders view occupies a somewhat strange position in debates regarding immigration. On the one hand, arguments for open borders are rarely heard in popular political discussion (which typically assumes the state's right to block migration). Even when the position is advanced in public debate (for example, by *The Wall Street Journal*), it is not seen as a serious policy option or engaged as anything more than fanciful provocation. Alternatively, it is no exaggeration to describe open borders as the dominant position among academics writing about justice and immigration. Indeed, here it is any *non*-open borders position that is seen as so much fanciful provocation. One author goes so far as to say that, although many arguments are employed by those who object to open borders, "there seems little reason to consider them all in detail, since all are fallacious: they are expressions of racist attitudes or general hostility to foreigners rather than the product of serious assessment" (Dummett 2001, 67). Whether or not one is antecedently sympathetic to the position, it is worthwhile to engage seriously and carefully with the arguments given in favor of open borders.

If nothing else, it is useful to think of open borders as the null hypothesis. Any restrictions that groups of individuals want to place on the movement of others must be justified with a set of reasons consistent with the equal status of all. The kinds of reasons one gives for rejecting open borders shape the types of restrictions (and so the type of immigration policy) that one can logically accept. For example, if open borders is rejected because of the importance of maintaining a given national identity (and we will examine arguments of this type in chapter 6), restrictions will be shaped so as to protect that identity. Other rationales for restricting immigration will set us on the course to very different kinds of immigration policies. Thus, even if it turns out that the open borders position is mistaken, it is nevertheless important to carefully consider the strength of the arguments that can be offered in its support.

Accordingly, this chapter and the next assess the case for open borders. The discussion is divided into two main sections, each of which plays an important role in challenging arguments for open borders. In this chapter I investigate claims regarding individuals' putative right to free movement.[2] I argue that while there is reason for international law to protect the right of some individuals to cross international borders, the claim that there is a *general* moral right to free movement depends on misunderstandings regarding different *types* of rights and the justifications on which they

[2] By a "right" to free movement, it is meant only that others have a duty not to interfere with their attempts to cross international borders. I will further discuss the scope of the right in question as we move forward.

hinge. The next chapter attempts to show that arguments for open borders based on distributive justice and claims of efficiency ignore the importance of self-determination even while they exaggerate the appropriate role for claims of equality of opportunity.

Notice that the arguments of both chapters claim only that advocates of open borders fail to convincingly demonstrate that justice *requires* the adoption of such a policy. None of this is meant as a claim that the United States may not, should it wish, *choose* to pursue a policy of open borders. Henry Sidgwick, for instance, argued both that a "state must obviously have the right to admit aliens on its own terms, imposing any conditions on entrance or any tolls on transit, and subjecting them to any legal restrictions or disabilities that it may deem expedient" (Sidgwick 1908 [1891], 248) *and* that "free admission of aliens will generally be advantageous to the country admitting them" (Sidgwick 1908 [1891], 310). Here, then, Sidgwick argues that though open borders policies are not requirements of justice, they are nevertheless optimal. I do not wish to rule out *this* kind of argument in favor of open borders. Hence, if the arguments in this chapter and the next succeed, we will see that the affirmative case for open borders fails to prove that such a policy is required by justice.

I RIGHTS TO FREE MOVEMENT?

It is often asserted that individuals possess a right to free movement that justifies a policy of open borders. For example, Darrel Moellendorf insists that "restrictive immigration policies appear to be a blatant violation of the right to freedom of movement" (Moellendorf 2002, 62). Likewise, Joseph Carens suggests that "liberal egalitarianism entails a deep commitment to freedom of movement as both an important liberty in itself and a prerequisite for other freedoms" (Carens 1992, 25). He supports a "right to go where you want to go" and speaks of free movement as a "basic human right" (Carens 1992, 36). Loren Lomasky argues that border control is "prima facie undesirable insofar as it hobbles the projects of individual actors," on which the justification for individual rights lies (Lomasky 2001, 70). And Roget Nett argues that "if we can justify any basic human right, freedom of movement is probably in that category" (Nett 1971, 219).

Rights-based arguments in favor of open borders typically hinge on one of two different types of consistency claims. The first says that insofar as one accepts that citizens have a right to free movement *within* their country, one thereby reveals oneself to be committed to a general right of free movement, the result of which is a commitment to open borders. Similarly, the second consistency claim says that if one accepts the right of the politically oppressed to exit their countries, then one reveals oneself to be committed to a right of free movement and, as a result, open borders. The idea is that these widely accepted rights claims logically entail a commitment to open borders.

Assessing these consistency claims requires a clear framework for thinking about the justification of rights in general as well as the shape of rights of free movement in particular (section II). Having laid out positions on these questions, we will then be equipped to understand the shape of, and relationship between, open borders arguments and the right of free movement domestically (section III). This will bring us to a discussion of subsistence rights and the importance of broadening the class of people given preferential treatment in terms of entry, from political refugees to the severely impoverished (section IV). I then attempt to clarify the grounds of the right of exit (section V). Altogether, this will put us into position to return to the consistency claims noted above and explain precisely how they go wrong (section VI). If the arguments of the chapter succeed, we will be able to better understand disputes regarding the ethics of immigration policy by having a handle on the limits of, and relationship between, different types of claims regarding rights to move across state borders.

II ASSESSING RIGHTS CLAIMS

Assessing the consistency claims on which the rights-based arguments for open borders hinge requires a bit of conceptual clarification. Accordingly, this section introduces an important, albeit familiar, distinction and explains how rights claims are justified.[3]

First, it is crucial that the reader keep in mind the important distinction between moral and legal rights. *Legal rights* are those rights protected by law, while *moral rights* represent interests so strong that "they are the conditions for a decent human life" (Buchanan 2004, 128) and thus impose moral duties (to do or forbear) on others.[4]

Second, I adopt an interest-based account of the nature of moral rights. On this view, justifications of rights must show that the interest in question

[3] It is perhaps worth mentioning that there are important limits to the depth of the inquiry undertaken here. Rather than pursuing the ultimate justification of moral philosophy or the practical business of public policy, this section takes up a middle level of analysis that tries to clarify the sense in which some common basic commitments fit together. For example, rather than attempting to argue with the ethical egoist, I simply assume that moral claims (including rights) exist and can be reasoned about. I borrow this characterization of the approach as "middle level" analysis from Nickel 2007, 3.

[4] The relationship between moral and legal rights is an area of substantial controversy (see, for example, Dworkin 1986; Finnis 1980; Fuller 1964; Hart 1961). Such disputes need not detain us here.

is of crucial importance to human well-being.[5] In Joseph Raz's words: X has a right when "an aspect of X's well-being (his interest) is a sufficient reason for holding some other person(s) to be under a duty" (Raz 1986, 166). That is, we say that an individual has a right when some important aspect of his well-being provides others with a duty to take, or avoid taking, some action. From this view of the nature of rights follows an account of the kind of argument needed to justify rights claims.

In particular: one "support[s] a rights statement" by "identify[ing] an interest that is especially important from a moral point of view" (Buchanan 2004, 25). Thus, in order to justify a rights claim one must "identify the interests to be protected and . . . make the case that they are of such moral significance as to warrant such extraordinary protection" (Buchanan 2004, 128). The claim has the necessary moral significance if it is "very difficult if not impossible for individuals to enjoy a decent human life" in the absence of the relevant good (Buchanan 2004, 128). While this framework obviously allows substantial indeterminacy, it at least guides our reasoning in a plausible way.

Indeed, this approach seems to be able to provide an explanation for why well-accepted rights are accorded such status. For example, a right not to be tortured protects an individual's interest in avoiding pain and suffering, disrespect and degradation, and worries driven by vulnerability. Thus, because being tortured threatens very basic interests of individuals, interests that are "constitutive of a decent life" and "necessary conditions for human flourishing" (Buchanan 2004, 127), these interests should be seen as justifying a basic moral right.

The interest-based account is helpful partly because it can demystify what it means to hold a right. While moral rights may seem like nebulous things, understanding them as a way of recognizing the restrictions our interests put on the actions of others (as in the torture example) allows us to see them as relatively familiar – the kinds of claims most of us recognize in our everyday behavior.

That an interest is of ample importance is a necessary, but not sufficient, condition for the justification of a moral right. A view that takes rights claims to be established *only* by identifying the centrality of the interest would conclude that many have a right to eternal avoidance of death. It is therefore important for the justification of a right to also include, in some form, an explanation of the putative right's feasibility and potential to guide

[5] Although there is some controversy regarding the appropriate way to go about justifying rights claims, rather than attempting to settle such controversies here, I instead work from a widely (though not unanimously) accepted position. Though this limits the interlocutors to whom I can speak, it also allows us to get to the heart of the political matter.

institutional reform. Buchanan, for instance, insists that in order for the relevant interests to rise to the level of a right, one must show "that institutional arrangements are necessary for protecting these interests and can be reasonably effective in doing so" (Buchanan 2004, 128). Without this feasibility constraint, it will not have been shown that the putative right differs from a high-priority goal (Nickel 2007, 29–32). The case of torture is again exemplary in that there are institutions (such as an explicit law code, due process, etc.) that can help protect an individual's interest in avoiding torture. Although giving specific substance to the feasibility constraint is highly contentious, our assessment of the two consistency claims can proceed without taking any particular position on this question.

III IS THERE A GENERAL RIGHT TO FREE MOVEMENT?

With the interest-based account of rights as well as the distinction between moral and legal rights in hand, we are now in position to investigate the first of the two consistency claims. Joseph Carens puts this claim as follows:

> Freedom of movement *within* the nation-state is widely acknowledged as a basic human right . . . If it is so important for people to have the right to move freely within a state, is it not equally important for them to have the right to move across state borders? The radical disjuncture that treats freedom of movement within the state as a moral imperative and freedom of movement across state borders as merely a matter of political discretion makes no sense. (Carens 1992, 27–28)

Here, Carens's strategy is to argue that accepting the relatively unobjectionable claim that individuals have a right to move within state borders logically forces one to accept that people have a general right to move freely across international borders. His claim is that consistency demands that if we accept a right to domestic freedom of movement, we must also accept an international right to free movement.

The first reason to be suspicious of this line of argument is that the underlying analogy is misleading. The right to vote is an important interest in the domestic case. Given this, we can ask – parallel to Carens's question regarding freedom of movement: If it is so important for people to have the right to vote in the elections of their state, is it not equally important for them to have the right to vote in the elections of other states? However, we do not typically think that – as a matter of consistency – individuals must have the right to vote in the elections of whatever state they wish. Instead, participation in a state's elections is typically seen as a privilege of citizenship. This should raise worries about Carens's position by casting initial doubt on the structure of the consistency claim. At the least, it shows that the argument cannot be made on grounds of consistency alone, and presses us to examine it further.[6]

More importantly, this type of argument – which suggests that we must either reject the commonly accepted claim that individuals have a right to relatively unconstrained movement domestically or accept an unconditional right to traverse national borders – rests on an inadequate consideration of the justification of claims to domestic freedom of movement. By failing to ask what justifies the claims that form their premises, proponents of such arguments misunderstand the shape of the core commitments from which they argue and, as a result, obfuscate our thinking about the ethics of immigration policy.

Having clarified the justification of individual rights, we are now in position to understand the inadequacy of Carens's claim of consistency. Again, in order for an interest to be elevated to the level of a right it must be the case that its "violation makes it very difficult if not impossible for individuals to enjoy a decent human life" (Buchanan 2004, 128). It is clear that in some cases freedom of movement is important for the construction of a decent life. For example, decent human lives are not built by individuals constrained for a lifetime to a single room. Few would deny that restriction of this type amounts to a rights violation.

However, there is no reason why this range of movement must extend indefinitely. Instead, we already recognize as legitimate all kinds of limits on movement: you are not free to move onto property owned by others, to climb onto the lap of the Lincoln Memorial, or even to move too quickly on an interstate. These restrictions seem quite *unlike* the one confining us to a single room. They do not seem to be rights-violating.

We can understand the difference in our intuitive responses to these two types of restrictions on movement by distinguishing between the need for a set of options *sufficient* for the creation of an autonomous life and an *optimal* set of options. According to this view, confining someone to a single room is a rights violation because it threatens their ability to live autonomously by undermining their access to a *sufficient* set of options. Alternatively, while stopping someone from climbing onto Lincoln's lap does restrict options, it is very unlikely to stand in the way of their having a sufficient set of options for an autonomous life. The restricted options are crucial neither in number nor importance.

[6] Those who accept the principle that "all affected" by government policy ought to have input in regard to its shape might welcome the consistency claim's extension of the franchise. Two points are worth making in response. First, the consistency claim does not say that all those affected by a policy ought to have a say, but says, instead, that individuals ought to be able to vote wherever they like. That said: as we have seen, the two may ultimately come to the same thing (see Goodin 2007). Second, I argued previously that there are good reasons to reject the all-affected view.

We are typically committed, then, to the right of free movement only in order to protect an individual's interest in living autonomously; and this requires, once again, the protection of a sufficient set of options.[7] Obviously, what counts as a sufficient set of options is a controversial matter of political judgment, but the difference between not being allowed on the Lincoln Memorial and being held captive in a single room suggests that there are nevertheless clear cases. Accepting the stronger claim that individuals have a right to an optimal set of options would force us to accept the odd view that justice requires us to live our lives only to maximize the set of options available for others. After all, any other course of action would limit their options.

Remember that Carens's claim was that if we accepted freedom of movement in the domestic case, we must also accept freedom of movement across state borders. In many cases (I discuss other types of cases below), however, legal protection of relatively free movement *within* a state is enough to protect this underlying interest; it is often enough to protect a sufficient range of options and so to satisfy one's underlying interest in a decent or autonomous life. Indeed, no such right is now protected but we typically agree that many people live decent lives. The overwhelming majority of individuals build such lives in one community, in which they stay throughout their lives.[8]

This explains why we ought to support a right to relatively uncontrolled movement domestically *and* why there is no hypocrisy in refusing to extend that right across international borders. The more minimal right is, in typical cases, enough to protect the relevant interest. Thus, being clear about the justification of a right to free movement allows us to avoid being seduced by the claim that accepting a domestic right to free movement logically entails a commitment to open borders.

While I have therefore argued that a moral right to movement across state borders does not follow from a commitment to domestic freedom of movement, there are at least two kinds of reasons why we must complicate this standard picture by recognizing that protecting the legal right to move across state borders is sometimes instrumentally crucial for the protection of other moral rights.

[7] Rawls suggests something similar in clarifying that it is only a "fully adequate scheme" of basic liberties (as opposed to a maximal scheme) that is lexically prior to non-rights-based concerns (Rawls 1993, 293).

[8] It is estimated that fewer than 2 percent of individuals migrate internationally (Castles and Miller 1998, 8–9).

IV SHOULD THERE BE A LEGAL RIGHT TO FREE MOVEMENT?

Although freedom of movement across borders does not itself qualify as a moral right, I shall argue that it is – in certain circumstances – instrumentally crucial to the protection of goods that should be seen as moral rights. Thus, in such cases freedom of movement ought to be protected by international law (even while we recognize that it is not itself a basic moral right).

It is widely (though of course not uniformly) held that there is a moral right to a basic level of subsistence.[9] For example:

> Everyone has the right to a standard of living adequate for the health and well-being of himself and of his family, including food, clothing, housing and medical care and necessary social services. (United Nations 1948, Article 25)

> Among the human rights are the right to life (to the means of subsistence and security). (Rawls 1999a, 65)

> The most basic human rights – those most important for the capacity to live a decent human life – include . . . the right to resources for subsistence. (Buchanan 2004, 129)

Although some dispute this claim and instead argue that only negative rights (rights against some kind of interference) are legitimate, there are at least two reasons to accept rights of subsistence and reject the putative distinction between positive and negative rights as overdrawn.

First, access to a certain level of material goods is uncontroversially necessary for the construction of a decent human life. Thus, if rights are indeed grounded in the interests of human beings, it is hard to see why individuals would have negative but not positive rights.

Second, securing *any* rights – positive or negative – requires positive effort on behalf of government. As Allen Buchanan notes:

> Even so-called negative rights . . . require much more than that individuals refrain from committing certain wrongs. They also require "positive actions" that are capable of absorbing almost as much resources as we are able to devote to them. For example, to establish a regime of negative rights to freedom from assault and violation of property rights requires resources for police, courts, prisons, etc. (Buchanan 2004, 184; also see Holmes and Sunstein 1999; Shue 1980, chapter 2).

Accordingly, "no right is simply a right to be left alone"; instead, "all rights are claims to an affirmative governmental response" (Holmes and Sunstein 1999, 44).

[9] For an influential argument in favor of such rights see Shue 1980.

Although I believe that – for these reasons – one should accept basic claims of subsistence as rights, I cannot here make a conclusive case for it. However, even if one denies the existence of subsistence rights, it is plain that they are instrumentally important for the exercise of any other right and, so, morally required for this reason. In what follows, I assume that subsistence rights are legitimate on their own accord. However, readers who disagree may substitute this instrumental argument for subsistence rights without damaging the arguments that follow.

There is no determinate answer to the question of what qualifies as subsistence (or, as noted above, what set of options is ultimately sufficient). However, because current public discourse focuses on the UN's $2 per day line, I accept this line simply to clarify discussion.[10] So, we can call territories in which the vast majority of individuals earn more than $2 per day *compliant* and those in which they fail to *non-compliant*. The main argument of this section is that:

If (a) individuals have a moral right to an income of $2 per day;
(b) the world's wealth is distributed geographically unequally such that (i) it is extremely difficult in some areas to reach that level of income and (ii) it is very easy to reach that level of income in other areas;

and

(c) individuals who move from non-compliant areas to compliant ones are typically able to take advantage of their location and earn incomes above $2/day;

then:

(d) recognizing a legal right to move across national borders is instrumentally valuable for the protection of individuals' moral subsistence rights.

Therefore, there is reason to grant legal rights of free movement to individuals residing in non-compliant economies. Such rights are *instrumentally* important for the protection of moral subsistence rights. This argument shows that, in certain circumstances, there is reason to accept that individuals in non-compliant territories should have a *legal* right to free movement.[11]

Already I have suggested (though, admittedly, not demonstrated) that we ought to accept (a); I will now suggest that there is good reason to think that (b) and (c) obtain in *our* world. If this is true, then not only *could* there be circumstances in which there is reason to protect a legal right to free

[10] The reader should feel free to substitute some other level or index, if s/he wishes.

[11] This instrumental case for the acceptance of a legal right to migration based upon the importance of subsistence rights is parallel to the justification of refugee status for those who suffer political persecution.

movement for individuals living in non-compliant areas, but there is *currently* reason to do so.

Recall that according to (b) the world's wealth is, in geographic terms, distributed extremely unequally such that in some territories it is very difficult to reach subsistence levels of income. This cannot be in any serious doubt. According to 2006 data, per capita GDP (in US dollars) was $536 in Benin and $80,676 in Bermuda, $925 in Dijibouti and $51,074 in Denmark, $346 in Uganda and $43,562 in the United States.[12] Rather than having a monopoly on talented individuals, the sheer capital possessed by wealthy economies makes it difficult to be poor (on the scale of the truly poor) there. Accordingly, one's income is *very highly* dependent on the geographic territory in which one lives. Indeed, both the world's very poor and very rich are heavily concentrated in particular geographic regions.

According to (c), individuals who move from non-compliant areas to compliant ones are typically able to take advantage of their location and earn incomes in excess of $2 per day. There is very strong evidence (based on the experience of those who have already moved from non-compliant to compliant areas) that this proposition is true. Lant Pritchett, for example, explains that wage gaps between compliant and non-compliant areas

> create pressure for migration because they are *not* primarily explained by differences in the characteristics of *people*. Wage rates are predominantly characteristics of *places*: People who move tend to have earnings much nearer the average wage of the country they move to than they are from, even in the short run. (Pritchett 2006, 6; also see Kapur and McHale 2006, 150–153)

This much seems obvious: transport an American to Uganda for a year and see, once she settles into a job, if she makes closer to $346 or $43,562. Our earnings depend much more on the wealth of the surrounding economy than on personal skills or characteristics. It is important to recognize that it does *not* need to be shown that immigrants from low-income countries will, having moved to compliant economies, earn as much as native individuals. Instead, as long as the move is likely to enable them to earn over the threshold demanded by rights of subsistence, the case for their right to move appears strong.

I have thus suggested that there is strong reason to accept that (a), (b), and (c) currently obtain. If the argument presented above is correct, there is thus instrumental reason to accept a legal right of free movement for those living in non-compliant economies. Accepting that such people have a legal

[12] This data is taken from the UN's website and can be accessed at http://unstats.un.org.

free right of movement is the consequence of a commitment to their subsistence rights. Indeed, there is *prima facie* reason to think that denying such people the legal right to move amounts to a denial of their basic moral right to subsistence. Though not always seen as one, the immigration of the impoverished is therefore a human rights issue. Having outlined the case for such a legal right, I now want to address several potential challenges to it.

Some may worry that it is pointless to grant a legal right of free movement to people who are so deeply impoverished. After all, international migration is a costly process and only a very small proportion of those entitled to the right will be able to claim it. Although I concur with the empirical claim behind this objection, I deny – for three reasons – that it undermines the case for the right in question. First, there are many legal rights that are not claimed by most people to whom they are available, and we do not typically regard this as reason to abandon the right in question. Many people do not exercise their right to vote or their right to worship, but we certainly do not think that this non-exercise of a right undermines the rationale for its existence. Second, the fact that few people manage to claim the right does not undermine its value for those who do. Third, to deny qualified individuals the legal right to immigrate makes one complicit in the violation of the subsistence rights in question. As Thomas Pogge explains, we "must not avoidably restrict the freedom of some so as to render their access to basic necessities insecure – especially through official denial or deprivation" (Pogge 2002, 67). Thus, even if it is true that few of the qualified individuals will be able to claim the right in question, this fact does not undermine the importance of legally recognizing it.

Connectedly, some might suggest that because it is impossible to overcome poverty-related problems through migration, it makes sense to address the issue via development rather than immigration policy. After all, about half of the world's population (approximately 3 billion people) live under the $2 per day poverty line while in recent years the United States – an "immigrant country" – has admitted about 850,000 legal immigrants annually. Because of these figures, it is hard to imagine that migration is a solution to world poverty. As Pogge remarks, "for every person we can persuade some rich country to admit, there will be hundreds, if not thousands, left in desperate need" (Pogge 1997, 14). Given an alternative that promises not just to help enrich some foreign individuals by incorporating them into our economy but to enrich foreign *populations* by contributing to the preconditions for development abroad, wealthy countries might rightly help protect the subsistence rights of the very poor abroad via means other than relaxed migration policies. If this is correct, it might seem as though protecting the subsistence rights of the impoverished demands an approach centered on development rather than migration.[13]

However, even if it is possible to transform developing economies through foreign aid, there is no doubt that the transformation of non-compliant economies will take time. During this transformational "hour," current individuals' subsistence rights provide strong reason to permit those individuals access to compliant economies. Moreover, there is substantial reason to doubt the ability of foreign aid efforts to transform the developing world. Indeed, William Easterly insists that donors "keep pouring in aid resources with the fixed objective of stimulating higher growth, although evidence does not support an effect of aid on growth" (Easterly 2006, 51). According to this view, development is a matter of getting the various institutions and incentives correct, and doing so is largely a matter of historical luck, too deeply embedded to be influenced in any straightforward or intentional way by well-meaning outsiders; aid, on this view, "cannot achieve the end of poverty" (Easterly 2006, 368; Knack 2001).

Thus, for two reasons development efforts cannot override the case for a legal right to free movement for those living in non-compliant territories. First, even if it is true that it is possible to transform the world's non-compliant economies, individuals in those economies have strong claims to a legal right of free movement until such a transformation occurs. Second, there is substantial empirical reason to doubt whether such transformation is possible. Thus, there is strong reason to think that existing transformational possibilities do not overcome the case for legal rights of free movement for those in non-compliant economies.

Here, it is worth pausing to note that advocating a legal right of free movement for individuals living in non-compliant territories amounts to a significant broadening of refugee status vis-à-vis the status quo.[14] Prior to World War II there was no legal distinction between refugees and immigrants, and until 1980 no comprehensive refugee law. Since World War II refugee policy has twisted and turned with American foreign policy, especially the Cold War (particularly in regard to interaction with Fidel Castro and events connected to US involvement in Southeast Asia). Here it is neither possible nor necessary to give an account of this history.[15] Rather, I will limit myself to saying a few words regarding classification.

[13] For related arguments, see Cavallero 2006; Pogge 1997; Wellman 2008; and Woodward 1992.

[14] However, the importance of recognizing the variety of ways (beyond political persecution) in which people's basic interests might be threatened has been increasingly recognized in international law in recent years (Price 2009, 5).

[15] For a helpful overview see Gibney 2004, chap. 5.

Since the 1980 Refugee Act all those fleeing a "well-founded fear of persecution" could – at least technically – qualify for special entrance to the country. This includes two groups of slightly different types. Refugees are individuals who, having fled their native countries, apply for entry from a country of first asylum, often from putatively temporary refugee camps. Alternatively, asylum-seekers apply from within or at the borders of the destination country. Again, in both cases successful claims depend on persuading officials that they are indeed fleeing fear of persecution. Thus, significant entry priority is granted to those who can demonstrate legitimate danger of political repression.

The distinction between run-of-the-mill immigrants and refugees is useful and important because it recognizes and responds to the fact that foreigners have disparate reasons for moving and that the urgency of their claims is not uniform. Surely this is preferable to – for example – the statist response to the refugees created by Hitler's call for Jews to emigrate up until 1941, when existing legislation saw "humanitarian considerations" as "irrelevant" and the United States "responded to the refugee crisis, as did most other countries, by creating barriers to entrance" (Zucker and Zucker 1987, 18). It is obvious that some, such as German Jews prior to the Holocaust, have particularly urgent claims to admission, and refugee law is useful in that it provides one way of recognizing this urgency.

However, as I have just argued, the distinction between refugees and immigrants – though useful as a first cut – is far too blunt to respond to the range of reasons potential migrants have for moving. Historically, we have given special preference to those fleeing political persecution but not those fleeing abject poverty, rampant disease, or incompetent governance because refugee policy was developed as a tool in the Cold War and sought to give priority to, and showcase those, fleeing Communist rule. For the reasons I have elaborated, however, it is doubtful that only those fleeing political persecution have very strong claims to entry.

Allowing that material subsistence is itself a right because it is an interest which, if unfulfilled, blocks individuals from living a decent life (or is instrumentally necessary for the exercise of political rights), forces us to accept a legal right of entry for the impoverished as well as the politically persecuted.[16] Again, it makes sense to recognize that some foreigners have

[16] It is possible that there are political reasons (related to the expressive function of asylum) to maintain a separate category for those fleeing political persecution, even while allowing admission to those whose basic interests are threatened for other reasons. For an account of the importance of the expressive function of asylum, see Price 2009.

much stronger claims to admission than others, but it is doubtful (to say the least) that the strength of one's claim is a function of and only a function of the probability of political persecution. We must broaden the concept of refugee so that it embraces both those fleeing political persecution and those trapped in abject poverty. Again, because both political persecution and severe poverty undermine core interests and threaten one's access to sufficient options, demands for admission from the severely impoverished raise – in a manner parallel to traditional refugees – important human rights issues.[17]

Moreover, it is important to emphasize that committing to upholding such a right is not costless. Matthew Gibney explains that:

> With the end of the Cold War and increasing ability for people to travel intercontinentally, there was pressure on the US government to find ways to restrict the granting of asylum. Indeed, by 1994 there was a backlog of 400,000 asylum applications and applicants regularly had to wait years for decisions. As a result, economic migrants saw that they could use the asylum system to gain temporary access to the economy. In response to these developments, the Clinton administration forced asylum applicants to wait 180 days before granting permission to work, made increasing use of detention centers for those in the process of application and strengthened its means of exclusion – visa controls, carrier sanctions and interdictions at sea.[18] (Gibney 2004, 163)

The upshot of such efforts is both that many entitled to asylum are blocked from reaching the country and that many asylum-seekers await decisions on their status for long periods of time, on meager funds, without the right to work, and while suffering constant humiliation (Dow 2004; Migrants Resource Center 2006; Moorehead 2006).

According to a Congressional report, in nearly 15 percent of the 6,000 studied cases in 2003, applicants waited over 180 days for a decision (USCIRF 2005, 343). During this time, "they can be stripped, searched, shackled, manacled, chained, and denied access to lawyers and to their families ... and, since September 11, increasingly so" (Moorehead 2006, 93). In 2007, US Immigrations and Customs Enforcement detained 311,000 aliens in their 300 detention facilities (Stana 2008).

While there are ghastly reports of abuse at some such facilities (Dow 2004), it is unclear how widespread are such practices. For example, Dow claims that "sexual abuse of prisoners is a common practice, and INS detainees are

[17] I am grateful to Michael J. Smith for a helpful conversation on this issue.

[18] The Supreme Court, in *Sale* vs. *Haitian*, ruled that interdiction is distinct from *refoulement* and, so, constitutional.

especially vulnerable for the simple reason that they can be deported" (Dow 2004, 52). The Government Accountability Office (GAO) reports that:

> The types of grievances at the facilities GAO visited typically included the lack of timely response to requests for medical treatment, missing property, high commissary prices, poor food quality and insufficient food quantity, high telephone costs, problems with telephones, and questions concerning detention case management issues ... At the time of our visits, we observed instances of noncompliance with ICE's medical care standards at 3 of the 23 facilities we visited. However, these instances did not show a pervasive or persistent pattern of noncompliance. (Stana 2008)

Unfortunately, the reliability of this information is unclear because the most widespread non-compliance was found with regard to the system in place to report complaints. For example, the GAO found that complaint hotlines were blocked at half of studied detention centers. This is consistent with anecdotal evidence suggesting that complaints are systematically ignored (Dow 2004, especially chapter 8).

A state honestly committed to asylum has an obligation to halt interdiction efforts and spend enough on asylum processing to ensure the humane and fair treatment of applicants. If detention centers are not eliminated, waits must be reasonable, detainees must be treated as innocent right-holders (rather than criminals), and conditions must be humane. Far preferable to detention centers is to hold hearings immediately or release applicants to sponsoring organizations until their asylum hearings. Refusing to undertake such efforts amounts to a refusal to recognize non-citizens as right-holders; it is tantamount to strong statism, which – as we have seen – cannot withstand scrutiny.

Having sketched the positive case for this legal right and addressed concerns regarding its power, I now address three potential worries. The worries discussed below accept the above argument, while raising questions about the *scope* that such a right ought to take.

First, while I have suggested that the right protects the ability of those in non-compliant economies to move to *any* territory with a compliant economy, it might instead be suggested that the right should only allow the relevant individuals to move to *particular* compliant territories (say, for example, the nearest one, the one in most need of foreign labor, the wealthiest one, or the one designated as most appropriate by an international committee on economic refugees). All of these institutional arrangements are plausible possibilities and I will not attempt to settle the dispute between them. Instead, I will only say that because it is so difficult for individuals with an income small enough to qualify for the right in question to migrate, it seems reasonable to suggest that any acceptable scheme will not turn qualified individuals back for showing up at the "wrong" compliant territory.[19]

Second, some will argue that the case for a legal right to free movement extends much further than I have suggested. In particular, if there are rights to resources beyond subsistence (as many cosmopolitan theorists have argued), then the legal right in question may be thought to extend to individuals living above subsistence but with access to far fewer resources than they might have were they working in a wealthier economy. The Mexican field worker is the salient example. Allen Buchanan at least suggests such a position, arguing that:

> An ideal moral theory of international law must include a prominent place for distributive justice, both as an individual human right and as a constraint on economic inequalities among states ... International law today can and should play a beneficial, largely indirect role in securing distributive justice ... by supporting efforts to liberalize immigration policies to increase economic opportunities for the world's worst off.[20] (Buchanan 2004, 193)

Before looking at the implications of rights to distributive justice, we should make sure we understand the justification of the rights in question, for this will affect their scope.

Indeed, I will argue that once we understand the justification of rights of distributive justice, it will become clear that the suggested extension of legal rights of movement is invalid.[21] Buchanan offers two lines of justification for the claim that there are rights of distributive justice. First, he argues that

> the most plausible and widely held human interest-based justifications for the basic civil and political rights also support rights of distributive justice. Our fundamental human interests in well-being and autonomy are served by freedom of speech and the right to political participation, but also by rights to basic health care and education. (Buchanan 2004, 197)

[19] It is also likely that a legal right of economic refuge of this kind will create a stream of migrants who do not quite qualify. It will, after all, be rather difficult to ascertain who does, and who does not, fall under the relevant level of resources. Nevertheless, given the basic moral right at stake for those who do qualify there is strong reason for states to err on the side of leniency in judging applicants.

[20] For at least two reasons, the extent to which Buchanan accepts the case for a legal right to free movement discussed here is unclear. First, the suggestion that international law support less restrictive immigration policy is vague. This is unsurprising since immigration is not a major focus of Buchanan's. Second, as I shall suggest, it is doubtful that his justification of rights to distributive justice supports the extension in question. In any case, it is more important to understand the issue correctly than to assess Buchanan's view.

[21] A similar argument, couched in terms of luck egalitarianism vs. relational egalitarianism, is advanced by Wellman (Wellman 2008).

This interest-based line of argument, however, establishes only that individuals have a moral right to a basic level of subsistence. It does not also show that individuals have rights of distributive justice in the more robust sense with which we are now concerned. That is, it shows that individuals have a right to some basic minimum, but it fails to show that in addition to this guard against *absolute* deprivation, individuals also have rights which protect them against *relative* deprivation.

Buchanan's second line of argument is meant to justify rights of distributive justice in this more robust sense; that is, in relation to relative deprivation. He argues that "rights of distributive justice are needed to constrain material inequalities among citizens so as to limit inequalities in the effectiveness of civil and political rights" (Buchanan 2004, 197–198). Here, Buchanan's argument is that if we are committed to equally recognizing the civil and political rights of individuals, then we must recognize the importance of achieving equality of a rough kind. In particular, there is a legitimate concern that in the absence of rough economic parity, members of a society will necessarily have quite unequal access to rights such as freedom of speech, religion, and assembly.[22] Substantial differences in income promise to render such rights ineffective.

Given, however, this account of the justification of rights of distributive justice it should be clear that they do not justify extending a legal right of free movement across international borders to individuals who, though living above subsistence levels, might earn much more in a wealthy economy. Instead, this argument provides reason to limit inequality within and between national economies (to the extent that members of different economies interact), but immigration is not a trustworthy way to pursue either goal. Encouraging the immigration of the poor (but not truly impoverished) from poor states to rich ones is, instead, likely to increase inequality in wealthy countries (Borjas 1999) and its effects on sending countries as well as inequality between nations are highly uncertain (Schiff 2006).[23]

In the absence of a specific and persuasive explanation of how such a legal right would significantly contribute to the realization of rough equality within and/or between national economies, there is no clear reason to think

[22] There is evidence that the US government is highly responsive to wealthy citizens and not at all responsive to poor groups (Bartels 2008; Gilens 2005).

[23] Remittances constitute a major source of income for some poor countries and migration can thus help alleviate economic inequality between nations. Alternatively, however, the flight of well-educated migrants from poor countries to rich ones can exasperate inequality between countries.

that extending a legal right of free movement to those living above subsistence would enhance equality within or between nations and, so, effectively empower individuals to exercise their political and civil rights.

The fourth potential objection to the scope of the above argument holds that if one accepts a legal right to free movement for all those living in non-compliant economies, then it is logically implied that we must make it possible for all such individuals to exercise this right. This line of response confuses the nature of the argument by mistaking the means for the end. The legal right to free movement is instrumentally required as a way to fulfill subsistence rights. The primary duty, then, is to fulfill the subsistence rights of all and not just to make it possible for individuals to move. We should pursue the fulfillment of subsistence rights in whatever way promises to be most efficacious.

So far I have argued that although individuals do not have a general *moral* right to move across state borders, there is nevertheless strong reason for international law to protect the *legal* right of individuals to leave countries in which their basic interests are jeopardized. There is, that is, strong reason not only to accept the claims of traditional refugees but also reason to widen the traditional conditions for qualification as a refugee by accepting that those living in severe poverty, like those subject to political persecution, are in a very strong position to demand entry.[24]

V RIGHTS TO EXIT

In rejecting the claim that those who accept domestic freedom of movement must also accept open borders we have thus been led to accept – and, indeed, broaden – the traditional right of exit. The idea that individuals have a moral right to exit is far more common than is the view that individuals have a general right of free movement. For example, Article 13 of the United Nations Declaration of Human Rights asserts that "Everyone has the right to leave any country, including his own" (United Nations 1948, Article 13). Michael Dummett insists that this claim is "manifestly correct" and "can be denied only by the comfortably situated and heartless" (Dummett 2001, 34).

We explained our acceptance of rights of exit by noting that accepting the interest-based account of rights forces one to accept the view that, when underlying basic interests (such as the freedom of speech, religion, or

[24] Others have defended a similar position by way of slightly different arguments. See, for example, Gibney 2004 and Shacknove 1985.

association) are at stake, freedom of movement takes on an *instrumental* or *derivative* importance. It is often thought, however, that accepting such a right of exit forces us, via the second consistency argument, to accept open borders. Consider the following arguments:

> One cannot consistently assert that there is a fundamental human right to emigration but no such right to immigration; the liberal asymmetry position is not merely ethically, but also conceptually, incoherent ... If it can be shown that the state *does* have the right to control immigration, it must follow that it also has the right to control emigration: the two stand and fall together. (Cole 2000, 46)

> The understanding is that people do have a right to move away from oppression and also have the right to move away from poverty if they can manage to do so. It takes but little extension of logic to suppose that people ought to have the right to move freely over the surface of the earth so long as they are willing to obey local laws and respect local customs. (Nett 1971, 219)

> The freedom of exit has come to be generally acknowledged as a desirable norm so that the states who violate it are ... on the defensive in relation to the international community. It is therefore startling that one cannot conceive of a similar consensus arising from what appears to be a concomitant principle: "Everyone has the right to enter any country." (Zolberg 1981, 6)

Each of these theorists suggests that an unlimited right to immigration is conceptually required given the "unproblematic" (Cole 2000, 43) claim that individuals have a right to exit their state. The question thus arises whether our escape from the first consistency-based argument for open borders nevertheless ensnares us in a second consistency-based argument for open borders by forcing us to accept a right of exit.

Once again: satisfactorily answering that question depends upon understanding the *grounds* of the widely recognized right to exit. Once we do this I think that we will again see that the initially attractive consistency claim on which the argument hinges is mistaken. Each of these arguments assumes that the acceptance of a right to exit logically *entails* a commitment to open borders. They thus seem to assume that the argument for a right to exit works as follows:

Premise: Individuals have a general right to free movement.
Conclusion: Therefore, individuals have a right to exit.

If this was the structure of arguments for the right to exit, then consistency claims of this kind would be convincing.

However, I have instead suggested that the argument for a right to exit works as follows:

Premise1: Individuals have a right to certain basic moral interests.
Premise2: In some cases, the protection of such interests requires exit.
Conclusion: In cases in which their basic interests are at stake, individuals have a right of exit.

It should be clear that there is no reason to say that accepting this argument commits us to saying that states do not have the right to control immigration. Instead, states are obliged to recognize a right of exit because of a commitment to a set of basic interests that does not present itself in typical cases of immigration. That is, because exit rights are justified only in cases in which they are instrumentally necessary for the protection of other rights, there is no reason to suggest that accepting them requires us to also set aside immigration restrictions in cases in which such interests are not at stake. Thus, the consistency arguments rest on a misunderstanding regarding the *grounds* of rights to exit.

Typically, we feel strongly about the importance of the right to exit because it protects one's ability to flee a tyrannical regime. Exit is of particular importance, the kind of importance that can rise to the level of a right, when it allows one to escape a situation in which basic moral rights are not protected. That is, the rationale for a right to exit depends upon it serving as a way to protect one's moral right to be free from torture and political persecution or allowing one to escape an environment in which basic moral rights (such as subsistence, freedom of association, speech, or religion) are not safeguarded. Thus, the right to exit is not itself a basic moral right, but instead deserves protection as a legal right because of its importance in securing interests that themselves qualify as basic moral rights. Besides being clear about the nature of a commitment to individuals' right of exit and casting doubt on rights-based arguments for open borders, this analysis has the further advantage of helping to clarify the legitimate *limits* on rights of exit.

While many commentators have expressed a concern that the development prospects of poor countries are hindered by the departure of well-educated individuals (Kapur and McHale 2005), proposals requiring that those who received their advanced training through public funding be required to spend a limited amount of time serving the community have met the objection that they illegitimately restrict the right of exit of such individuals. The above analysis demonstrates the inadequacy of this rationale for objecting to limits on the movement of professionals whose training has been funded by the community.

If it is correct that the right of exit is not itself an important moral right, but instead that it is instrumentally important as a way of protecting various civil liberties and other basic rights, then the relevant individuals cannot claim that restrictions on their movement based on concerns about brain drain are rights-violating. So long as the relevant basic moral rights (freedom from torture, freedom of speech, freedom of religion, etc.) are not in jeopardy, it is wrong to claim that restrictions on their movement violate any *right* of exit.

Instead, there is a strong case to be made for thinking that by pouring their resources into the training of such individuals, the political community obtains a kind of partial claim to the skills of that individual and thus may restrict their exit for limited periods of time. If the political community jointly pours resources into training programs in an attempt to improve the quality of public services provided, it thereby gains a limited claim over the future activities of the individuals trained with that money. Of course, that accepting public training will bring along with it temporary limitations on movement ought to be made clear prior to acceptance of the training (for a similar position, see Carens 1992, 33). No right is thereby violated.

So, this analysis helps dispel what some theorists have thought is an important quandary. In particular, according to probably the most common position in public debate, individuals have a right to exit their countries, but no equivalent right to enter whatever country they wish. As we have seen, however, this "liberal orthodoxy" (Cole 2000, 43) has been criticized as incoherent:

> One cannot consistently assert that there is a fundamental human right to emigration but no such right to immigration; the liberal asymmetry position is not merely ethically, but also conceptually, incoherent. (Cole 2000, 46)

The claim that it is incoherent to accept one side of the free movement claim without the other forms the center of Cole's argument that "there are no coherent liberal arguments that can establish the state's right to control immigration" (Cole 2000, 46). Recognizing, however, that neither rights of emigration nor rights of immigration are basic moral rights, but are instead of instrumental value because of their ability to (sometimes) protect interests that *do* rise to the level of moral rights, dispels the notion that there is any incoherence in the traditional view.

VI LIMITS AND CONCLUSIONS

With a better understanding of the sense in which individuals can be said to have rights of free movement, the difficulties with consistency-based arguments for open borders ought to be clear. For example, we have seen that Roger Nett explained that

> the understanding is that people do have a right to move away from oppression and also have the right to move away from poverty if they can manage to do so. It takes but little extension of logic to suppose that people ought to have the right to move freely over the surface of the earth so long as they are willing to obey local laws and respect local customs. (Nett 1971, 219)

Nett draws on two legitimate intuitions: that individuals ought to be able to (a) flee tyrannical rulers; and (b) move from territories with non-compliant economies. Unfortunately, he wrongly assumes that such rights must be justified by an underlying *general* moral right to free movement. This, as I have tried to show, is more than a "little extension of logic."

The argument suggests that if one accepts a right to flee tyrannical rulers, one must therefore accept an unqualified right of free movement. This is a mistake because the right to exit that we typically affirm is not a special case of a general right to free movement, but instead justified instrumentally. It is an implication of a commitment to basic political and subsistence rights. Once we understand the justification for rights of exit and subsistence, it becomes clear that accepting them does not provide reason to accept a general right of free movement.

Thus, seeing that rights of free movement are not basic moral rights, but instead are instrumentally important for the protection of other such rights allows us to better adjudicate arguments regarding the appropriate shape of immigration policy. It shows, in particular, that rights of movement ought to be protected where they are instrumentally necessary for the fulfillment of moral rights (such as freedom of speech, religion, or basic claims of subsistence). Understanding the shape and justification of such rights therefore helps resist the claim that rejecting open borders is importantly akin to rejecting rights of exit for the oppressed or impoverished.

There remains an important question about the cost that receiving countries are obliged to incur in order to protect the rights in question. This issue combines two difficult and unsettled questions:

1. What priority ought to be given to the protection of rights when such protection comes at the cost of the general welfare?
2. What are the limits on obligations imposed by the duty to rescue?[25]

Clearly, neither of these important questions is specific to debates over immigration, and both raise very difficult questions that cannot be addressed without traveling very far afield.

[25] Most of the literature on this question revolves around Singer's classic argument against any important limits on the duty to rescue (Singer 1972). For an important argument against that position, see Murphy 2000.

The first question is one that we face in important domestic issues as well. We could – for example – spend infinitely ensuring the protection of the right to vote or the freedom of speech. Indeed, the idea of the lexical priority of rights – made famous by Rawls, but adopted as well by many others – suggests such a position (especially in the formulation used in *A Theory of Justice*). Likewise, Ronald Dworkin notes that

> there would be no point in the boast that we respect individual rights unless that involved some sacrifice, and the sacrifice in question must be that we give up whatever marginal benefits our country would receive from overriding these rights when they prove inconvenient. So the general benefit cannot be a good ground for abridging rights. (Dworkin 1977, 193)

Applying this view of rights to our question would suggest that the rights of potential migrants could not be rightfully restricted until doing so legitimately threatens the protection of the individual rights of current citizens.

The problem with this argument is the jump from the claim that there would be no point in individual rights if we were not prepared to protect them even when doing so would impose *some* cost in terms of the general welfare and the claim that "the general benefit cannot be a good ground for abridging rights." Although it is surely correct that a commitment to individual rights would have little meaning if such rights were sacrificed for *any* general benefit, it does not follow that a meaningful commitment to rights entails the claim that the general benefit – no matter how sizable – can *never* provide grounds for abridging rights.

Taking the priority of rights too seriously condemns us to spending infinitely to secure such protections.[26] Surely, we could spend without end attempting to provide an infrastructure for elections that ensured that the votes of all would be counted and that fraud would be impossible. However, such precautions are unacceptable in that they call for an inordinate (indeed, limitless) sacrifice of the general welfare for the protection of individual rights. They take the priority of rights too seriously.

What is needed, in regard to our first question, is a principle that prioritizes rights by giving them a special, but not absolute, weight. Unhappily, specifying that principle is a task I can only leave to a better mind. For us, the important point is only (once again) that those from non-compliant territories should – like traditional refugees – be granted priority admissions, and there is an obligation to grant entry to such individuals at least up to the point where allowing more to enter promises to generate significant costs.

[26] In later work, Rawls more carefully specified the priority of liberty partially in order to avoid this worry (Rawls 1993).

In regard to the first question, we saw that while a commitment to individual rights surely demands at least some willingness to sacrifice the general welfare, it is much less clear how far this willingness to sacrifice must go. Likewise, in regard to the question of the limits of a plausible duty to rescue, it seems clear that we ought to be willing to accept *some* sacrifice. Consider the following example:

> You are preparing dinner for an evening date (the other person has yet to arrive) when you hear a faint knock at the door. Opening the door reveals a severely bloodied individual. It is clear that the person requires immediate transportation to the hospital.

In this case, I think it is clear that there exists a duty of assistance to stop preparations for your date and aid the individual. It would be morally unacceptable to explain, while gently shutting the door, that you have a risotto going on the stove that will surely be ruined – along with the rest of your evening – if you leave. While assisting the person requires you to accept some cost (rescheduling or delaying your date), it nevertheless seems incumbent upon you to do so.

We might, then, agree that there is a duty to rescue that requires accepting some limits on the pursuit of our own interests (Singer 1972). Nevertheless, the extent of such limits remains unclear. Contrast our first case with the one that follows:

> An individual in Nazi Germany, overcome by the plight of her Jewish compatriots, decides to secretly hide Jews and help them escape the country. She does this despite recognizing that her chance of pulling off the task without eventually being detected and punished accordingly is small.

This case is importantly different from the first one. We regard the Schindlers of the world as heroes. They, because of the risk they undertake, leave the world of moral requirements and embark upon the supererogatory. While we perhaps hope that – faced with such a situation – we might reveal ourselves to be of the same character, those who fail to do so, instead neither contributing to nor preventing atrocities, are not blameworthy. Instead, they reveal themselves to be mere mortals rather than heroes.

The primary reason for our different reactions to the cases is that the individual in the second case assumes a serious burden or cost. If caught, she faces severe and costly punishment above and beyond the mere inconvenience of a missed date. We can see this by fancifully revising the first case so that rather than one bleeding individual there are 2, then 8, then 100, then 1,000, and so on. As the numbers increase, so too do the demands imposed on he who would provide assistance. What was at first a sacrificed date becomes a sacrificed weekend which, in turn, becomes a holiday from work and eventually the forgoing of significant life projects. The difference between the required action and the saintly action seems to lie in the degree of self-sacrifice.[27]

These distinctions, though far too rough, set the parameters of the debate: when refuge can be provided at minimal cost, it is surely required. When the cost imposes important risks or constraints on our lifestyle, it begins to enter the category of supererogatory. Candidly, I do not know how to further specify this condition (for example, how much risk or self-sacrifice is one *obliged* to take on?), and so we are left with a much too vague directive: allow economic refugees (those from severely impoverished areas) until it begins to have an important effect on the political community's standard of living. At such a point, there is still reason, albeit no longer dispositive, to allow further entry. While I wish that I could say something more specific about this guiding principle, I doubt whether we can get to a more precise conclusion from widely accepted premises or shared intuitions.

Despite not having adequate answers to these questions, we have enough to – at least for the moment – guide our thinking about immigration policy. In particular, there is reason to significantly liberalize restrictions on those from severely impoverished areas and to continue to do so, step by step, until there is good reason to think that substantial costs are thereby being imposed. While these costs can – in principle – be either material or in the form of radical and abrupt cultural changes (as discussed in chapter 6), I see no reason to think that current levels of immigration from very poor regions impose anything like such costs. And, again, even once significant costs begin to be imposed by the entry of economic migrants, there nevertheless remains reason to continue to grant entry. Such reason is just no longer clearly dispositive. Thus, at present, there seems to be good reason to admit far more individuals from economically failing (or non-compliant) states. Accepting this, however, does not require accepting open borders.

27 Although there is a difference between the revised first case and the second case in that the second case involves danger and not just a sacrifice of the pursuit of one's interests, I do not see why this disanalogy should be important.

CHAPTER 5

Distributive justice and open borders

In the previous chapter, I argued that there is no general moral right to free movement and that, as a result, it is a mistake to suggest that the case for open borders can be established simply by reference to rights of free movement. Nevertheless, two strategies for arguing for open borders remain: those based on overall productivity and those based on distributive justice. In this chapter, I assess these remaining strategies, arguing that neither line of argument is capable of justifying open borders.

I EFFICIENCY, DISTRIBUTIVE JUSTICE, AND OPEN BORDERS

Sometimes, more often among economists than political theorists, the case for open borders hinges on claims regarding the potential for enormous gains in productivity. Although not themselves advocating open borders, Caglar Ozden and Maurice Schiff explain that "by allowing workers to move to areas where they are more productive and valued, migration leads to a direct increase in global output and income" (Ozden and Schiff 2006, 6). On this view, open borders ought to be adopted because of the potential gains in efficiency.

Such calculations have been made by a number of economists (Hamilton and Whalley 1984; Martin 2004), and are typically based on simple estimates derived in the following way:

> Imagine that per capita income is $2,000 in country X and $22,000 in country Y. Now, imagine that we increase the flow of workers from X to Y by 100,000. If the main differences in income between X and Y arise from differences in capital between the two economies (rather than differences in the skill sets of the individuals), then we can calculate the net economic benefits for the increased migration by multiplying the difference in wages by the number of individuals who will benefit from exposure to the capital-rich economy. $20,000 ·× 100,000 = $2,000,000,000. Thus, according to

> our rough calculation, potential gains from increased migration are enormous (and concentrated among the migrating individuals).

The efficiency argument stresses the gains from potential migration and attempts to represent them as so large that no further discussion is required.

It is worth noting that such estimates exaggerate the benefits of migration in two ways. First, a significant increase in the supply of laborers will decrease the cost of labor. These costs may be spread geographically throughout the country as native workers respond to decreased demand for their labor in areas of heavy immigration by migrating elsewhere or refusing to migrate to areas to which they otherwise might have (Borjas 1999, 62–86; for an opposing view, see Card 2001). So, the efficiency argument exaggerates potential gains by failing to take into account the decrease in average wages in destination countries.[1]

Second, such an influx of workers will impose costs. Most importantly, such individuals make demands on public services – from highways and hospitals to law-enforcement institutions. Indeed, the mere presence of large flows of people across borders presents a cost in terms of wear on publicly provided goods (transportation, police, and medical infrastructure). However, because such costs are not easily estimated in the way that gains from migration are, they are often put to the side. This is especially so because the "costs of migration tend to be deferred, especially if the first migrants are workers whose families arrive later ... Costs also tend to be dispersed widely and are much harder to measure" (Martin 2004, 473). These considerations suggest that the estimated gains in efficiency available from selecting an open borders policy may not be as sizable as sometimes claimed.

Much more importantly, however, the sense in which such arguments show that citizens are obliged to open the borders is unclear. It is hard to see why increased productivity, on its own, provides reason to liberalize movement across borders. What is missing, then, is an explanation of why citizens ought to see increased productivity as dispositive reason to open the borders.

Proponents of the productivity line of argument attempt to answer this charge by suggesting that "the overall net economic gain from immigration is positive, and that the receiving country would still be better off if the losers from migration were compensated" (Martin 2004, 446; see also Chang 2008). That is, the policy yields a Hicks–Kaldor improvement: those who gain as a

[1] Notice also that average income is at least a doubly misleading measure. There is no guarantee that a country's émigrés will accurately reflect the home population; indeed, the poorest individuals do not have the resources to emigrate. Moreover, it appears that larger gains are made by highly educated immigrants, who are better equipped to take advantage of a capital-rich economy (Jasso *et al.* 2000).

result of the policy, gain by so much that they would be able to compensate those who are made worse off by the policy and nevertheless remain better off than they would have been without opening borders in the first place.[2]

This argument misses the point because it fails to explain why those made worse off by a policy should care that they would be better off *if* compensated given that such compensation is unlikely. In what sense, that is, is the Hicks–Kaldor claim a genuine justification to those who will lose from increased immigration (native-born workers with skill sets similar to admitted immigrants)? Most of us generally accept a host of restrictions that block Hicks–Kaldor and even Pareto-efficient transactions (the sale of votes, for instance). If your employer suggested that your working overtime would produce a big enough surplus to satisfactorily compensate you for the work, would you be satisfied or might you hold out for the *actual* transfer of (part of) the surplus?

The difficulty is that reason has not been provided to explain why citizens are obliged to follow the path of increased efficiency; and in particular, reason has not been provided to explain why it is the increased efficiency of the world as a whole as opposed to the citizenry that is the appropriate criterion. In an excellent discussion of the issue, Gillian Hadfield explains that to approach questions related to the justice of an immigration policy from the perspective of "a social welfare function that reflects the well-being of men alone or current workers alone is to assume away the ethical issues involved" (Hadfield 1995, 205). The point here is that the issue cannot be settled simply by appeal to claims of efficiency, for what is needed is a defense of the dispositive relevance of efficiency claims (as well as a defense of *whose* interests must count in the efficiency calculation).

The most influential attempts to explain why citizens are obliged to pursue gains in overall efficiency hinge on an appeal to the role such gains may play in advancing equality of opportunity. The world's wealth is distributed in a highly inegalitarian fashion (such that one's country of citizenship is a very important predictor of wealth).[3] As a result, if one is committed to some form of equality of opportunity for all individuals, then one must allow individuals to "move to

2 This line of argument is misleading because it relies on an estimate of the benefits without, as we have seen, factoring in the costs. That is, the assertion that the liberalization of borders is Hicks–Kaldor efficient is groundless (even though possibly correct). Without knowing the size of the various costs, we cannot be confident that the improvement really is Hicks–Kaldor efficient. Indeed, this is another instance of the benefits of increased migration being taken out of the context of the necessary qualifications.

3 In this sense, citizenship can be seen as a classic example of a Walzerian dominant good in that "individuals who have it, because they have it, can command a wide range of other goods" (Walzer 1983, 10; and Hartogh 1999, 494 and 510).

where the opportunities are in order to take advantage of them" (Carens 1992, 26). On this view, open borders ought to be supported because they "contribute to a reduction of political, social and economic inequalities" (Carens 1992, 26). Here, the argument for open borders has shifted from grounds of efficiency to grounds of distributive fairness. Because I think that the appeal of the efficiency argument ultimately lies in its connection to these distributive concerns, I will focus directly on the distributive argument.

In a number of pieces, Joseph Carens argues that a commitment to distributive justice requires open borders.[4] His suggestion is that:

> The exclusion of so many poor and desperate people seems hard to justify from a perspective that takes seriously the claims of all individuals as free and equal moral persons. (Carens 1992, 26)

The distributive argument works roughly as follows:

P1. We must "treat all human beings as free and equal moral persons" (Carens 1992, 25).
P2. A necessary condition of respecting the equal moral status of individuals is providing them equal opportunity of some type.
P3. Restrictive immigration policies are an obstacle to equality of opportunity because they stop individuals from moving to pursue opportunities.
C. In the pursuit of equality of opportunity we should open borders.

The main intuition lying behind this position is thus that there is an injustice in individuals having different life prospects simply as a result of the arbitrary fact that they are born into different political communities.[5] Like Carens, Charles Beitz insists that members of a political community cannot be entitled to its relative wealth because the community to which one is born is "morally arbitrary" and "hence unacceptable" as a "standard for distribution" (Beitz 1979, 163).

[4] While in some later work Carens may seem to move away from advocacy for open borders, this "contextual" turn marks a change in perspective, a promise not to ask the question about open borders (Carens 1988, 59), rather than an abandonment of the open borders position (Carens 1999).

[5] David Miller rejects the import of this appeal to arbitrariness by pointing out that although a handicapped child is "not morally responsible for having the disabilities that she now has," she may nevertheless be entitled – as a result of these arbitrary differences – to extra resources from the state (Miller 2009b, 296). He concludes from this example that we should discard the view that one cannot be entitled to goods as a result of arbitrary differences. The problem with this line of argument is that those who advocate giving more resources to those with special needs can justify this as a move *toward* equality (properly understood) rather than away from it. On this view, while it might be the case that the handicapped individual will be entitled to more resources *from the state* than others, the justification of this will be to ensure that this person's overall package of resources is as close to equal as possible (for the classic account along these lines, see Dworkin 2000, chap. 2).

This is a powerful and important argument. Indeed, when I started this project, I began – having read some of Carens's work – from the assumption that something along these lines must ultimately be correct. Although I no longer believe this to be the case, I certainly appreciate that there is a reasonable, intuitively powerful, and internally consistent case for open borders that flows from the distributive argument. The attraction of the distributive argument for open borders runs deep. Certainly, those of us born to wealthy political communities must recognize that this good fortune is just that: good *fortune*. Moreover, because of this good fortune we may well want our political community to be one that welcomes outsiders and gives them an opportunity to benefit from the accumulated wealth of the community. Although I understand and share this inclination, it strikes me as best understood – for reasons that I hope shall become clear – as a type of beneficence rather than a requirement of justice. As I shall explain, I doubt that all good fortune requires justification or that all inequalities are cases of injustice.

The remainder of this chapter explains why we ought to reject the distributive case for open borders. I do so by challenging P2 (the claim that respecting the equal status of outsiders mandates equality of opportunity) in two ways. First, I argue that a commitment to equality of opportunity conflicts with claims of associative ownership (section II). Second, I argue that equality of opportunity is not in fact a necessary condition of respecting the equal moral status of individuals (section III). My hope is to draw attention to the difference between the claim that it would be benevolent to adopt a policy of open borders (which may be true) and the claim that justice *requires* open borders (which I will obviously deny). Finally, I will close by discussing a powerful rhetorical tool commonly relied upon by advocates of the distributive argument and explain why I think that it is misleading (section IV).

II SELF-DETERMINATION AND THE DISTRIBUTIVE ARGUMENT

Although in what follows I will thus challenge the general applicability of equality of opportunity, I want to first make clear that even if we insisted that all inequalities in opportunity are unjust, we would nevertheless have to face a conflict between different types of justice claims. In other words, even if it were true that equality of opportunity was a requirement of justice, it would not follow that it was the *only* valued goal. In chapter 2, we saw that groups of individuals may possess claims of collective ownership that, in turn, underlie claims of self-determination. However, a commitment to self-determination includes allowing groups to pursue their chosen ends and, at least to some extent, to reap the benefits or suffer the consequences that follow. Thus, a commitment to self-determination conflicts with the position that all inequalities are unjust.

However, as we have seen, we regularly recognize the legitimacy of arguments regarding self-determination in other areas of collective life. For example, within the Jewish community, it is very common for charitable donations to be directed toward the Jewish Federation. Such federations are umbrella organizations bringing together social agencies, educational organizations, political advocacy and volunteer programs. Together the groups provide a range of important services, from aid to vulnerable individuals to education programs and political advocacy.

We typically think that the Jewish Federation and similar organizations are justified both in controlling access to the organization and the distributing the benefits that go along with it. To say, instead, that all who wish to benefit from the efforts of contributors to the Federation must be included is a mistake because it would make it impossible for contributors to guide the organization according to their preferences. If all were entitled to the benefits of the group, it would be impossible for the group to maintain the orientation toward Jewish causes that is its reason for being. The Federation is a way for Jewish individuals to exercise collective ownership and create a set of mutually beneficial institutions that give voice to their interconnected destinies. Thus, it would be odd to say that *all* must have access to such services (as a result of a concern with eliminating inequality of opportunity). Such a position would undermine the collective endeavor – itself an important aspect of justice – of Jewish contributors.

Notice that this is *not* to say that contributors to the Jewish Federation are exempt from the general demands of justice. Instead, they are – of course – obliged to meet the background demands of distributive justice (by, for example, paying taxes). Private donations to the Jewish Federation are made on top of mandatory compliance with the demands of justice. However, the benefits that accrue as a result of the Jewish Federation's work should not be seen as available to all as a matter of distributive justice. Although the Jewish Federation may not serve the *most* vulnerable individuals and may provide benefits to those who cannot be said to deserve them, this seems acceptable given that contributors meet whatever obligations they have to outsiders. To disagree would be to say that a concern with distributive justice can never be satisfied and, so, must dominate our lives, leaving no room for the collective life and association that is also an important aspect of acceptable lives.

As a result, however, one cannot *both* accept the importance of self-determination *and* insist that individuals have a right to (a) demand membership in any association they choose; or (b) dismiss all advantages gained from membership as unacceptable as a result of their arbitrary nature. Attempts to eliminate the benefits individuals collect as a result of characteristics that are arbitrary from a moral point of view promise to undermine the possibility of self-determining groups. Imagine that I show up at the Jewish Federation headquarters and say:

> I want access to the funds that you have raised through the effort and accomplishment of your staff and contributors. Moreover, it is unfair for you to deny me that access. Of course, you – and your predecessors – have worked hard to establish the institution as a successful one, but the skill and motivation powering that hard work is not something that you deserve. As a result, you ought to recognize that the success that you have had is arbitrary from a moral point of view and, so, not hoard the benefits that result.

This request strongly conflicts with basic intuitions about entitlement and ownership. Even if the qualities of the participants that led to the enterprise's success are arbitrary from a moral point of view, their use of these characteristics was *ex hypothesi* consistent with the other duties they had to outsiders.

Moreover, accepting the view that schemes of mutual benefit should be open to all because they are the product of talents and motivations arbitrary from a moral point of view undermines incentives to build such schemes.[6] If individuals know that any time they join together to create a set of benefits, all those who did not likewise contribute will show up after the hard work is done and demand inclusion in the scheme (pointing out that participants in the scheme do not *deserve* the talents or motivation that led them to contribute), incentives for creating beneficial enterprises will suffer. Thus, taking seriously the arbitrariness objection destroys payoffs for building such institutions.

It is clear, for example, that in a society in which successful organizations for mutual benefit are forced to publicly distribute their proceeds, there will be few such organizations. In this way, a norm insisting that because of the arbitrariness of all accomplishments all those who desire membership must

[6] For a similar line of argument see Miller 2007, 70.

be accepted is self-defeating, for it predictably destroys the motivation to build the very institutions to which it seeks to guarantee access. It undermines the creation of the very benefits that it seeks to distribute more fairly.

Note here that this aspect of the response to the arbitrariness objection is but a special form of the general argument in favor of some level of inheritance. Although it is true that allowing inheritance provides some with advantages that they do not deserve in any deep sense, laws protecting inheritance may nevertheless be justified because (a) they protect the ability of givers to use their resources as they like; and (b) they create more resources in society by giving individuals reason to produce beyond what they can consume.[7]

Just as we might want to limit inheritance in domestic society in order to (say) ensure that the needs of the least well-off are attended to or to prevent levels of inequality that threaten political equality, we might also want to limit the extent to which the associative ownership claim empowers political communities to "hoard" their resources. Even if this is so, we should still allow that the associative ownership claim is one important consideration in arguments about immigration and provides a reason of some weight in favor of restrictions (once again, it may very well be a reason that will be *outweighed* by the claims of some migrants, especially those with legitimate claims to asylum).

If this is correct, advocates of the distributive argument face the following difficulty: they must either reject the perfectly quotidian claim that the Jewish Federation has at least some legitimate entitlement to the fruits of their efforts or explain why their view applies to state institutions but not private associations. The former option is, I believe, implausible. Rather than saying more in regard to it, I will leave it to advocates to explain how the position might be made plausible.

In regard to the latter option, one might try to argue that there is an important difference between membership in private associations and membership in public schemes of mutual benefit. However, the resistance to seeing states as associations stems from the fact that its institutions are coercively imposed on citizens and, as I argued in chapter 2, this difference does not seem to call into question claims of ownership. Accordingly, it remains to be explained why the private–public distinction is significant here.

[7] For an argument against inheritance that denies the claim that abolishing inheritance will erode incentives for production, see Haslett 1986. To my mind, this denial is implausible, but it is ultimately an empirical matter about which I present no evidence.

As I have been trying to suggest, then, this line of argument can be extended to the state. While the distributive argument suggests that *everyone* is entitled to the fruit of citizens' labor in constructing mutually beneficial institutions, I find it difficult to understand why this would be so. To show why, it is helpful to look at Bruce Ackerman's version of the distributive argument. Though its language is unusual, conceptually it is paradigmatic. He asks us to imagine:

> that there are two spaceships – Explorer and Apollo – engaged in the task of discovery. Each contains an equal number of people who satisfy the necessary conditions for liberal citizenship. The Explorer, however, lands first, and the Commander of that ship gives each member of her landing party a single grain of manna with which to begin life. A split second later, the Apollonians arrive and demand equal standing in the burgeoning liberal polity:
>
> APOLLONIAN: I want half your manna.
> EXPLORER: Sorry, but I need all of it – and more – if I am to attain my ends in life.
> APOLLONIAN: But I need it too! If personal need is a good reason for your getting manna, why shouldn't it count in my case as well?
> (Ackerman 1980, 89)

The considerations raised in this dialogue lead Ackerman to conclude that

> analogy to a private club is misconceived. In ideal theory, *all* people who fulfill the dialogic and behavioral conditions have an unconditional right to demand recognition as full citizens of a liberal state. (Ackerman 1980, 88)

So, in Ackerman's view (and, more generally, that of those who embrace the distributive argument for open borders), resources and membership should be equally available to all capable of liberal citizenship. Nothing about the members of the two groups, he suggests, can distinguish their entitlements.

The problem with this argument is that it obfuscates the situation by denying that there is any relationship between the existence of the goods and those who are claiming entitlement to them. However, the goods typically at stake in arguments about immigration are politically or socially created. Effective pension programs (for example) are built rather than stumbled across. Likewise, the establishment of law and order, an effective market, and basic infrastructure are hard-fought accomplishments – accomplishments that hinge on the collectively coordinated and authorized decisions, labor, and contributions of group members.

Associational benefits are the product of the coordinated collective decisions, labor, and contributions of group members. When associations bring the relevant institutions into being through their collective decisions and contributions, as they often do, they may claim special entitlement to them. Such institutions are not manna, sitting waiting to be claimed by whoever happens across them. Instead, they are owned by the political community in the same way that, for example, the Jewish Federation has a kind of ownership claim over the institutions and resources that exist as a result of their contributions and efforts. As a result, it would be odd to suggest that *everyone* must, as a matter of justice, be granted access to the accomplishments of the community just as a result of their personhood.[8]

As Robert Nozick so forcefully reminded us, our world's resources are not just there waiting to be claimed and divided; instead, justice "is historical; it depends upon what actually has happened" (Nozick 1974, 152).[9] I take this to be a relatively uncontroversial claim that even most proponents of "patterned" views can accept because in saying that justice depends on what has actually happened, I do not mean – with Nozick – that justice depends *only* on what has actually happened.[10] As we have seen, one can accept the associative ownership view even while allowing that some distributions may be objectionable regardless of how they came about because, for example, of the people they leave severely impoverished.

This difficulty is present even in the positions of those who take a somewhat more moderate view than does Ackerman. For instance, Barbieri argues for the "categorical right of all settled residents to political membership" (Barbieri 1998, 115, also at 137 and 157; similarly, see Carens 2005) on the grounds that "acknowledging individual consent is important for membership policies, for denying the possibility of consent would constitute a form of domination" (Barbieri 1998, 141). He says also that "few would deny that changes in citizenship status should not be imposed, but rather should reflect the will of the persons affected" (Barbieri 1998, 152). As with Ackerman's argument for open borders, these arguments for the right of all living in a territory to have access to citizenship makes sense only if the goods connected to citizenship are like manna dropped from heaven.

[8] This position is roughly consistent with Stephen Nathanson's description of "moderate patriotism" (Nathanson 1989).

[9] Here, it is worth noting that libertarians who embrace rights-based arguments for open borders implicitly tolerate the redistribution of collectively owned property (in the form of publicly provided goods) from citizens to non-citizens. It thus appears that rights-based arguments for open borders conflict with the strong property-rights claims that are basic to libertarian political morality.

[10] Notice, for example, that Rawls's view is both historical and patterned. It is important that the people at the top of the distribution are the people whose efforts have benefited the rest of society. Otherwise, the inequality will not work to the advantage of all.

Given, instead, that such goods are built by a community over time, members of that community come to have at least some special claims upon them. Seeing this allows us to recognize that a commitment to the consent of those affected or against the imposition of membership changes on the unwilling requires us to take into account the claims not just of *potential* citizens, but also the claims of *current* citizens. That is: not explained is why we should place such strong weight on the consent of non-members, but none at all on the consent of members. Rather than eliminating the non-consensual imposition of membership changes on affected parties, this proposal only shifts it from non-citizens to citizens.

A position that stresses that political self-determination is itself an important value is – I think – the best way to understand the example that Rawls proffers in support of the idea that duties of distributive justice across state borders should have a target rather than applying "continuously without end" (Rawls 1999a, 117). Rawls asks us to consider two countries with the same level of wealth and population size:

> The first decides to industrialize and to increase its rate of (real) saving, while the second does not. Being content with things as they are, and preferring a more pastoral and leisurely society, the second reaffirms its social values. Some decades later the first country is twice as wealthy as the second. Assuming, as we do, that both societies are liberal or decent, and their peoples free and responsible, and able to make their own decisions, should the industrializing country be taxed to give funds to the second? According to the duty of assistance there would be no tax, and that seems right; whereas with a global egalitarian principle without target, there would always be a flow of taxes as long as the wealth of one people was less than that of the other. This seems unacceptable. (Rawls 1999a, 117)

Here, Rawls argues that a society can have at least some entitlement to the wealth that amasses as a result of its collective decisions. This is a consequence of the idea that a political community is "an ongoing and independent association, whose members expect it to continue into the indefinite future" (Cohen 1989, 21).

I want to briefly resist the worry that this example is somehow too strange or odd to usefully employ in argument. Consider the case of Singapore and Malaysia, which I will – very roughly and briefly – recount. Both countries were British colonies prior to World War II. In the wave of self-determination movements that followed the war, both gained independence. After becoming a state in the summer of 1958, Singapore set about working to overcome ethnic tension by building a national identity. They worked to industrialize the country, increasing spending on education from

S$600,000 in 1960 to S$10 million in 1963 (Lepoer 1989, §10). And, finally, they preached the crucial importance of merger with Malaysia.

The highly influential minister of finance Goh Keng Swee insisted in 1960 that "major changes in our economy are only possible if Singapore and the Federation are integrated as one economy. Nobody . . . believes that Singapore alone, in isolation, can be independent" (quoted in Lepoer 1989, §10). After a brief period of merger, Malaysian political leaders – suspicious of Singapore's political leaders and worried about ethnic tension – unilaterally ended the union. Famously, Lee Kuan Yew – the prime minister of Singapore – announced Singapore's independence in tears, allowing that "it is a moment of anguish. All my life, my whole adult life, I have believed in merger and unity of the two territories" (quoted in Lepoer 1989, §10). Singapore was thus thrust into independence with significant worries about the viability of the project.

The country then embarked upon a project of national unification and economic development that included a renewed commitment to education, the construction of an advanced infrastructure, and the recruitment of substantial foreign investment. "Since independence, Singapore's economy has consistently posted the region's highest growth rates, sometimes expanding as much as 11 percent per year" (Neher 2000, 128). In 1965, Singapore's per capita GDP (in 1990 international Geary–Khamis dollars) was $2,667 and Malaysia's was $1,804. However, as a result of the success of Singapore's project of economic development and construction of political community, in 2001 the figure for Singapore was $21,011 while Malaysia stood at $7,756 (Maddison 2003, 185). Likewise, in 2008, the World Bank reported that Singapore's per capita GDP corrected for purchasing power parity was $49,288 (higher than that of the United States) and Malaysia's was just over $14,000 (just lower than Mexico) (World Bank 2009).

Although this account could not be more compressed (and the theoretical point obviously does not depend on any particular account of the events in Southeast Asia), it nevertheless serves to highlight the key point. Namely: whereas the advocate of the distributive argument holds that Singapore's success generated an injustice (by increasing the inequalities between its citizens and Malaysia's) that must be rectified by allowing open access to these economic and social gains, the associative ownership position insists that the development of Singapore was a triumph and that the political community that generated these gains has at least some special entitlement to them.

As I have been at pains to make clear, this is not to say that the citizens of Singapore do not have obligations to individuals falling below some specified minimum, that their entitlement overrides injustices they may have committed in the pursuit of development, or that they are not obligated to fairly share the benefits of international social cooperation; but it is to say that part of what it means to see – as we typically do – political communities as ongoing and independent associations is to recognize that they have some level of entitlement to the goods that result from their collective efforts. Alternatively, advocates of the distributive argument are forced to conclude that citizens of Singapore – after having been unilaterally excluded from federation with Malaysia – are now morally obliged to open their borders to the citizens of that country in order to redress the inequalities generated by the success of their collective endeavor. It is this conflict between the idea of political community as an ongoing project of self-determination and an unbounded principle of equality of opportunity that provides the first reason to doubt the distributive argument.

By ignoring the role political associations play in the creation of the valuable goods at stake in arguments about immigration (from basic public goods to public pension, healthcare, or education programs), advocates of open borders treat the goods to be distributed as "manna from heaven." They fail to recognize the special claims that political associations (and, through them, citizens) have over the goods at stake. There is, then, a deep conflict between the possibility of the self-rule of political communities and claims of equality of opportunity.

Unfortunately, this point is too often missed. For example, Ayelet Shachar speaks approvingly of the idea of self-determination, saying that

> members of bounded polities may wish to endorse a particular vision of the common good through the enterprise of shared citizenship (for example, by prioritizing the separation of state from religion; endorsing liberal democratic values; supporting a relatively robust welfare system; or preserving a distinct culture or way of life). (Shachar 2009, 78)

Indeed, Shachar rejects open borders because she (rightly) sees it as conflicting with the "important prerogative of sovereign authority and democratic self-governance" (Shachar 2009, 75). However, she also severely criticizes any system that tolerates "an inequality of starting points" that depends on one's citizenship (Shachar 2009, 43). The trouble with this position is that it fails to recognize that part of what it means to commit oneself to the idea that members of a polity ought to be able to make their own decisions about the future of their communal life is that individuals will necessarily be born to different societies, with at least somewhat different life expectations, sets of opportunities, and the like. Because equality of opportunity and self-determination conflict with one another, insisting on wholehearted support for both is platitudinous.

Indeed, this conflict is precisely what makes questions surrounding immigration vexing. In an effort to instead take the conflict seriously, I will now suggest some reasons for thinking that it is best navigated by jettisoning the unbounded commitment to equality of opportunity.

III INEQUALITIES AND INJUSTICES

Key to the distributive argument is the claim (P2) that treating others as equals entails their having equal opportunity. This raises the question of whether there is necessarily an *injustice* in the existence of groups of people with different life expectations or whether, instead, as Rawls says, "inequalities are not always unjust" (Rawls 1999a, 113). I will argue that (a) there are four main kinds of cases in which inequalities in life prospects might be rightfully considered an injustice;[11] and (b) the intuition that lies behind P2 (and so powers the distributive argument) mistakenly sees equality of opportunity as a fundamental value instead of recognizing as instances of injustice only those cases that feature said inequalities. The appeal of the distributive argument hinges on the intuitive objection to these four objectionable types of inequalities, but – as we shall see – the associative ownership position has the resources to object to such inequities, without embracing an unbounded commitment to equality of opportunity.

The first kind of case in which the fact that different groups have different opportunities should be seen as an injustice is one in which the worse-off group falls below some minimal standard of decent living even while the better-off group enjoys an excess. Many iterations of the distributive argument hinge on an appeal to this kind of inequality. Recall that Carens introduces the intuition behind the distributive argument by insisting that

> the exclusion of so many *poor and desperate* people seems hard to justify from a perspective that takes seriously the claims of all individuals as free and equal moral persons. (Carens 1992, 26 emphasis added)

Likewise, he begins a well-known article by reminding us that

[11] It is likely that other categories of objectionable inequalities could be identified, but for our purposes these are most important.

> borders have guards and the guards have guns. This is an obvious fact of political life but one that is easily hidden from view – at least from the view of those of us who are citizens of affluent Western democracies. To Haitians in small, leaky boats confronted by armed Coast Guard cutters, to Salvadorans dying from heat and lack of air after being smuggled into the Arizona desert, to Guatemalans crawling through rat-infested sewer pipes from Mexico to California – to these people the borders, guards and guns are all too apparent. What justifies the use of force against such people? (Carens 1987, 251)

These passages suggest that much of the appeal of the view hinges on the juxtaposition of the desperately poor with those who enjoy an excess. The difficulty with appeal to these kinds of examples is that they do not necessarily support P2 (the claim that we must institute a regime of equality of opportunity in order to respect the equal status of all). Instead, such examples cannot help adjudicate between open borders and views (such as the associative ownership view) which hold that admission ought to be granted to those who fall below some minimum or subsistence level.

In other words: insofar as these arguments hinge on an appeal to the interests the desperately impoverished have in admission, we can accept their power without also accepting open borders because the importance of admitting such individuals is compatible with a view that accepts a duty to rescue along the lines described in the previous chapter. An argument for open borders faces a much stronger justificatory burden: in particular, advocates of open borders must show that *any* inequality in life prospects is an injustice.

Distributive arguments for open borders that hinge on the injustice of excluding the severely impoverished are inadequate because we can accept the claims of such individuals without also accepting open borders. Indeed, the associative ownership position does just that. Thus, we can accept the claim that there is an injustice in some individuals falling below a given threshold while others benefit from superabundance without also saying that *all* inequalities are unjust.

The second kind of case in which an inequality in life prospects will signal an injustice is when the inequality is a direct result of the illegitimate actions of the better-off group. So, for example, if Country A is wealthy and Country B poor *because* A (for example):

- enslaved the citizens of B and forced them to build a highly effective industrial infrastructure;
- stole the natural resources to which citizens of B were entitled; or
- imposed upon B an unfair structure of international trade or economic rules,

then, the inequality is important because it points us to the underlying injustice.

Certainly, in such instances (which are obviously not merely hypothetical) there can be a case for rectification and, so, for alleviating these *particular* unjust inequalities.[12]

For the reasons discussed previously, this raises an extremely difficult topic in political theory regarding when injustices must be rectified and when we can understand them as having been, in Waldron's words, superseded (Waldron 1992). I do not mean to take any particular position on this separate controversy. Instead, my point is only that distributive arguments for open borders ought not to rely on the claim that some particular historical injustices require rectification because any view – including the associative ownership position – can accept *that* point. Just as concerns about severe poverty do not commit us to unrestricted equality of opportunity, so too concerns regarding particular historical harms are not sufficient to establish the unbounded importance of equality of opportunity.

Third, inequalities might be unjust not because of their source or because of the existence of unnecessary deprivation, but because of their effects. If individuals stand in certain kinds of personal and political relationships with one another, inequalities might bring forth injustices of other kinds. This is perhaps most important in the case of political relationships. For example, it is often claimed that it is necessary to maintain a certain level of substantive equality between citizens in order to ensure that their political interactions are fair. For example, Rawls worries that

> historically one of the main defects of constitutional government has been the failure to insure the fair value of political liberty. The necessary corrective steps have not been taken, indeed, they never seem to have been seriously entertained. Disparities in the distribution of property and wealth that far exceed what is compatible with political equality have generally been tolerated by the legal system. (Rawls 1999b, 198–199)

Likewise, as we have seen, Buchanan argues that a commitment to distributive justice is "needed to constrain material inequalities among citizens so as to limit inequalities in the effectiveness of civil and political rights" (Buchanan 2004, 197–198). According to these views, when individuals share a political relationship it is necessary to impose certain kinds of constraints on material inequality in order to ensure that their interactions are fair. The extent to which this claim is true is a matter for debate since we

[12] There is no immediately obvious reason why open borders would be a suitable rectification for these kinds of injustices (although nothing I say rules out that possibility).

might maintain the fair value of political liberties in a number of other ways (including mandatory voting laws and public funding of elections).

A related point is that the mere fact that individuals interact personally with one another may speak in favor of ensuring that – when they do so – they can meaningfully confront one another as equals, and this may require limits on allowable inequalities. That is: there may be limits to the kind of inequality that can be countenanced among those who share a political and social association if – when they interact – they are to do so in a way that makes manifest their equal status. Too much material inequality challenges the possibility of personal interaction on an equal playing-field and risks creating an environment in which some are treated with undue deference – as dons, doyens, or lords. Such interaction is not consonant with making manifest the equal moral status of all.

Having said that, it is worth noting that although this line of argument for concern with distributive justice is most often applied to those who share a domestic government, it is at least conceptually possible for such considerations to bear on international relationships as well. In our world, interactions are far from limited to compatriots and one might hold, in a parallel manner, that we need rough equality between nations in order to guarantee that states interact fairly with one another. Notice that this may be true without forcing us to accept the same *degree* of concern with inequality internationally as we do domestically; instead, concern with inequality might vary with the type or density of interaction.

However, it is important that concern with inequality among those interacting with one another does not speak in favor of open borders (at least not in any obvious sense). This is because open borders does not necessarily reduce inequalities between nations. Although it is likely to help those members of poor countries who immigrate to rich countries gain access to more opportunities, its effect on the relevant inequality (that is, inequality between *countries*) is highly uncertain. Moreover, it may introduce a new source of inequality to receiving countries. Because of this, there is no clear reason to think that international interaction can be made more fair by accepting open borders. Thus, even if we accept the claim that fair interaction requires some level of material equality, we have an argument in favor of redistribution across borders (if achievable), but not an argument for open borders.

The fourth type of inequality that raises concerns of injustice hinges on the idea that when one plays a role in imposing a scheme of governance upon others and that scheme distributes rights, opportunities, wealth, and income in a particular way, others are owed a justification for why that particular scheme – as opposed to feasible alternatives – is being imposed. The core idea here is that being party to the imposition of an economic and political scheme of mutual benefit carries with it the demand that that scheme fairly treat the individuals subjected to it. This is especially important when the scheme in question has a pervasive effect on the well-being of participants and is imposed non-consensually. Although there are a number of ways to give shape to this requirement, it is not necessary (or possible) for us to try here to adjudicate between rival possibilities.

Instead, I am here mainly interested in expressing the core idea, which is also reflected in Rawls's remarks about the circumstances of justice. The circumstances of justice are the circumstances that give rise to, or make legitimate, claims of justice. Rawls describes these as "the normal conditions under which human cooperation is both possible and necessary" (Rawls 1999b, 109):

> There is an identity of interests since social cooperation makes possible a better life for all than any would have if each were to try to live solely by his own efforts. There is a conflict of interests since men are not indifferent as to how the greater benefits produced by their collaboration are distributed, for in order to pursue their ends they each prefer a larger to a lesser share. Thus principles are needed for choosing among the various social arrangements which determine this division of advantages. (Rawls 1999b, 109)

The basic thought is that individuals engaged in a cooperative enterprise can structure the rules for that enterprise in a number of ways, and the differences will have important distributive effects for participants. Given that cooperation is non-consensual, the particular shape of social cooperation must be justified to participants.

According to this view, a robust principle of distributive justice is not merely a reflection of the moral status of individuals *qua* human, but instead a demand that – among the possible ways of organizing social cooperation – a set of rules be chosen that organizes the benefits of such cooperation fairly. For example, Rawls explains that the demand for the difference principle arises because the basic structure of society provides a framework for social cooperation, and implicit in the idea or practice of cooperation are two elements:

> The first is a shared notion of fair terms of cooperation, which each participant may reasonably be expected to accept, provided that everyone else likewise accepts them. Fair terms of cooperation articulate an idea of reciprocity and mutuality: all those who cooperate must benefit, or share in common benefits, in some appropriate fashion judged by a suitable benchmark of comparison ...

> Now the appropriate notion of fair terms of cooperation depends on the nature of the cooperative activity itself . . . What is distinctive about the basic structure is that it provides the framework for a self-sufficient scheme of cooperation for all the essential purposes of human life. (Rawls 1993, 300–301)

On this interpretation, considerations of distributive justice are relevant among participants in a shared scheme of self-sufficient social cooperation, and *not* humans (or even interacting humans) more generally speaking (Rawls 2001, §39).

One way of understanding this line of argument is by saying that the ideal of equality of opportunity holds only in very specific contexts. We are not obliged to give others equal opportunities to be our friends, our business partners, our lovers, or the like.[13] Instead, if an inequality is to be an injustice, it must be because of the particular context in which it arises. The objectionable inequalities that I have discussed are circumstances that might make it the case that an inequality can be seen as an injustice. Again, this includes cases in which (a) the worse-off fall below a level of sufficiency while others enjoy an excess; (b) the better-off enjoy their status as a result of illegitimate interaction with the worse-off; (c) the parties share a close relationship of interaction such that relative equality is a necessary condition of maintaining equal status; and (d) inequalities reflect an unfair parceling out of the advantages of social cooperation. However, in the absence of any such circumstances, we are without reason to conclude that an inequality is an injustice.

These considerations should help us distinguish between two different kinds of questions that are too often confused. One question relates to what is owed to those with whom we *already* – through no fault of their own – share a strong social relationship; while the other is about those who *wish to enter* such a relationship. One can treat those of the former type equally only by ensuring that the shared cooperative framework in which we are non-consensually enmeshed makes manifest the equality of all participants by fairly dividing the benefits of ongoing social cooperation. This underlies the objection to caste societies and explains why it is a mistake to suggest that because they contribute less to government, poorer members of a society ought to have less say over the ends it pursues.[14]

[13] I have benefited from discussion with Sam Scheffler on this point. He addresses these issues very helpfully in "What is Egalitarianism?" (Scheffler 2003).

[14] This does seem to be an implication for associations that are started by individuals *within* the confines of the state. So, for example, if we start a business together and I contribute 75 percent of the start-up capital, I should have a proportionate say in the future of the business. However, the same does not seem to be true for the state, because what each of us brings to the table to contribute to the

Alternatively, for those who stand outside that social relationship (and do not have the kinds of urgent reasons for entry held by legitimate asylum-seekers), being treated as an equal may involve nothing more than non-interference and – if desired – fair intermittent interaction. The latter is a non-option for those with whom we already find ourselves enmeshed in a project of social cooperation. This explains why claims of associative ownership may be adequate to justify the exclusion of distant outsiders even while they are easily outweighed in discussions regarding the appropriate treatment of internal minority groups who – for one reason or another – are not thought to have contributed significantly to the political community.

This line of argument suggests, moreover, that some inequalities that arise out of social cooperation may be objectionable or unjust in a way that the *same* inequality – were it to occur among individuals not enmeshed in non-consensual social cooperation – would not be. Considering the following examples may help illustrate this thought (cf. Nozick 1974, 185–186; Beitz 1979, 165; and Blake 2001):

- There are two islands on which political communities live. The two communities have no contact with one another. Although both groups industrialize and provide perfectly adequately for their populations (such that nobody can make claims of need), over time one group accumulates substantially more wealth. Is there an injustice here that is only discovered and potentially remedied once the two groups learn of each other's existence?
- If we discover a booming civilization of human-like creatures on another planet living an even more bountiful existence than ours, does this mean that we are somehow the victims of a terrible injustice (when just before we learned of their existence we thought that we were in fact the picture of justice)?

Although it is possible to think – in the second example – that one would prefer to have been born on this distant paradise of a planet, and even that, in some cosmic sense, the situation is unfair, it is difficult to identify an *injustice.*

Who committed it? How? If we demanded a justification for the even greater wealth of those on the other planet (or island), wouldn't it be

association is itself a product of the social cooperation made possible by the state and the particular shape of social cooperation that is settled upon (Rawls 1993, Lecture VII). Accordingly, the appropriate question is not about how much different individuals contribute to upholding the state, but instead whether the social cooperation facilitated by the state fairly distributes the product of social cooperation (Murphy and Nagel 2002, esp. 31–37).

adequate for those individuals to respond that the inequalities between us (a) are not such that we are condemned to lives of poverty while they live in great excess; (b) are not the result of past injustices inflicted on us by them; (c) do not – given our lack of association – belittle us in any important way; and (d) do not amount to an objectionable parceling out of the advantages of social cooperation? Why not?

One way of responding to these kinds of arguments is via the argument that the society into which one is born is arbitrary (see, for example, Barry 1989, 238–239). I hope that the discussion in this section and the previous one make clear how I would like to respond. The main claim is that not all arbitrary inequalities are injustices; instead, arbitrary inequalities become injustices when they are experienced in certain contexts, have certain histories, or interfere with certain relationships. I have tried to provide reason to think that this way of understanding justice – rather than simply seeing justice as a way of responding to arbitrariness – rests more easily with considered convictions.

Notice that I use the above examples as hypothetical possibilities in order to illustrate the broader conceptual point, and *not* as direct analogies to the relationship between citizens of a state and non-citizens in our world. Instead, of course it is true in *our* world that there is substantial interaction among citizens of different states. As Jeremy Waldron colorfully remarks, we live in a world where it is easy for an individual to refuse "to think of himself as *defined* by his location or his ancestry or his citizenship or his language," so that though one may live "in San Francisco and be of Irish identity, he does not take his identity to be compromised when he learns Spanish, eats Chinese, wears clothes made in Korea, listens to arias by Verdi sung by a Maori princess on Japanese equipment, follows Ukranian politics, and practices Buddhist meditation techniques" (Waldron 1995, 95). As Waldron illustrates, we are not in the position of having simply learned of each other's existence on a distant and unconnected planet. Rather, we are tied together through a dense series of economic interactions, cultural exchanges, and – to some extent – political institutions.

Notice, however, that the line of argument employed above for equality of opportunity did not depend on the density of consensual economic interactions. Instead, the relevant question is to what extent the circumstances of justice apply. Or, more specifically: to what extent are the riches of the developed world the result of the imposition of a scheme of social cooperation that allows such states to unfairly hoard the results of such cooperation? Empirically, this is a complex question – one that we will not easily sort out. Part of the complexity lies in the fact that the appropriate answer is surely between the easy extremes.

Our relationship with foreigners is clearly unlike the hypothetical examples above. As Thomas Pogge has convincingly argued, there are clear senses in which the international "community" enforces norms on participating states in a way that affects how the benefits of social cooperation are distributed (Pogge 2002). For example, according to Pogge the fact that the global order allows rulers (regardless of the fragility of their claims to legitimacy) to borrow money in the name of their citizens and to take ownership of the state's natural resources facilitates "oppressive rule and greatly encourage(s) coup attempts and civil wars in the developing countries" (Pogge 2002, 22). To the extent that (a) this is true; (b) these rules are so basic to international interaction that individuals are subsumed under them non-consensually; and (c) these rules structure a system of mutually advantageous cooperation, then there is a strong case to be made that the inequalities generated by such rules are objectionable or unjust. Moreover, it should be obvious that the processes of globalization affect the extent to which this argument applies and, so, the extent to which relationships of distributive justice obtain across borders.

Still, our relationship with foreigners is also unlike – in the relevant respects – our relationship with fellow citizens in the *extent* to which our relationships are marked by these kinds of non-consensual mutually beneficial interaction. As Liam Murphy and Thomas Nagel insist, the institutions that fellow citizens subject us to make possible even the basic necessities of a decent life:

> In the absence of a legal system supported by taxes, there couldn't be money, banks, corporations, stock exchanges, patents, or a modern market economy – none of the institutions that make possible the existence of almost all contemporary forms of income and wealth. (Murphy and Nagel 2002, 32)

Murphy and Nagel's (Hobbesian) point is that the cooperative venture of the state – imposed upon us by fellow citizens – makes possible all the wealth that we enjoy above a very grim baseline. The same cannot be said for the kind of cooperative ventures that we share willy-nilly with subjects of other states.[15] Similarly, Samuel Freeman insists that

[15] The same point is made in a slightly different way by David Reidy. He says that

> individual human persons literally come to be as persons or moral agents only within and through social cooperation. They are not born, but rather are made. And they are made only through cooperative social institutions ... Nature permits these capacities; it does not deliver them ... Matters are different with respect to peoples. Peoples can both come to be and persist over time as corporate moral agents apart from any cooperation with other peoples. *(Reidy 2004, 298–299).*

> social cooperation is the most profound and influential relationship that humans can have; it is the fundamental precondition for our developing our distinctly human capacities and achieving a status as free agents with a capacity for practical reason and a conception of our good . . . Without cooperation with *other societies*, we lose the economic and cultural benefits of commerce with other peoples. Without social cooperation with *other persons*, we lose civilization and all its essential benefits. (Freeman 2007, 422)

The significance of this framework of social cooperation in making possible civilized life forms the precondition for claims of equality of opportunity. It is the centrality of the benefits of social cooperation that make such claims obtain, for fairly sharing the benefits of *this* social cooperation means fairly sharing the possibilities for a decent life that it brings forth.

Unfortunately, the question of the *extent* of the benefits that flow from cooperative ventures that ensnare individuals beyond political borders is a complicated and messy one. Accordingly, I will not even attempt to offer an estimate or assessment of the exact extent to which systems of international cooperation call forth duties of distributive justice. Instead, for our purposes it is only necessary to say that even if we allow that some inequalities may be objectionable when they arise from a process that unfairly shares the benefits of social cooperation, it remains quite unclear that this demand brings forth a legitimate claim of equality of opportunity. For that to be true, it would at least need to be the case that – as with the state – the cooperative venture makes possible all forms of profitable interaction that take us beyond a Hobbesian state of nature. Because the benefits brought forth by mutual cooperation with fellow citizens are so basic and all-encompassing, the fair distribution of them may call forth a demand for a strong concern with the relative distribution of goods (manifesting, perhaps, in equality of opportunity or the difference principle) that will have no basis among those whose social cooperation is less thorough.

Accordingly, it is not necessary to answer the empirical question regarding the extent of relevant social cooperation between non-citizens in our world in order to conclude that the distributive argument is wrong to insist that treating individuals as equals *requires* that we intervene to ensure that they have opportunities equal to us. Although it perhaps remains possible to somehow show that existing international cooperation brings forth a requirement to ensure the equality of opportunity of all participants, that this claim does not simply follow from the equal moral status of all individuals follows from the conviction that we at least sometimes treat others as equals simply by leaving them alone.

In a wonderfully helpful article on the scope of distributive justice, Arash Abizadeh objects to this kind of social cooperation argument for limiting the scope of distributive justice. In particular, Abizadeh insists that "the problem with this suggestion is that it ignores" the background argument for distributive justice according to which "one of the roles of applying principles of distributive justice is precisely to ensure that it is possible, in the long run, for individual transactions and exchanges to be fair" (Abizadeh 2007, 337). Here he has in mind Rawls's claim that

> the conditions necessary for background justice can be undermined, even though nobody acts unfairly or is aware of how the overall result of many separate exchanges affects the opportunities of others. There are no feasible rules that it is practicable to require economic agents to follow in their day-to-day transactions that can prevent these undesirable consequences. (Rawls 1993, 266 cited by Abizadeh 2007, 328)

In Abizadeh's view, it is a mistake to suggest that robust demands of distributive justice kick in only among those sharing a cooperative relationship that is more involved than mere economic interaction, because even simple interaction raises the concern that individual exchanges will cumulate in a way that has unpredictable and unacceptable long-term consequences. In other words, "one of the roles of applying principles of distributive justice is precisely to ensure that it is possible, in the long run, for individual transactions and exchanges to be fair" (Abizadeh 2007, 337). This is supposed to show that it is a mistake to insist that demands of distributive justice are only applicable among those who share in some type of robust social or political cooperation (as opposed to mere economic interaction).

The problem, in my view, with this line of argument is that it hinges on the assumption that the "conditions necessary for background justice" are *independent* of the relationship in which agents stand to one another. The concern, however, with background justice is a concern about the effect inequalities that build up over time can have on individuals. But, again, such worries are *most* powerful if individuals stand in certain relationships (especially political relationships) vis-à-vis one another.

Again: there is special reason to be concerned about the relative distribution of wealth among compatriots because such inequalities might interfere with the possibility of fair political interaction and the maintenance of the social bases of self-respect (Rawls 2001, 161). As Rawls says: "the appropriate notion of fair terms of cooperation depends on the nature of the cooperative activity itself" and the relationship of those involved in dense social cooperation is special because it provides the prerequisites for "all the essential purposes of human life" (Rawls 1993, 301). The worry is that inequality among those who share an ongoing scheme of social cooperation "may arouse widespread attitudes of deference and servility on one side and a will to dominate and arrogance on the other. These effects of social and economic inequalities can be serious evils and the attitudes they engender great vices" (Rawls 2001, 131). Alternatively, there is much less reason to worry about the long-term cumulative effects of interactions between two people who are not later going to meet in the public sphere as putative equals.

Once again: although I do *not* want to claim that concerns of background justice are irrelevant among those who do not share a strong political relationship, I *do* want to say that the extent to which the background argument provides reason for us to worry about inequalities depends on the relationship in which individuals stand vis-à-vis one another. If this is correct, it is a mistake to say that because of the importance of the background argument, interaction of *any* kind calls forth uniform demands of distributive justice (or equality of opportunity).

Although we often take a commitment to equality of opportunity as a bedrock principle of political morality, I have argued instead that equality of opportunity draws its appeal from legitimate worries about four particular kinds of unjust inequalities. This includes those that

- force some to live below a minimum standard of subsistence while others enjoy an excess;
- exist only because of the illegitimate actions of the (now) better-off group;
- undermine the fairness of interaction; and
- result from the unfair distribution of the benefits of social cooperation.

Thus, although there *is* a range of reasons to be concerned about inequality (even across borders), none of these concerns lends support to the view that *all* inequalities are injustices and, so, it is unclear why we should accept the claim (P2) that we are bound by justice to create a universal regime of equality of opportunity.[16]

To illustrate these concerns, it may be helpful to consider an argument put forth by Ayelet Shachar. She repeatedly portrays inherited citizenship as

[16] For arguments along similar lines from which I have benefited, see especially Anderson 1999 and Frankfurt 1987.

a betrayal of our commitment to equality of opportunity by pointing out that in our world a tremendous number of people live below any plausible line of subsistence. For example, she argues that

> more than a billion people live on less than a dollar a day; about 2.7 billion live without access to adequate sanitation and more than 800 million are seriously malnourished ... When our citizenship laws effectively become intertwined with distributing shares in human survival on a global scale – designating some to a life of relative comfort while condemning others to a constant struggle to overcome the basic threats of insecurity, hunger, and destitution – we can no longer accept this situation. (Shachar 2009, 11–12; also see pp. 22, 24, 96, 98, and 105)

Although the tremendous still-existing poverty reflected by these figures is indeed tragic, it should by now be clear that this judgment does not uniquely support the conclusion that we must embrace an unbounded principle of equality of opportunity. Again: we can accept that there is an injustice in certain inequalities without also accepting an unlimited principle of equality of opportunity. Insofar as advocates of unbounded equality of opportunity rest their case on these kinds of objectionable inequalities, we are left to guess what might be the justification for concluding that *all* inequalities are cases of injustice.

For instance, it is natural to reflect on the fact that the United States has a gross national income (GNI) per capita of nearly $46,000 whereas the figure in Sierra Leone is $660. No American can reasonably claim to *deserve* this advantaged position. Surely, there is an injustice in some having to survive in a war-torn country on a pittance. The question we face is how to appropriately describe this injustice. One way to think about the question is to imagine that we discover

> a small island with a thriving population and a GNI per capita of $92,000. Thus, the difference in GNI/capita between the newfound island and the United States is just barely more than is the difference between the United States and Sierra Leone. Are the citizens of the United States now, although they heretofore did not know it, mired in a life of injustice?

If you are like me, you will be inclined to think that discovering a culture with a much higher standard of living is interesting (and perhaps even inspiring). It is difficult, however, to see why this information should lead me to think that my life – which seemed perfectly adequate before – is now marred by injustice. To the extent that this judgment is shared, it provides reason to think that what is truly worrisome about the original pairing is not the inequality, but instead the fact that so many individuals (for example, the citizens of Sierra Leone) fall below some standard of sufficiency in a world that showers extravagances on those of us fortunate enough to be born within the "right" political lines.

Thus, an argument (such as Shachar's) that rejects the transfer of wealth via citizenship because of the existence of terrible poverty fails because one can hold (as the associative ownership position does) that the transfer of wealth via citizenship is only acceptable if it does not feature unjust inequalities. Insofar as Shachar's argument (a) hinges on appeal to unjust inequalities; (b) fails to recognize the conflict between self-determination and equality of opportunity; and (c) does not inquire about the appropriate grounds and scope of equality of opportunity, it does not cast doubt on the associative ownership position.

My overall claim is twofold. I have argued (1) that equality of opportunity is at odds with a commitment to associative ownership/self-determination; and (2) that the associative ownership view can respond to unjust inequalities. Once we incorporate a concern with these unjust inequalities, the distributive argument loses its appeal. Thus, the distributive justice argument's single-minded commitment to equality of opportunity seems to pursue the elimination of unobjectionable inequalities at the expense of important elements of political morality (namely, associative ownership and self-determination). Advocates of the distributive argument thus bear the burden of explaining why we should bear an unlimited obligation to ensure equality of opportunity.

IV THE ANALOGY WITH FEUDALISM

Before closing this discussion, it is worth discussing one prominent argument by analogy that is often used by advocates of the distributive argument. In particular, advocates often present the distributive argument as a generalization of the conclusion that feudalism is unjust. For example, Joseph Carens argues that

> citizenship in the modern world is a lot like feudal status in the medieval world. It is assigned at birth; for the most part it is not subject to change by the individual's will and efforts; and it has a major impact upon that person's life chances . . . Limiting entry to countries like Canada is a way of protecting a birthright privilege. (Carens 1992, 26)

Here, Carens's strategy is to convince the reader that if one objects to medieval feudalism, then one must also object to border restrictions of any kind. Because the analogy between feudal status and immigration restrictions is common and rhetorically powerful, I want to briefly explain how the arguments adumbrated above cast doubt on its applicability. In particular, I want to suggest that feudalism is unjust precisely because the inequalities that it sustains are objectionable in *all four* of the potential ways noted above.

First, we object to medieval feudalism because of the impression that it left serfs below a minimally acceptable standard of living even while lords lived a life of (relative) luxury. Second, we object to the practice of feudalism because of the way it structures interpersonal relations. As Marc Bloch explains in his classic study, feudalism makes one "the man of another man" and thus "emphasizes the subordination of one individual to another" (Bloch 1961, 145). This is most clear in the institution of homage:

> Imagine two men face to face; one wishing to serve, the other willing or anxious to be served. The former puts his hands together and places them, thus joined, between the hands of the other man – a plain symbol of submission, the significance of which was sometimes further emphasized by a kneeling posture. At the same time, the person proffering his hands utters a few words – a very short declaration – by which he acknowledges himself to be the "man" of the person facing him ... The superior party, whose position was created by this act, was described by no other term than the very general one of "lord." (Bloch 1961, 145–146)

This practice – which "could not be offered or accepted by proxy" (Bloch 1961, 147) – is neither consistent with the equal status of participants nor fair interaction between the parties; instead, it served precisely to personally and vividly express the subordination of serf to lord. Third, these differences in status were often the direct result of injustices (such as the "usurpation of authority, often by violent means" (Bloch 1961, 148)) committed by the stronger parties. Fourth, the practice of feudalism seems to quite unfairly distribute the benefits and burdens of social cooperation. Thus, inequalities in the feudal world were objectionable in each of the ways noted above: they juxtaposed great need with relative excess; they were the direct result of the illegitimate action of the advantaged parties; they created a relationship of inequality that undermined the equal standing of the less well-off; and they inappropriately divided the benefits of social cooperation.

This is important because it shows that positions (such as the associative ownership view) that reject inequalities with these features, but stop short of accepting an unbounded principle of equality of opportunity, can accept the injustice of medieval feudalism even while holding that some restrictions on immigration are not unjust. Thus, the problem with arguments that hinge on the feudalism analogy is that they do not succeed in giving us reason to favor open borders over other views that have the resources to explain resistance to feudal practices. Unfortunately, this point is obscured by the tactic's rhetorical appeal. It would be preferable if advocates of open borders instead relied on arguments that helped distinguish their view from plausible alternatives.

V SOME CONCLUDING REMARKS

We have seen that arguments based on efficiency or distributive justice do not provide reason to grant citizenship to all comers. *Efficiency Arguments* hinge on the overall economic benefits that might be gained from allowing widespread access to wealthy economies. However, they fail to explain *why* increases in efficiency should be taken as dispositive reason in favor of open borders. Instead, I believe that the intuitive attractiveness of the position depends on its connection to concerns of distributive justice.

Meanwhile, *Distributive Justice Arguments* hinge on the obligation to equalize the opportunity of all individuals. However, such claims ignore (a) the importance of political association, particularly the role of the citizenry in developing the goods that advocates of open borders would freely distribute; and (b) the way in which positions short of open borders can respond to objectionable inequalities. Although it is perhaps short of conclusively demonstrating that seeing others as equals does not require an unbounded regime of equality of opportunity (and so demonstrating the inadequacy of P2 in the distributive argument), I have suggested that such a view conflicts with other core elements of political morality (including the idea of self-determination) and depends for its appeal on rhetoric that can be made sense of by positions that reject an unbounded commitment to equality of opportunity.

My hope is that this line of argument at least shows that advocates of the distributive argument for open borders bear the burden of more clearly explaining why it is that acknowledging the equal status of all requires that we also accept an unbounded principle of equality of opportunity. Without convincing further explanation along these lines, the distributive argument for open borders is inadequate.

CHAPTER 6

The significance of national identity

Perhaps the most common type of argument put forward to defend the state's right to restrict immigration hinges on the putative importance of shared national identity. Historically such concerns have played an important role in public discourse surrounding immigration policy. Although, as noted above, the country's early years saw little restriction of immigration, this lack of legislation was not a reflection of the public's lack of interest. Instead, concerns about the identity of the fledgling nation were of immediate significance. Several anti-immigration and anti-Catholic riots took place in New England during the 1830s and 1840s (Daniels 2004, 10). Likewise, the infamous Know-Nothings built a strong following, even entering Millard Fillmore into the 1856 presidential election and holding forty-three House seats between 1855 and 1857 (Tichenor 2002, 62).

About a century after independence, the first major piece of immigration legislation, the 1882 Chinese Exclusion Act, banned the entry of Chinese laborers (but not merchants) for ten years.[1] President Cleveland justified such restrictions by insisting that the

> experiment of blending the social habits and mutual race idiosyncrasies of the Chinese laboring classes with those of the great body of the people of the United States [has] proved by the experience of twenty years ... in every sense unwise, impolitic, and injurious to both nations. (quoted in Daniels 2004, 20)

Likewise, in Senate debate Chinese migrants were described as "hordes of heathens that swarm like rats in a cellar" and "aliens in blood, aliens in faith, and clogs to the free movement of the wheels of Christian civilization and enlightened progress ... A degraded people" with "nothing in their civilization that has an elevating tendency" (quoted in Calavita 2000, 11). Debates about the cultural differences of immigrants have been prominent

[1] For an interesting exploration of the difficulties surrounding enforcement (especially distinguishing between laborers and merchants) see Calavita 2000.

(even if the terms in and groups towards which such concerns are expressed has shifted somewhat).

Initial passage of the Chinese Exclusion Act proved to be but the tip of the iceberg. Extended in 1892, it was not repealed for more than fifty years and, even then, was replaced by the token acceptance of barely over one hundred Chinese immigrants annually. Moreover, from 1882 to 1921 a succession of other exclusions succeeded in barring almost all Asians. For instance, in 1907 the "Gentlemen's Agreement" reached with Japan guaranteed that Japanese authorities would block the emigration of their citizens as long as the United States agreed to refrain from disrespectfully banning Japanese immigrants. This increasing exclusion of Asian immigrants led employers to systematically recruit Mexican immigrants for the first time and, indeed, the years after the "Gentlemen's Agreement" saw the first significant influx of migrants from Mexico. It was as a result of these laws that "a federal bureaucracy was created to control immigration and immigrants, a bureaucracy whose initial raison d'être was to keep out first Chinese and then others who were deemed to be inferior" (Daniels 2004, 3). Simply put: worries regarding the cultural or ethnic makeup of the American people are a perennial feature of immigration debate.

Such concerns continue to play an important role in arguments about the appropriate goals for immigration policy. Indeed, the state is often seen not just as a set of coercive institutions or a framework for social cooperation, but as the protectorate of a *nation.* It is seen, in other words, as the institutional manifestation of a community of individuals sharing a distinct identity. Accordingly, it is often thought that there are arguments – related to the value and maintenance of this shared identity – that may justify substantial restrictions on immigration. This chapter seeks to assess the legitimacy of three such arguments.

First, according to the *cultural authenticity* view, cultural groups have a legitimate interest in the future flourishing of a form of life that is distinct to the group, and providing for this may require certain kinds of restrictions on immigration. Second, according to the *instrumental argument,* individuals have an interest in the preservation of their culture because it provides a context of choice that enables one to live autonomously. According to this view, the protection of national identity is important because of its instrumental importance in the successful pursuit of individual autonomy. Third, according to the *social trust view,* justice requires certain kinds of redistributive institutions which people will only be willing to support if they see themselves as sharing a political identity with those who benefit from them.

My objective in this chapter is to investigate the legitimacy of these three lines of argument.[2] Although the diversity of arguments that fall under the national identity aegis render it difficult to say anything that applies to all such arguments, there is one important point that applies across a wide range of such arguments. In particular, advocates of such views must explain why members of the cultural majority are entitled in the first place to make decisions about the future cultural composition of the country. It is not obvious that the mere existence of cultural similarity could by itself justify this claim. Instead, it seems likely that any persuasive explanation is going to hinge on the historical role members of the culture in question have had in constructing the institutions to which access is at stake. For example, an apt assessment of the right of Israeli Jews to take steps to preserve the cultural integrity of their country surely depends on the prior legitimacy of their claim to the relevant territory.

Partly for this reason, I hope to suggest that the relationship between citizens and their political institutions is better understood as a claim of entitlement justified via associative ownership. According to this view, arguments related to shared identity are best seen as reasons to invoke this antecedent entitlement rather than reasons that may justify it in the first instance. So, I shall argue that the relevance of national identity in justifying restrictions on immigration is often greatly exaggerated and, in fact, faces very significant limits.

I THE CULTURAL AUTHENTICITY ARGUMENT

The cultural authenticity argument insists that maintenance of a cultural form has a certain kind of value in itself. Johann Fichte was one of many late eighteenth- and early nineteenth-century philosophers who advocated such a position:

> Those who speak the same language are joined to each other by a multitude of invisible bonds by nature herself, long before any human art begins; they understand each other and have the power of continuing to make themselves understood more and more clearly; they belong together and are by nature one and an inseparable whole. Such a whole, if it wishes to absorb and mingle with itself any other people of different descent and language, cannot do so without itself becoming confused, in the beginning at any rate, and violently disturbing the even progress of its culture. (Fichte 1968 [1806], 190)

[2] It should not be surprising that those who argue for restricting immigration as a result of concerns related to national identity often combine the lines of argument to be considered in this chapter. Nevertheless, for analytical purposes it is useful to distinguish them.

Although this view is less prominent in contemporary philosophical dialogue, something akin to it is often the driving force behind culture-based arguments for restrictions on immigration in the public debate. Peter Brimelow, for instance, announces that

> race and ethnicity are destiny in American politics. The racial and ethnic base of America is being radically altered through public policy ... Essentially, a nation is a sort of extended family. It links individual and group ... in ways that reach beyond the rational to the most profound and elemental in the human experience. (Brimelow 1995, xvii and xix)

On this view, there is a parallel between a commitment to the claim that individuals have the right to develop their own authentic individual identity and the rights of nations to do so. Herder's insistence that "a *Volk* should be true to itself, that is, its own culture" (Taylor 1994, 31) is – according to this view – legitimate in the same way as is Polonius's plea to Laertes in *Hamlet*: "to thine own self be true."

According to this view, nations, like individuals, are entitled (perhaps within the constraints imposed by the basic rights of others) to articulate and maintain into the future their identity. The idea is to ensure "that there is a community of people here in the future that will want to avail itself of the opportunity" to be members of the culture in question. This requires that nations "actively seek to *create* members of the community" by adopting policies that assure "that future generations continue to identify" as members of the culture (Taylor 1994, 58–59). In sum, the demand is that "we let cultures defend themselves" because the continuing survival of the culture is thought to have value in itself (Taylor 1994, 64).

Like Taylor, David Miller defends the claim that individuals have an interest in controlling the shape of cultural change in their country. He suggests that

> the public culture of their country is something people have an interest in controlling: they want to be able to shape the way that their nation develops, including the values that are contained in the public culture. (Miller 2005, 200)

This claim is meant to be stronger than the instrumental argument considered below because it holds that individuals not only have an interest in having a relatively stable cultural context from which to pursue an autonomous life, but also "a reason for wanting to stay in control of the process" of inevitable change to that cultural context (Miller 2005, 201). In particular:

> They may certainly have good reason to try ... to maintain cultural continuity over time, so that they can see themselves as the bearers of an identifiable cultural tradition that stretches backward historically. (Miller 2005, 200)

It is important to be precise about what is at stake here. The question that faces us is whether immigration restrictions can be justified on the grounds that they are necessary to tie *future* generations to a cultural shape valued by present members. "After all," Taylor remarks, "if we're concerned with identity, then what is more legitimate than one's aspiration that it never be lost?" (Taylor 1994, 40).

I want to try to argue – partly by way of historical example – that it is a mistake to think that people's having such a desire (real enough though it may be) can justify restrictions aimed at ensuring the future survival or success of their cultural way of life.

In 1965 the United States instituted a set of reforms which eliminated the quota system, replacing it with hemispheric limits and a system that gave priority to the family members of current citizens. Resulting changes in the distribution of immigration visas are displayed in figure 1.

As we can see, these reforms, together with changes in the global economy, shifted the origin of immigrants from Europe to Latin America and Asia. Peter Brimelow warns that this reform

> risks making America an *alien nation* . . . in the sense that America will become a freak among the world's nations because of the unprecedented demographic mutation it is inflicting on itself . . . in the sense that Americans themselves will become alien to each other, requiring an increasingly strained government to arbitrate between them. (Brimelow 1995, xix)

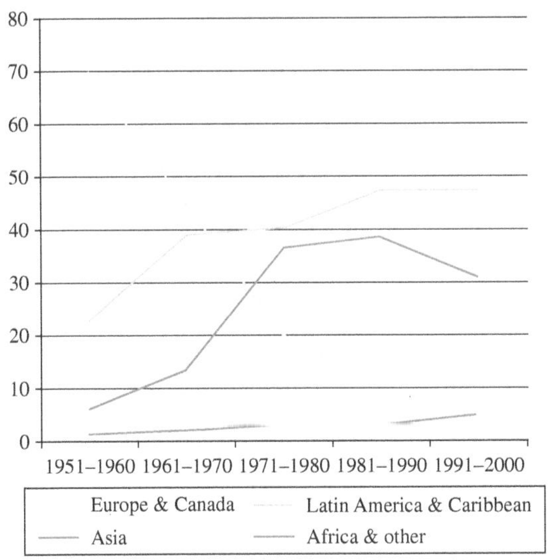

Figure 1 Regional origins of immigrants (by percentage) to the United States, 1951–2000

Unquestionably, the move from a quota system to a system of family preferences altered the ethnic composition of the United States by substantially increasing the number of immigrants from Asia and Latin America while slowing immigration from Europe.

That the abandonment of quotas had significant ramifications for the ethnic background of the United States would not have surprised those who designed the quota system. Indeed, quotas were precisely an attempt to *ensure* the future success and survival of a distinctive ethnic composition. The policy was developed in the wake of – and in response to – a substantial increase in the number of Southern and Eastern Europeans coming to the United States. While in 1882 only about 13 percent of European immigrants came from Southern and Eastern Europe, by 1907, 81 percent of such immigrants hailed from these regions (King 2000, 50–51). These changes led legislators to believe that control over the shape of American cultural life was being lost, that a distinctively American way of life was being forfeit.

In response, a quota system was introduced that allowed 3 percent of a nationality's population in 1910 to enter each year (granting 360,000 quotas in all). The approach – which was also adopted by other receiving countries in the 1920s – was "non-discriminatory" in that it brought annually "an installment of European immigration reproducing in miniature the American composite" (Senate Judiciary Committee, quoted in Graham 2004, 52). Indeed, the expert advisor to the House Committee on Immigration explained that, in order to "keep America American … after we determine what the American race is, and the biological components of it in the proper proportion, then our immigration policy should be to recruit each element of these races" (quoted in King 2000, 135). Originally, the quota system applied only to Europeans. Immigration from the Western hemisphere remained unlimited (largely because legislators in the West and Southwest insisted on the importance of Mexican laborers), and Asians were largely excluded. The expiration of this law brought, in 1924, a revised version based on the 1890 census (adopting the earlier date gave further preference to Western Europeans over their Southern brethren). The American experiment with a quota system, then, was precisely an attempt by current citizens to ensure the future survival or success of their culture.

My supposition is that Miller and Taylor would object that the quota system was flawed because of the explicitly racial interpretation of culture and, thus, the particular cultural shape that advocates sought to protect. The problem, according to this view, was not the attempt to protect culture, but the particular understanding of the culture that the quota system sought to protect.

Despite its initial attractiveness, I think that this view is mistaken. Reasons to object to the quota system run deeper than the way in which advocates understood culture, the shape of the culture they sought to protect, or the hubris and implicit claim of infallibility involved in institutionally protecting the future existence of one's culture.

There are also objectionable costs imposed by efforts to institutionally embed a cultural shape. Rather than treating individuals as equals, the quota system treated individuals as simple reflections of their racial heritage. While I do not want to attribute such a view to Taylor or Miller, I worry that any attempt to institutionalize an immigration policy that seeks to encode and ensure the future survival of a particular cultural form is likely to travel a road similar to the quota system. This is because national identity is an amorphous concept, and attempts to operationalize it are likely to turn toward the racial and national traits favored by the quota system.

David Miller describes shared nationality in terms of "a common public culture." He explains:

> There must be a sense that the people belong together by virtue of the characteristics that they share. It is not so easy, however, to pin down precisely what this entails ... If what matters to nationality is that people should share a common public culture, this is quite compatible with their belonging to a diversity of ethnic groups ... All that matters is that the melding together of different "races" should have produced a people with a distinct and common character of its own. (Miller 1995, 25–26)

The difficulty is that demographic information is not sorted by "common public culture" and, as Miller admits, it is not clear how we might do so. Officials have no way of assessing whether potential immigrants have the desired cultural commitments (or of ensuring that citizens do).

There is a real concern that the concept of a "common public culture" conceals more than it illuminates by allowing advocates to, in rather *ad hoc* fashion, declare the existing citizenry of any state an essentially unique cultural group. Without a clearer description, such claims are terribly difficult to assess. It is unclear what it would mean to adequately challenge or defend the claim that a people share a distinct and common character. Moreover, given this difficulty and the readily available nature of demographic information based on ethnic and racial distinctions, there is an ever-present danger that attempts to protect a "common public culture" will soon slip into the quota-era practice of determining the standing of individuals by reference to their national and racial backgrounds. Indeed, social scientists interested in testing Miller's claims have unhesitatingly (and, indeed, given the lack of clear alternatives, understandably) fallen back on racial and ethnic data (Soroka *et al.* 2006).

It is tempting to respond by characterizing culture – much more thinly – as a commitment to democratic political institutions and a willingness to learn the language(s) of the public sphere. This is a plausible description of what the otherwise incredibly diverse citizenry of the United States does actually share.[3] The problem with this response is that it fails to provide reason to restrict those who agree to, and are interested in, integration into this political culture.

This, however, includes the vast majority of potential immigrants. Recent evidence suggests that while only 41 percent of first-generation Hispanic immigrants are either bilingual or primarily speak English, the number increases to 92 percent in the second generation, and 99 percent in the third generation (Citrin *et al.* 2007, 37). This is not an accident; instead, 93 percent of Hispanic immigrants interviewed in Spanish in 2002 agreed that it is important to learn English. Moreover, because systems of education and employment are built around the language, "learning English is virtually inevitable for the children and grandchildren of immigrants" (Citrin *et al.* 2007, 37; also see Alba and Nee 2003, 225–228). Likewise, attachments to the symbols and values of the country are as strong or stronger among native-born Hispanics than they are among white citizens (Citrin *et al.* 2007, 41–43). Because the vast majority of potential immigrants internalize the culture in at least the thin sense of learning the language and being committed to the country's political institutions, this argument seems unable to justify the kind of *carte blanche* control over immigration that advocates of the position intend; instead, even if correct, the line of argument could only justify limits on the *rate* of immigration when necessary to ensure the continuous survival of the language and support for democratic institutions.[4]

We have seen that advocates of the cultural authenticity view argue that cultures have the right to protect the future flourishing of their cultural practices. However, I have tried to explain that advocates of this position face the following dilemma. On the one hand, they can embrace a thin interpretation of culture (according to which the country's shared culture can be understood mainly in terms of a shared language and commitment to democratic political institutions). Indeed, it is unclear in what other sense we could give meaning to the idea that the hugely diverse citizenry of the

[3] For a review of evidence on the shared commitment of US citizens to democratic institutions, see Klosko 2000, chap. 5.

[4] Because this position is more strongly supported by the instrumental conception of the value of culture, I will discuss this farther in the section that follows.

United States importantly shares a cultural identity. However, even if one allows that groups have the right to protect the future practice of their culture in this thin form, the overwhelming tendency of immigrants to learn English and embrace the country's political institutions suggests that immigration is a threat to this thin conception of the culture only at the margins and, so, the argument can only provide reason to slow immigration to a manageable rate. It cannot justify the broad restrictions on immigration called for by so many of the advocates of this position.

Alternatively, advocates of the cultural authenticity view can embrace a more robust conception of culture. This allows them to make it more plausible that immigrants in fact present an important threat to the cultural integrity of the country. However, attempts to operationalize this more robust conception of culture typically hinge on objectionably identifying people as simple reflections of their racial or ethnic backgrounds. Especially given the US government's history of condemning people because of racial and ethnic characteristics, there is important reason to avoid a justification of immigration restrictions that turns on the claim that those from different ethnic or racial backgrounds are, because of those backgrounds, inferior candidates for citizenship. In sum: a thin conception of cultural similarity cannot justify significant restrictions on immigration while a thick conception of cultural similarity (a) cannot be justified given the great diversity of American citizens; and (b) risks assigning rights and duties based on racial and ethnic background. We will see in the next section that advocates of the instrumental view face a similar dilemma.

II THE INSTRUMENTAL ARGUMENT

It is often argued that national culture is significant – not in itself – but because of the instrumental contribution it makes to individual well-being or autonomy. For instance, Avishai Margalit and Joseph Raz argue that membership in pervasive cultures is of "great importance to individual well-being" and, as a result, individuals have an important interest in the prosperity of their culture (Margalit and Raz 1990, 449).[5] Similarly, Will

[5] The relevant cultural groups are large social groups that have a substantial impact on the identity and lifestyle choices of members in a large range of personal decisions. More specifically, encompassing groups have "a common culture that encompass[es] many, varied and important aspects of life"; influence those who grow up in their midst in "profound and far-reaching" ways; distribute membership according to mutual recognition; form a salient part of members' social identities; do not distribute membership according to achievement; and "are anonymous groups where mutual recognition is secured by the possession of general characteristics" (Margalit and Raz 1990, 443–447).

Kymlicka contends that "freedom is intimately linked with and dependent on culture" because cultures provide "members with meaningful ways of life across the full range of human activities" (Kymlicka 1995, 75–76).

So, according to this view, an individual's culture is of value because it provides a context through which to make sense of a range of options and possibilities:

> The argument simply says that cultural membership is important in pursuing our essential interest in leading a good life, and so consideration of that membership is an important part of having equal consideration for the interests of each member of the community. (Kymlicka 1989, 168)

Culture provides a lens through which life can be interpreted, understood, and meaningfully pursued.

It is sometimes said that this line of argument – according to which we assess cultures by the value that they have for their members – involves an objectionably individualistic view of culture. Culture is, after all, a social good. However, it is important to recognize that one can accept that culture is valuable to the extent that it benefits individuals even while recognizing – as Charles Taylor rightly insists – that culture is an "irreducibly social good" (Taylor 1995, 138). Culture could not be supplied by a single individual, no matter how fabulously wealthy; instead, its existence depends on the mutual understanding of a number of individuals, and such "common understandings are undecomposable" (Taylor 1995, 139). Although culture is a social good in the sense that it cannot be *provided* by a single individual, once provided we can nevertheless assess its value by asking how it affects the lives of the various individuals upon which it touches.

For instance, although baseball is a social good, there is no reason to think that we cannot estimate its worth by thinking about the value it adds to individual lives. Of course, part of enjoying baseball is regaling with other fans or players in the group's accomplishments. The game of baseball, much less its significance, can only be understood dialogically. Without understanding the game's history and connection to particular communities, the game is seemingly reduced to the very odd event of a man swinging a stick at a small sphere hurled at him by another man. In the absence of social context, the event is silly.

However, despite the moment's meaning and value relying so heavily on this web of social creations, I see no reason to think that its *value* cannot be assessed (though certainly not in some very precise manner) by thinking about the value of the event to those individuals involved (for example, the utility of the experience for fans, the business it created for nearby bartenders, etc.).[6] It is hard to conceive of what value it might have that does not in some sense reside in the effect it has on individuals. It is this thought, and the connection between culture and individual autonomy, that underlies the instrumental argument.

If the existence of an encompassing national context is a precondition for individual well-being or autonomy, it seems to follow that individuals have reason, though not necessarily decisive reason, to exclude those who threaten to undermine the prevailing culture and prefer potential immigrants who share cultural similarities with the broader encompassing group. This much follows from a commitment to individual autonomy or well-being. Indeed, a number of political theorists advance arguments along these lines:

> Limits on immigration can be justified if we recognize that liberal states exist, not only to protect standard rights and opportunities of individuals, but also to protect people's cultural membership. (Kymlicka 1995, 126; also see Coleman and Harding 1995)

The implications of this line of argument are that the citizenry's interest in living within cultural groups justifies (a) excluding immigrants who threaten to undermine existing unity; and (b) preferring immigrants who are culturally similar to the current population. While this instrumental argument generates reasons of a legitimate type for restricting immigration, it faces competing concerns that severely limit its relevance.

Most importantly: this line of argument provides no reason to exclude immigrants who are of similar cultural background to citizens and little reason to exclude those who are not of similar cultural background but wish to integrate into the culture of the receiving country. After all, immigrants of either of these types do not pose important threats to the culture's ability to provide a meaningful context of choice for citizens.

This once again raises the question of what it means to say that co-nationals share a similar cultural background. As in the previous discussion, we can distinguish between strong and weak views. According to the strong view, sharing a common cultural background requires that citizens share a particular ethnic background, religious views, and a particular set of norms and values. This, however, cannot be the kind of similarity at stake because citizens in the huge modern states in question (such as the United States) clearly have a great diversity of norms, ethnic backgrounds, and religious views.

6 Charles Taylor denies this, saying that cultures are "worth fostering, not as contingent instruments, but for themselves" (Taylor 1995, 137).

Instead, for the argument to get off the ground, the cultural similarity in question must be much thinner. It must refer to what citizens of enormous and diverse modern democracies can be plausibly said to share. This can credibly include little more than a common language and commitment to the fairness of basic democratic institutions and procedures. Indeed, the cultural context that Kymlicka has in mind in advancing the instrumental argument "involves a common language and social institutions, rather than common religious beliefs, family customs, or personal lifestyles" (Kymlicka 2001, 25). He goes on to explain that

> societal cultures within a modern liberal democracy are inevitably pluralistic, containing Christians as well as Muslims, Jews, and atheists; heterosexuals as well as gays; urban professionals as well as rural farmers; conservatives as well as socialists. Such diversity is the inevitable result of the rights and freedoms guaranteed to liberal citizens, particularly when combined with an ethnically diverse population. This diversity, however, is balanced and constrained by *linguistic and institutional cohesion*. (Kymlicka 2001, 25, emphasis added)

So, the instrumental argument hinges on the existence of a shared culture in this weaker – linguistic and institutional – sense. It refers to the existence of a particular cultural context and not a culture of a particular shape (Kymlicka 1989, chapter 8). It must do so, for it is only in this weaker sense that citizens of modern democracies can plausibly be said to share a culture.

However, once we appreciate this point, we must conclude that there are quite significant limits to the ability of the instrumental argument to justify restrictions on immigration. The argument does not provide reason to exclude English-speaking immigrants who are committed to the legitimacy of democratic institutions. Likewise, although it may provide some reason to slow entrance of immigrants who wish to integrate into the culture, it does not seem to provide reason to reject them altogether. After all, we have already seen that the tendency of immigrants to learn English and accept basic democratic political norms is very strong. The instrumental argument only seems to provide reason to (a) reject those immigrants who wish to resist integrating, preferring instead to continue speaking their native language and rejecting the legitimacy of democratic institutions; and (b) restrict immigration to levels that ensure that any change in the culture is gradual enough so as not to disrupt the consensus on democratic institutions and widespread use of English. The point here is not that the instrumental argument is unsound, but only that its implications are much more limited than its advocates typically allow.

I should expand a bit more on the claim that the argument can only justify slowing the *rate* of immigration. If nationality gains its significance by making autonomous life possible, individuals have a strong interest in a context that they can make sense of and so succeed in providing a range of meaningful choices. However, this does not show that changes to the cultural context (so long as they are manageably gradual) are an important affront to the autonomy of individuals within it. The point here is that even if individuals have an important interest in a cultural context that follows from a commitment to individual autonomy or well-being, it does not follow that they have a claim to an *unchanging* cultural context.

Unfortunately, this point is often lost in debate. For instance, Samuel Huntington argues that "a bifurcated America with two languages and two cultures will be fundamentally different from the America with one language and one core Anglo-Protestant culture that has existed for over three centuries" (Huntington 2004, 324). Likewise, it is not uncommon to hear concerns about the "degradation" of the culture to which they have become accustomed. Although Huntington may be correct that such a culture will be different than what has existed in the past, this observation cannot be used to support the instrumental line of argument because there is no reason to think that citizens are incapable of living autonomously in a slowly evolving culture or a culture different in important ways from some traditional ideal.

People are dynamic creatures, capable of communicating across language divides and learning as well as communicating in multiple languages. A gradually changing cultural context poses a challenge rather than a threat; in a Millian sense, it provides opportunities for self-development and the exercise of autonomy in different and unexpected directions. Accordingly, the worry that immigration may lead to the gradual change of a country's cultural context is ultimately a concern not about culture's ability to play an instrumental role in contributing to the autonomy of citizens, but instead an appeal to the cultural authenticity argument. Such a response must therefore answer to the difficulties faced by that line of argument (section I).

In order to justify the kind of *carte blanche* control over immigration typically claimed by states and affirmed by advocates of the instrumental position, the instrumental argument would have to hinge on a much thicker conception of shared culture. However, any appeal to such a conception ought to be rejected because countries such as the United States do not feature a shared culture in this thicker sense.

Although there are other important limitations to the instrumental line of argument, they have been explored in detail elsewhere (see, for example,

Johnson 2000; Scheffler 2007; and Waldron 1995), and, as a result, I limit myself to rehearsing two such qualifications.

First, the value of the local culture cannot be ensured in the absence of competing alternatives. Jeremy Waldron has pointedly insisted that one can only

> make his choice a genuine *evaluation* to the extent that the culture he is scrutinizing is vulnerable to challenge and comparison from the outside ... To preserve a culture – to insist that it must be *secure*, come what may – is to insulate it from the very forces and tendencies that allow it to operate in a context of genuine choice ... We cannot guarantee at the same time the integrity of a given community and say that its culture (or the fate of its culture) can *tell* people about the value and viability of this particular way of life. (Waldron 1995, 109)

Legally protecting a given cultural shape precludes individuals from choosing differently, it prohibits them from fashioning cultural materials in ways that cohere with individual projects. Once we legally protect a certain cultural form we forfeit evidence of its putative value (Hart 1963). The point here is that we need the challenge presented by sincere advocates of other cultures or modes of life in order to be confident that our own ways are indeed valuable.

Accordingly, although protecting the radical change of one's cultural context might well contribute to individual autonomy or well-being, protecting culture from exposure to alternative possibilities is an important *threat* to that same individual autonomy or well-being. We must, then, tread carefully when considering the possibility of restricting cultural change for the good of individual autonomy. Unfortunately, when it comes to changes to a cultural context, what counts as dislocatingly abrupt rather than acceptably gradual promises to be contentious. While this ambiguity cannot be eliminated, I doubt that the United States has reached a point where this line of argument will justify further clamping down on immigration.

While it is true that the current *number* of immigrants is higher than ever (with over 9 million entering between 1991 and 2000), the *percentage* of foreign born individuals in the United States (11.1 percent in 2000) is lower than it was from 1860 to 1930 (when it ranged from 11.6 to 14.7 percent) (see figure 3 below). Moreover, as a point of comparison, seven OECD countries report higher percentages of foreign-born populations than the United States – with Canada, New Zealand, Australia, and Switzerland all hovering near 20 percent.[7] This suggests that substantial immigration and probably

[7] See http://www.oecd.org/dataoecd/7/49/24994376.pdf, accessed June 5, 2010.

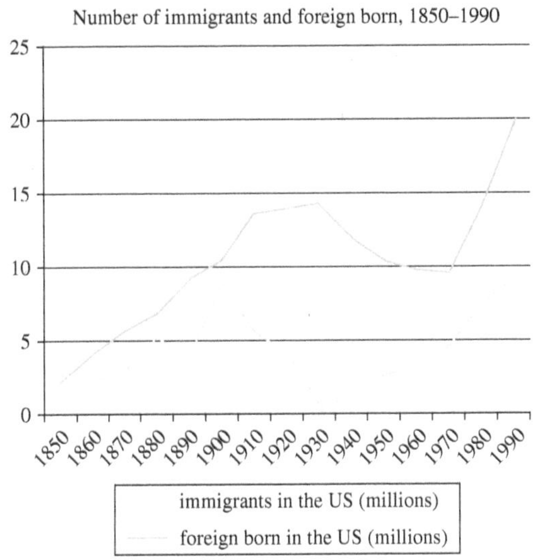

Figure 2 Number of immigrants and foreign born, 1850–1990 (source: Daniels 2004, 5–6)

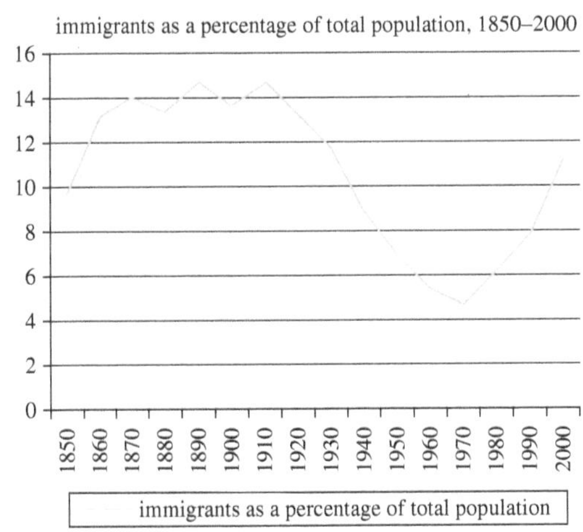

Figure 3 Immigrants as a percentage of total population, 1850–2000 (source: Daniels 2004, 5–6)

substantially *more* immigration are consistent with the maintenance of the thin culture that is – however loosely – shared by citizens.

It is sometimes objected that today's immigrants are largely from Asia and Latin America while those of the previous era were largely from

Southern and Eastern Europe and, thus, the newer immigrants pose a larger threat to the country's cultural integrity. One commentator, for example, notes that "nearly 90 percent of all immigrants now come from continents and countries whose peoples have never been assimilated fully into any Western country" (Buchanan 2006, 5). By itself, this argument is not compelling. Required is a specific and plausible account of how immigrants from Asia and Latin America are a threat to American cultural integrity that will importantly endanger the ability of citizens to use their culture as a tool for autonomous life. In entertaining such accounts, we should be alive to the fact that those arguing about immigration in the era that brought us quotas saw Southern Europeans (bolstered by eugenics evidence) as threatening in just the same way that today's restrictionists see those from Latin America and Asia as constituting a threat (King 2000; Lee 1998, 41; Ngai 2004, chapter 1).

The main account hypothesized in the literature, at least in regard to Mexican immigration, is the claim that Mexicans' tendency to live among their compatriots and continue to interact in Spanish undermines the centrality of English in US political life. For instance, Samuel Huntington says that "throughout American history English has been central to American national identity," and warns that

> without a common language, communication becomes difficult if not impossible, and the nation becomes the arena for two or more language communities whose members communicate far more intensely with the members of their group than with those of the other group. [In such countries] divorce is always a possibility, and historically these countries have in large part held together by fear of more powerful neighbors. (Huntington 2004, 159)

Here, then, is an account of the specific danger presented by at least some of these new immigrants. It is true that to the extent that immigration threatens to undermine the possibility of democratic government by corroding the common currency in which debate and deliberation occurs, there is reason to restrict it.

However, the evidence does not seem to substantiate at least Huntington's strongest concerns. For instance, Jack Citrin and his colleagues report that although Mexican immigrants arrive with less English than other immigrants, this gap is closed relatively quickly such that "the gap between people of Mexican ancestry and others is very small: 86 percent of those with families originally from Mexico speak only English or speak English very well, compared to 94 percent of people of Asian origin" (Citrin *et al.* 2007, 35). Against the view that there is something fundamentally different about these immigrants, they conclude that "the trajectory of their progeny's assimilation resembles that of their European predecessors of a century ago, and their rate of linguistic assimilation is on par with or greater than those of other contemporary immigrant groups" (Citrin *et al.* 2007, 35).

Likewise, Kymlicka points out that the kinds of movements that tear countries apart culturally require much more than a simple increase in numbers. Instead, he emphasizes how "onerous efforts at cultural reproduction" are:

> Sustaining a societal culture in the modern world is not a matter of having yearly ethnic festivals, or having a few classes taught in one's mother-tongue as a child. It is a matter of creating and sustaining a set of public institutions which enables a minority group to participate in the modern world through the use of its own language . . . The minority must . . . engage in its own competing form of state-sponsored nation-building . . . And they must use the same tools that the majority nation uses in its program of nation-building – i.e. standardized public education, official languages, including language requirements for citizenship and government employment, etc. (Kymlicka 2001, 159)

Together with the evidence of integration among immigrants from Mexico, the difficulty of developing and sustaining a minority nation provides reason to be skeptical about worries along the lines suggested by Huntington.

The second qualification to the instrumental view is that the interest citizens of destination countries have in a reasonably stable cultural context does not necessarily override the interests or claims of potential immigrants (Margalit and Raz 1990, 451; Hampton 1995, 81; and Perry 1995, 116). For example, it is hard to see how claims based on cultural context will outweigh requests for asylum (even very generously interpreted). Thus, the strength of this line of argument depends on the competing claims posed by potential immigrants and here dovetails with the previous discussion regarding the expansion of amnesty.

Potential immigrants from the EU (or other parts of the developed world) may have less compelling competing claims. However, as we have seen, it also seems likely that the argument is limited in its ability to justify restricting immigration from the EU because of the similarity in public culture between the EU and the United States. Residents of the EU grow up in democratic cultures that take seriously (or similarly seriously) individual rights, the separation of church and state, religious tolerance, and the like. Thus, the instrumental line of argument faces limitations in terms of, on the one hand, the competing claims presented by potential immigrants from the developing world and, on the other, the similarity of cultures (in the thin sense) across the developed world.

Another way in which the instrumental argument sometimes arises is in regard to concerns of population density. David Miller, for example, argues that

> those of us who live in relatively small and crowded states experience daily the way in which the sheer number of our fellow citizens, with their needs for housing, mobility, recreation, and so forth, impacts on the physical environment, so that it becomes harder to enjoy access to open space, to move from place to place without encountering congestion, to preserve important wildlife habitats, and so on. (Miller 2005, 202)

Certainly, the density of a community's population affects the kind of life members can live and so seems to be a relevant consideration in thinking about justice and immigration.

It is important, however, to recognize the kinds of limitations this line of argument faces, especially in regard to the United States.[8] This is because, comparatively speaking, the United States far from faces a land shortage.

The United States has less than 30 percent of the population density of the EU. To the extent, then, that concerns regarding population density provide reason to limit population, the justification cannot be the claim that there is simply no room for additional people.

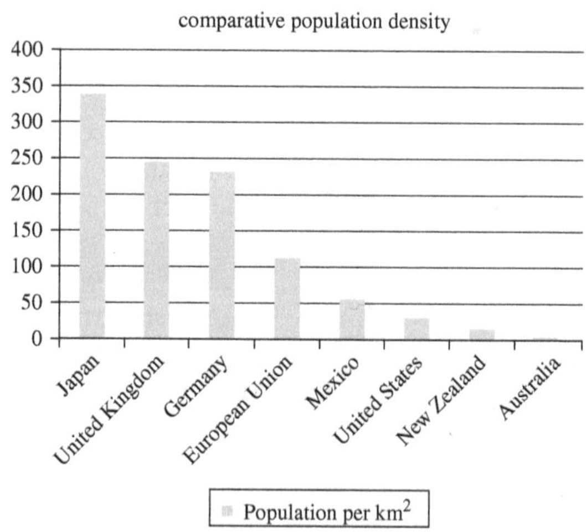

Figure 4 Comparative population density
(Source: United Nations 2006)

[8] Of course, my particular focus on the United States is not shared by Miller, and so these comments must not be taken as direct criticism of his claims.

Rather, the claim must be that current citizens prefer the lifestyle afforded by living in a country with a relatively low density of population. Although there is nothing objectionable – on the face of it – about this claim, we should recognize that ultimately it is a claim about the type of lifestyle citizens wish to lead and not an absolute claim about the amount of room available in the territory. The claim has to be that those of us who are here have grown accustomed to this particular lifestyle and our potential autonomy has come to depend on the type of context for choice provided by it.

This argument is subject to all of the qualifications relevant to this general class of argument. Namely, as we have seen, it must be balanced against the claims of outsiders, and provides reason to prevent sudden change to the existing lifestyle framework, but not to resist change altogether. Thus, in the US case, considerations regarding population density have rather limited consequences.

One way of reformulating this concern regarding population density to reflect a more powerful set of concerns is to connect increased immigration to environmental concerns. Along these lines, some environmentalists have argued vehemently for immigration restrictions. Because birthrates among native citizens in the United States (and generally throughout receiving countries) are quite low, population growth in these countries is now mainly driven by immigrants – both by their arriving in the country and their subsequently having more children. Moreover, it is this population growth that has driven increases in the CO_2 emissions of the United States:

> Between 1990 and 2003, US *per capita* CO_2 emissions increased 3.2 percent, while *total* US CO_2 emissions increased 20.2 percent. Why the discrepancy? During that same period, America's population increased 16.1 percent. More people drove more cars, built more houses, etc. Population growth greatly increased total emissions, and it is *total* emissions, not per capita emissions, which quantify our full contribution to global warming. (Cafaro and Staples 2008, 12)

This leads the authors to conclude that

> a growing population increases America's large environmental footprint beyond our borders and our disproportionate role in stressing global environmental systems. To seriously address environmental problems at home and become good global environmental citizens ... we should limit immigration into the United States to the extent needed to stop US population growth. (Cafaro and Staples 2008, 5–6)

There are actually two arguments here, and it is helpful to distinguish them. First, immigration increases the country's environmental footprint and, so, worsens the contributions of the United States to global environmental problems (such as global warming). Second, increased domestic population makes it more difficult to address local environmental issues (such as urban sprawl and the preservation of local wilderness areas and wildlife).

The idea that we ought to restrict immigration in order to reduce the country's contribution to global environmental problems is surely a mistake. To see why, imagine that there was a natural disaster that eliminated half of the population of the United States:

> At this point, a surviving politician advocates a loosening of environmental restrictions, pointing out that this can be done responsibly. Thanks to the deaths of his compatriots, it is in his view now possible to *both* increase the country's per capita consumption by 50 percent and still decrease its overall footprint by 25 percent.

Although the politician's calculations are correct, surely the judgment that so long as the country stays within its prior footprint it is acting environmentally responsibly is mistaken. In view of the change in population, the prior footprint is an irrelevant standard. What matters is not the country's total emission, but global emissions. Thus, drastic changes in the population of the country bring with them different expectations about what the country can responsibly emit.

By the same token, if a country's citizens emit at a responsible rate (whatever that might be), and it adds immigrants who adopt similarly responsible lifestyles, we ought not to be concerned about the increase in the country's overall emissions. It is global emissions, rather than country-by-country emissions, that are significant. To be responsible global citizens, perhaps the United States will have to cut back on emissions, but this is the case regardless of immigration. Thus, the claim that the United States ought to restrict immigration in order to become a more responsible global citizen is based on confusion. It would suffice if US citizens – whether immigrant or native – adopted responsible lifestyles.

The second line of argument suggests that immigration, by increasing domestic population, puts pressure on domestic resources and, so, makes it more difficult to control urban sprawl, and maintain both local species diversity and wilderness territory. A policy of open borders – or, as I have advocated, a significant broadening of the classification of refugees to include the severely impoverished – indeed promises to put substantial pressure on the local environment (in terms of biodiversity, urban sprawl, and the maintenance of wilderness areas). These are important concerns.

That being said: because of the enduring and extreme poverty of our world, it is likely that such an argument would have to prioritize domestic environmental issues (such as "livable, uncrowded cities," urban sprawl, and "sharing the land with the full complement of its native flora and fauna" [Cafaro and Staples 2008, 6]) over the provision of basic necessities for potential immigrants. Again: while it is of course true that immigration is unlikely to be a panacea for global poverty, it *does* effectively resolve the problem for those able to migrate. This is of no small importance. Thus, as long as we live in a world marred by severe poverty and are without the capacity to quickly and effectively eradicate that poverty via development policies alone, limiting immigration for the sake of local environmental concerns elevates issues such as urban sprawl and the maintenance of sufficient wildlife above the basic interests of potential migrants.

Although in my view such an ordering is perverse, this is a judgment that hinges on claims regarding anthropocentrism and perhaps the value of future people that I am not prepared to defend. These are enormously difficult and contested philosophical issues. Instead, here I will have to rest content with merely pointing out the relevant issues. In particular, while it is a mistake to advocate restrictions of immigration as a solution to global environmental problems, there are valid arguments regarding local environmental conditions that could speak in favor of the restriction of immigration.

However, the soundness of such arguments hinges on their ability to outweigh the very strong interests many potential immigrants have in migrating. In my view, this puts environmental arguments for the restriction of immigration on a rather weak footing. Instead, I am tempted to think that the environmental problems we face reflect more basic challenges to the way we organize our lifestyles, challenges that ought not to be confused with, or pinned on, the largely separate issue of immigration.

In this discussion, I have introduced the instrumental argument for the importance of shared national identity and rehearsed four objections to it. By way of summary, we can say that a reasonably stable cultural context is a prerequisite for an autonomous life and that, as a result, individuals have an important interest in it. However, this interest (a) does not provide reason to restrict the entry of those who either already share a similar cultural background or are willing and able to integrate; (b) does not require the absence of cultural change; (c) cannot be adequately protected by legally entrenching a particular conception of the culture; and (d) may be outweighed by the interests of potential immigrants. Thus, the most that the shared identity argument entitles us to say is that citizens may object to floods of new residents that outrun the capacity of the society to integrate them.

Moreover, as I insisted at the outset, even this line of argument makes sense only if it can be explained why citizens have some special connection to the territory and institutions in question that justifies their making decisions in regard to it. It is not clear that a group's cultural similarity can justify restrictions on the movement of others unless the group has a prior rightful claim to control access to the territory or institutions in question. Insofar as this entitlement is best explained by appeal to the contributions citizens have made to such institutions, it makes sense to see the instrumental argument as dependent upon a prior commitment to the associative ownership view.

III THE SOCIAL TRUST ARGUMENT

A third line of argument related to the importance of national identity holds that concerns regarding social trust may justify restrictions on immigration. Indeed, it is commonly argued that immigration restrictions are justified because a nationally unified community is a necessary prerequisite of various redistributive programs (themselves required by justice).[9] According to this view, to the extent that immigration threatens a community's enabling unity, it may be legitimately restricted. Many influential analysts endorse such a view:

> Just states "require a common public culture that in part constitutes the political identity of their members, and that serves valuable functions in supporting democracy and other social goals." (Miller 2005, 199; also see Miller 1995, 96)

> Liberal egalitarian principles can only be realized in communities where relations among citizens are characterized by solidarity and trust, relations that are often sustained by a shared culture and can be jeopardized by large, short-term changes in membership. (Gibney 1999, 174)

In addition to academic proponents, public debate in many receiving countries revolves around concerns about integrating immigrants into the public political culture in a way that does not threaten valued political and social institutions (Geddes 2003).

The social trust position is constituted by the following set of claims:

P1. A commitment to justice entails the support of a welfare state.[10]
P2. The welfare state has costs (in terms of a higher tax rate).[11]

[9] For opposing views see Abizadeh 2002; Habermas 1995; and Mason 2000, chap. 5.

[10] I interpret "welfare state" in a broad way so as to include not just TANF (Temporary Assistance to Needy Families), food stamps, or other means-tested redistributive programs, but also the much larger "universal" programs such as social security, public education, and Medicare.

[11] According to some analysts, the welfare state is – setting aside its redistributive effects – desirable because of its relative efficiency in supplying widely desired goods and services (Barr 2001). According

P3. Citizens will only be willing to pay such taxes if they share a sense of common identity with fellow citizens.[12]

Conclusion: Because admitting immigrants disrupts the shared identity of the citizenry,[13] erodes support for the welfare state, and, so, obstructs the realization of justice, there is good reason to restrict immigration.

For our purposes, we can simply assume that P1 is true. Given P1, P2 is unobjectionable: if programs are required, they will have to be paid for. Having accepted P1 and P2, a rejection of the social trust view must hinge on challenging the validity of P3 and/or the relevance of P3 to the conclusion.

In recent years, empirical evidence has been presented which suggests that increasing diversity is linked to reduced provision of public goods (Alesina *et al.* 1999; Easterly and Levine 1997) and that increasing migration stunts the growth of the welfare state (Soroka *et al.* 2006). It is commonly thought that such findings "vindicate Miller's worries about threats to the national basis of the welfare state" (Soroka *et al.* 2006, 279) and that, as a result, we must recognize that increased immigration is inconsistent with such redistributive programs. I dispute this claim in two ways. First, I review evidence that challenges the validity of the empirical claim (section A). Second, I argue that the claim is not just an empirical one, but hinges also on an implicit, but dubious, normative component (section B).

A The empirical claim

The first reason to resist the social trust view is that the empirical claim on which it hinges is (at least) not unambiguously supported by the evidence. Against the view that diversity necessarily undermines the provision of public goods, many analysts argue that the trust on which the welfare state relies depends more on the shape of the institutions than on the identity of the population that they serve.

to this view, market mechanisms will be less efficient in circumstances marked by certain kinds of risk and lack of information, conditions that characterize markets for goods such as healthcare and pensions. If widely seen as true, this would – at least to some extent – undermine the plausibility of the social trust view by persuading individuals (including the wealthy) that it is costly to *refrain* from supporting such institutions.

12 For an important formal and empirical challenge to this claim see Shayo 2009.

13 Even if sound, the argument only works against potential immigrants who do not also possess the relevant characteristics or identity. Thus, throughout when I refer to immigrants, the entry of non-national immigrants it at stake.

For instance, Kumlin and Rothstein argue that the negative effects of diversity are "by no means cut in stone" and have the "potential to wither away as a consequence of positive experiences of social interaction and institutional fairness" (Kumlin and Rothstein 2007, 5 and 23; also see Collier 1998). Likewise, Bo Rothstein contends that:

> In designing our political institutions, we also in large part determine the normative attitudes citizens hold about welfare policy. If citizens regard the prevailing welfare programs as designed in accordance with principle of justice [*sic*], if they consider the implementation of such programs to be fair, and if they believe all citizens (or almost all of them, at least) pay their due share of the costs incurred, then the political support for the universal welfare policy will in all likelihood endure. Otherwise not. (Rothstein 1998, 222)

This institutional view is important because it suggests that support for the welfare state depends primarily on features of *institutions* rather than on characteristics of the population (see, for example, Habyarimana *et al.* 2006; Svallfors 1993 and 1997). On this view, the effects of diversity depend on the institutional context in which it is experienced.

If so, welfare programs will maintain support if they incorporate immigrants in a way that current citizens see as fair (especially by taking the precautions necessary to stop immigrants from free-riding on the benefits of such programs) (Nannestad and Svendsen 2005). Just institutions, according to this view, generate their own support: they (a) create incentive-based trust by providing people with incentives to comply; and (b) change the citizenry in ways that *create* the very unity on which they putatively rely.[14] Even if no empirical view on the source of social trust is undisputed (Cook and Cooper 2003, 235), the institutional view at least suggests that the link between diversity and lack of redistribution is more complex than social trust advocates typically allow.

The scope of the claim is also worth questioning. Underlying P3 is the assumption that the required common identity must be supplied by *national* groups. Because immigrants typically do not arrive sharing the nationality of their new society, they are seen as threatening the required shared identity. However, scholars of nationality argue that identification with such communities is socially constructed; it is (at least partly) the result of institutionally created shared experiences, stories, and myths (Anderson 1991; Gellner 1983; Hobsbawm 1990; Miller 1995). Rather than being a

[14] Likewise, there is evidence that education has a substantial effect in generating tolerant attitudes toward trade and other elements of globalization. These effects cannot be explained simply in terms of expected benefit from globalization (Hainmueller and Hiscox 2006).

natural feature of the pre-political world, the extent to which a set of people identifies with one another may be influenced by the way in which political institutions are designed (Hardin 1995; for a challenge to this view see Rice and Feldman 1997 and, more moderately, Uslaner 2008).

This is important because if (a) a shared identity is an empirical prerequisite for redistribution; (b) a shared identity can be engineered through the design of political institutions and/or imposed through a public mythology; and (c) redistributive programs are a requirement of justice, why not create the communities of shared identity needed to maintain a just distribution of resources? Why not engineer that shared identity which best satisfies the antecedent requirements of distributive justice?

To render the issue less abstract, consider the relationship between the EU and the social trust view. To begin, I reject the claim that the EU straightforwardly falsifies the national orientation of the social trust view by facilitating redistribution transnationally in the absence of a common identity. Instead, the EU has not yet acted as a sufficient source of redistribution to issue a substantial challenge to the social trust view. Without claiming that the EU is non-redistributive, there are significant limits to its capacity in this regard. Fully substantiating this claim would take me far afield, but two points merit brief mention.

First, the EU lacks a common set of social policies (such as a unified pension program) and a single financial/credit market, but these are the devices that would allow unification to beget redistribution (Galbraith *et al.* 1999). Second, it lacks the resources that would be needed to generate significant transnational redistribution. To give an idea, projected EU expenditure for 2007–2013 is 862 billion euros (for a population of nearly 500 million) while US federal expenditure (for a population of roughly 300 million) is $2.8 trillion for 2007 alone. Indeed, the EU controls only 1 percent of the GDP of its member states. Thus, it currently lacks the capacity to generate significant redistribution.

However, the EU could *come to* issue a challenge to the national orientation of the social trust view in a slightly less direct way: EU leaders may gradually instill a common European identity in members that will eventually support redistribution across member states. There is no reason for shared identity to be constrained to national communities; instead, groups of any size may come to experience the required identity. If so, the social trust view may provide reason to *create* the shared identity that best facilitates just redistributive institutions rather than – as typically claimed – justifying the maintenance of whatever identities *currently* facilitate redistribution.

These points both insist that the way in which institutions structure our lives affects how we conceive of our political relationships and, in this way, opens the door (in ways I shall explain) to questions about the argument's ability to justify restrictions on immigration. In the section that follows, my objective is to call into question the *relevance* of the social trust thesis by demonstrating that the position rests on a dubious normative claim.

B The normative claim

While I previously suggested that the empirical claim underlying P3 is vulnerable to challenge, it is crucial to recognize that the claim is not just an empirical one. Instead, there is also a normative component to the social trust view that requires clarification and is susceptible to challenge. In recent years increasing migration has "provoked widespread public opposition in industrialized countries" (Cornelius and Rosenblum 2005, 99) and, as Stephen Macedo remarks, this opposition may "tend to lower public support for social welfare and redistributive programs" (Macedo 2007, 67). At issue, however, is whether worries about immigration's effect on public support for the welfare state may *justify* restricting immigration. In this section, I (a) deny that the argument provides justification for restricting immigration; and (b) show that it is incapable of providing the type of reason advocates suggest.

Imagine that there are two societies: in X, P3 obtains empirically; in Y, it does not. Would we then want to say that X is justified in restricting immigration while Y is not?

> *X says to those seeking entrance*: "We cannot allow you to enter because doing so will erode the support of our current citizens for the welfare state. Our citizens will be unwilling to support the necessary institutions knowing that such institutions will partially benefit you. Thus, admitting you would undermine our welfare state and we are – as a matter of justice – committed to such institutions."
>
> *Alternatively, Y says to those seeking entrance*: "We will grant you access to our institutions because we trust that you will see that they are fair and will, thus, be moved to support them. Likewise, we trust that our citizens will welcome you (even if you make demands on the state) because they trust that if the state accepts your requests, they must be legitimate ones."[15]

Citizens of X thus claim that their *own* unwillingness to contribute to the welfare state may justify restrictions on immigration.

[15] Notice that this response mirrors the institutional view explained above.

This line of argument wrongly depicts the will of citizens "as *just* a sociological fact" (Cohen 1991, 308). So, P3 is an empirical claim buttressed by the judgment that we must accept it as a fact about the world and not, instead, as an alterable claim about the people making it. However, it is objectionable to allow citizens to use predictions about *their own* future behavior to rule out policies, because they control their future behavior. That this is true is obvious in other situations. Imagine that all of a society's surgeons insist that if their pay is not increased, they will jointly refuse to provide many needed operations. Though the surgeons' claim clearly provides a reason (albeit a threatening and coercive one) to give them a raise, what it does *not* provide is justification.

One might object, however, that there is an important dissimilarity between the surgeons and citizens in receiving countries. The surgeons intentionally manipulate future behavior in order to gain benefits, whereas, advocates of the social trust view might suggest, those in receiving countries are only responding to diversifying immigration reflexively and with no preconceived ill-intent. The advocate of the social trust view may maintain that it is just an empirical fact about people in general that their support for a welfare state will decrease if some of the resources they contribute will benefit those of a different nationality. It is not a fact about particular people, but a putatively *general* finding of social science.[16]

This line of objection is not without force. It demands that we distinguish between premeditated threats and reflexive responses to changed circumstances. Let us, then, reformulate the surgeon example:

> In an effort to render important services more widely accessible, a new government healthcare plan caps the amount surgeons are allowed to charge for a given procedure. Unfortunately, this intervention backfires. At the reduced rate, many of the country's surgeons are unwilling to perform needed operations. Some reduce their working hours, choosing to spend more time on non-work activities; others retire early; and still others move into the more lucrative business of cosmetic services. The result of these uncoordinated decisions is that many patients are forced to go without services that they desperately need.

It is clear that these surgeons are less culpable than those in the previous example (Cf. Cohen 2002 and Estlund 1998). Here their actions are regrettable, but not premeditated and coercive. However, acknowledging the

[16] One way of accounting for this reflex would be that individuals of different nationalities prefer different sets of public goods and, thus, have trouble realizing a robust provision with nationally different others. For example, a Protestant-dominated national group might prefer publicly provided education while a Catholic one prefers a private system.

force of this worry does not denude objections to the relevance of the claim. Even if the reactions (in providing surgery or failing to support redistributive programs) are not premeditated there remain reasons to doubt whether they can provide normative justification.

It is not clear that the surgeons in the second example are irreproachable. Regrettable social occurrences (such as causing a traffic accident), despite a lack of conscious choice or ill-intent, demand regret, and often recompense. Likewise, the surgeons (despite the lack of preconceived ill-intent) might, once made aware of the situation, have some duty to work out a scheme for providing the necessary operations. Similarly, it may be the case that evidence showing that support for the welfare state decreases with an increase in the diversity of recipients provides reason to rectify the problem rather than justifying the response (and the institutional view suggests that such a change is possible). Indeed, it is hard to see how such evidence could provide justification unless it somehow proved such decreased support to be an *inescapable* human response to increased diversity.[17]

Thus, the objection remains important both because it further increases the empirical burden of justification shouldered by proponents of the social trust view and because it suggests that the reason it provides is pragmatic rather than justificatory. Advocates must now demonstrate not just that there is some correlation between national homogeneity and strength of redistributive programs, but that it (a) does not depend on institutional context; (b) is robust across otherwise diverse eras and cultures; and (c) is a necessary reflexive response rather than an instance of conscious threat-mongering. However, all of these claims are susceptible to challenge.

As we have seen, it is likely that the effects of diversity are mediated by the institutions in which it is experienced. Just as the effects of diversity are not "cut in stone," so too what constitutes diversity is subject to change. For instance, the superintendent of the 1870 and 1880 US censuses insisted that immigrants from Southern and Eastern Europe were "degraded below our utmost conceptions ... beaten men from beaten races, representing the worst failures in the struggle for existence" (quoted in Ngai 2004, 30). Likewise, when Congress passed a 1921 law with the effect of limiting immigration from Southern and Eastern Europe, a House Report explained that such individuals were "abnormally twisted," "unassimilable," and "filthy un-American" (quoted in Calavita 1996, 187). While such remarks reflected

[17] However, once we adopt this strong view of the deterministic nature of human action, arguments regarding what constitutes legitimate restrictions on immigration miss the point, for they depend on the assumption that the potential set of feasible policies includes at least some policies other than the status quo.

common opinion (Lee 1998, 40–44), Southern and Eastern Europeans are no longer typically seen as distinct from other Europeans. As a result,

> one cannot rule out in the long run that even perceptions of physical difference – that is, of a racial distinction – will change ... Some of the major European immigrant groups – the Irish, Italians, and Jews are the best-documented cases – were viewed as racially different from native-born whites ... perceptions of, and social values attached to, different physical features changed over time. (Alba and Nee 2003, 63)

Likewise, Robert Putnam explains that social policy can dramatically affect "salient line[s] of social division" (Putnam 2007, 160). The social trust view hinges on the claim that responses to and characterization of diversity are inalterable facts about humanity, but there is evidence that such responses depend on the institutions in which diversity is confronted.

Moreover, in at least some of the empirical literature supporting the social trust view, the explanation includes individuals' unwillingness to benefit others who are perceived as different. For instance, Alesina and his colleagues suggest that one reason that ethnic fragmentation makes the provision of public goods more difficult is that "the identity of the beneficiaries of the public good directly influences the utility level of each individual" such that, for example, if "a white person perceives that a public good is enjoyed mostly by black citizens, he would oppose it precisely for that reason" (Alesina *et al.* 1999, 11). Likewise, in 2003 a Swiss anti-immigration party garnered a plurality of votes with a platform based on the slogan "The Swiss are becoming Negroes." In cases in which a refusal to contribute to redistributive programs hinges on the fact that some of the benefits will go to racially different others, the fact cannot be taken as *justification* for restricting immigration.

The important point is that it is worth being clear about the type of reason that the social trust view (even if correct on all counts) provides. The surgeon example shows that rather than a moral justification, the reason is an instrumental or pragmatic one. Of course, this does not make it unimportant, but it is worth bearing in mind that – just as those who benefit from a monopoly may bitterly (and from a powerful perch) protest policies meant to ensure competition – so too just immigration reform is likely to evoke significant reaction. The mere fact of powerful opposition to a policy ought not to be taken as justification for its repudiation. Especially given evidence for the institutional view, rather than succumbing to the tendency for diversity to undercut redistributive programs, we have reason to work toward institutions that help overcome that tendency. As a result, we should reject the claim that the social trust view can *justify* restrictions on immigration.

IV CONCLUSION

We have seen that commentators have suggested that states may restrict immigration for three different types of reasons connected to national identity. There are – as we have seen – important differences between these lines of argument. Here, however, I want to set aside such differences and instead reiterate in general form the dilemma that faces arguments for restrictions on immigration based on the importance of a shared cultural identity.

Often such arguments hinge on an ambiguity between thick and thin conceptions of shared culture. We can dismiss appeals to the importance of maintaining a shared culture in the thick sense because modern democracies do not feature shared cultures in this sense. Instead, the combination of the protection of basic liberties (such as freedom of speech, press, religion, and assembly) and the sheer size of such states ensures that the cultures that inhabit them are extremely diverse. Instead, to the extent that we can say that these states feature shared cultures, we must focus on a thin conception of culture revolving only around a shared language and commitment to democratic political institutions.

However, as we have seen, modern democracies are quite effective in inculcating this thin culture in new residents. Schools teach the publicly shared language and the labor market provides strong incentives for immigrants to become adept in it. Likewise, immigrants have an extremely strong tendency to internalize a commitment to the norms and institutions of democratic political systems. It would of course be wrong to suggest that the ability of states to assimilate immigrants to this thin conception of culture is unlimited, and so culture-based arguments perhaps provide some reason to limit the *rate* of immigration. Still, such arguments fall far short of justifying the *carte blanche* power that it is typically assumed states have in selecting or rejecting potential immigrants.

Moreover, even the argument regarding rate depends on thinking that existing citizens have some prior rightful claim over the institutions and territory in question. Accordingly, arguments based upon the importance of shared identity hinge on a prior explanation of the citizenry's right to control access to territory and institutions. Such explanation is best provided by the associative ownership view. Arguments based on shared identity are better seen as providing reason to *invoke* the right to impose some restrictions on the rate of immigration rather than *justifying* in the first instance the right of citizens to do so.

CHAPTER 7

Applications

This chapter applies the associative ownership framework to several important policy debates including the claims of resident non-citizens and the legitimacy of attempts to militarize the border (section I). After rejecting the leading approaches to such problems, I argue that the difficulties raised by illegal immigration may be well addressed by the development of a certain type of guest-worker program (section II). Finally, I offer some brief concluding remarks on the overall argument (section III).

I NON-CITIZEN RESIDENTS

There are two popular positions in regard to illegal immigration: the treatment of non-citizen residents; and border control. First, many analysts – call them *integrationists* – argue that justice requires that all illegal immigrants permanently residing in the territory be fully, and even automatically, integrated into the political community. Second, *restrictionists* – especially in the country's public debate – have generated widespread support for militarizing the border and refusing to tolerate the presence of illegal immigrants.[1]

A Opposing integrationism

Integrationists insist that all long-term residents of a territory – including illegal immigrants – are entitled to full membership in the body politic. Ruth Rubio-Marín, for example, argues that

[1] Many scholars avoid using the term "illegal immigrants." It is often viewed as excessively "laden" in a way that promises to "prejudice" analysis (Carens 2008, 164). I do not follow suit. It is clear that some immigrants arrive in violation of the existing legal code, and are therefore illegal immigrants. However, that an immigrant is illegal is merely a comment on their standing relative to existing law, and ought not to be taken as a normative judgment or expression of approval for the law. To forfeit the use of the term "illegal" in favor of "irregular" is just to muddy the issue. Either "irregular" simply means and stands in for "illegal" or its meaning is unclear. It is thus preferable to use "illegal," but be clear that labeling something "illegal" is a comment about its status relative to existing law and not a normative expression of disapproval.

all those who live on a permanent basis in a liberal democratic state ought to be considered members of that democracy and thus share in the sphere of civic equality with the equal recognition of rights and duties. (Rubio-Marín 2000, 6)

And likewise insists:

States claiming to be committed to liberal democracy ought to regard as full members of their organized political community, all those who reside in their territory on a permanent basis, being subject to the decisions collectively adopted there and being dependent on its protection and recognition for the full development of their personalities . . . after a certain residence period, permanent residents ought to be automatically and unconditionally recognized as citizens of the state. (Rubio-Marín 2000, 20)

The position is motivated by the claim that "membership is first, and above all, a social fact, determined by social factors such as living, working or raising a family and participating in the social and cultural life of a community" (Rubio-Marín 2000, 21, also see Carens 2009). In this section, I argue that the integrationist demand undermines the political community's interest in self-determination and the community's ownership of the political institutions that exist as a result of their contributions.

According to the integrationist view, recognizing membership as "a social fact" commits us to granting full membership to all permanent residents because the autonomy of long-term residents is tied up in the society in a manner that cannot be justified without granting such individuals a role in determining the political community's shape (Gibney 2004, 66–67). For instance, Rubio-Marín argues that long-term residents'

direct subjection to the laws justifies the need for them to be able to participate in the democratic process . . . It founds the individual's stake in the overall society and hence in the political system shaping and defining its present and future functioning.[2] (Rubio-Marín 2000, 33)

The integrationist position gains its appeal by abstracting, in two ways, from relevant historical information.

First, it ignores how permanent residents arrived. In the case of illegal immigrants, by entering the country illicitly such individuals took their place in the community without the consent of the citizenry. Although it is true that – after a number of years – such individuals are likely to find themselves in a situation in which they are subject to the law and have an

[2] The claim is therefore a variant of what we can call the "inclusivity principle" or the idea that all affected by a set of institutions are entitled to an equal say in how such institutions function. See chapter 2 for discussion.

important stake in the future shape of the political community, it is important that they put themselves in this situation without the consent of the citizenry. As such, it is unclear why that community should be required to pass ownership of their institutions to illegal immigrants.[3]

There are three reasons integrationists may suggest why the lack of consent of the political community ought not to carry the importance I attribute to it. First, it might be thought that the vulnerability of the circumstances under which illegal immigrants make the decision to migrate may justify their claims to integration. Already, however, we have allowed that those who qualify as political *or* economic refugees are entitled to full citizenship (except in the rare instances in which the circumstances that qualify them as refugees are likely to be very short-lived). The illegal immigrants whose status is at stake in this discussion are, therefore, individuals whose basic human rights are, *ex hypothesi*, reasonably secure.[4] Although they will almost certainly be fleeing political or economic circumstances less favorable than those obtaining in the receiving country, we have seen that they neither have a right to admission nor a right to conditions better than the ones they seek to flee.

The second way in which integrationists might resist the claim that the consent of the citizenry is important is by insisting that because illegal immigrants contribute to the provision of important public goods (through tax payments), they are entitled to full status within the community. This line of argument, however, ignores the fact that illegal immigrants enter without the consent of the citizenry. Imagine the following parallel case:

> A group of childhood friends each month wire money into a bank account under an agreement that when they reach the needed sum of money, they will together purchase a vacation home which they will then share. John, who is not a friend of the group, seeks access to a vacation home but cannot afford one on his own. Hearing of the above scheme, he begins to wire money into the bank account without the agreement of the group. After the group has raised the requisite amount of money and purchased the home, John steps forward – produces receipts documenting his contributions – and demands an equal place in the group.

Although it is true that John has contributed to the group's goals and now their collective decisions will affect his interests, it would seem quite strange

[3] This is not to say that they *may* not, should they so choose.

[4] In an excellent article, Robert Mayer argues that the question of exploitation does not arise for those choosing from a position of sufficiency (Mayer 2005).

to say that John has a *right* to inclusion in the group. Instead, the members might say to John: If you wanted a share in the scheme, you ought to have approached us, and worked out a mutually agreeable solution (or, in the case of immigration, complied with the procedures for legal immigration). But to simply contribute to the scheme and expect membership ignores the obvious: we are the *owners* of this scheme and have a *prima facie* claim to make decisions about membership as we see fit. To insist that contributions alone entitle one to membership ignores the prior claim individuals have over the institutions that they create or have passed down to them.

This example can be challenged on a number of grounds, and so it is worth thinking about a bit more. One might think, for example, that though the basic claim is correct, it is also true that members of the group ought to return John's money. Although I am unsure whether or not such an obligation indeed exists, it would only show – if true – that citizens ought to return money collected from illegal immigrants for services for which they are not eligible (such as social security). This much, however, I have already granted; it is not in dispute. Granting this falls well short of establishing the integrationist claim that the contributions to and residence under the citizenry's scheme obliges them to grant illegal immigrants full membership.

Another way in which the example might be challenged is via the insistence that the example is not properly analogous to government provision of goods because the vacation home is not non-rival.[5] Although some government-provided goods (such as clean air and defense) are indeed non-rival, this is not true of the whole range of claims to which illegal immigrants would lay claim if we accepted the integrationist view. The granting of full citizenship to all illegal immigrants would involve, for example, including them in programs of mutual cooperation such as public pension, healthcare, and redistributive programs. However, such inclusion – unlike in the case of non-rival goods – has a clear cost. So long as it is the case empirically that illegal immigrants have fewer resources than average citizens, full inclusion of illegal immigrants has costs for existing citizens. The issue is analogous to the vacation home in that at least some of the goods at stake are not non-rival. Additionally, we can imagine that John agrees not to use the house when others would like to, and promises not to cause any damage and to cover the costs of any wear. In this case, his use of the good

[5] Non-rival goods are ones whose use by one individual does not threaten their availability for others. Clean air is non-rival because my breathing clean air does not threaten its availability for others. Alternatively, a piece of cake is a rival good. My eating the piece of cake renders it unavailable for others.

would be akin to the use of a non-rival good. Still, I think that the group could rightfully reject John's use of the home.

Third, it is sometimes claimed that it is a mistake to suggest that the political community does not consent to the presence of illegal immigrants. For example, Rubio-Marín argues: "The alleged lack of consent becomes suspicious, when there has not been any serious attempt to prevent illegal entry or to deport illegal aliens before they consolidate their existence in the new society" (Rubio-Marín 2000, 83). Of course, there is truth to the claim that members of the political community, and even the political community itself, have played a role in creating the pattern of illegal immigration. Clearly, part of the reason that halting illegal immigration has proved difficult is that politically powerful employers welcome the cheap and exploitable labor and, moreover, longstanding state policies (especially the Bracero Program) encouraged employment-driven migration between the USA and Mexico. Thus, there is some force to the view that the political communities' lack of consent has been ambivalent.

To say, however, that this ambivalence amounts to consent is a mistake. Consent involves a positive acceptance, rather than a lack of protective measures. Just as the individual who refuses to hire a security guard for their home does not consent to robbery, the mere fact that the political community prefers not to fully pursue the extraordinarily expensive measures that would be required to block all illegal immigration and, especially, to find and deport those present is certainly not equivalent to consenting to the presence of such individuals.[6] Likewise, if I work as a waiter and do not report my tips as income, the fact that the political community does not succeed in discovering that I do not contribute sufficient taxes does not suggest that they consent to my cheating. Instead, it implies only that the community has decided that it can better spend its resources elsewhere. Moreover, even if falsely construed as consent, it would only be consent to the presence of illegal immigrants *as* illegal immigrants and not somehow consent to their presence as full members of the political community.

For these reasons, it seems most accurate to say that although the political community has not consented to the presence of illegal immigrants (in terms of positively accepting their presence rather than merely declining to take sufficient protective measures against it), many members of that community have encouraged and contributed to the widespread presence of illegal immigrants. The ambivalence noted above is, in part, a reflection

[6] Rubio-Marín ultimately weakens her position and at least considers accepting this claim (Rubio-Marín 2000, 92).

of disagreement within the political community. It reflects conflicts of interests between different parts of the community as well as deep disagreements on what constitutes a proper response to migration pressures.

Thus, although I am sympathetic to the integrationists' concern, the claim that there is consent here goes much too far. A more plausible assessment instead suggests that the existence of a historical relationship between Mexico and the United States (in terms of border disputes, encouragement of illegal immigration, and Mexican contribution to the development of the US economy) provides reason to find a less exploitative and, indeed, mutually agreeable resolution to the forces underlying the phenomenon of illegal immigration. Unlike the integrationists, who read consent into a quite conflicted political response (part of which involves very explicit rejection of illegal immigration, including substantial expense dedicated to preventing it), this view responds to the evident ambivalence of the political community.

A guest-worker program (argued for in section II) refuses to simply ignore the contributions of Mexican workers and the US role in creating and attracting this flow of workers (as would restrictionists), but does so without exaggerating the consent of the US political community (as would integrationists). Here, as elsewhere (such as between open borders and statism), the associative ownership view opens up a middle ground between extreme and ultimately unpersuasive options, which are too often offered in public debate as the only choices.

The second (and connected) major problem with the integrationist position is that it ignores how the relevant political communities – and the benefits that correspond to membership – arose. Because the supporting arguments for this claim have been developed in the preceding chapters, I will not repeat them at length here.[7] The basic point, which should by now be familiar, is just that citizenship entitles one to a set of benefits that arise from institutions collectively developed through a historical process of collective contributions made by the citizenry. Through such contributions, the citizenry comes to have special claims to the benefits of the operation of such institutions. One way of denying this claim is to argue, with integrationists, that all who make their way into a territory – consensually or not – have a right to the fruits of this labor. Maintaining this, however, requires denying that working to build institutions gives one a special claim over the benefits that result.

[7] That objections to integrationists mirror objections to advocates of open borders is no accident. Instead, the two positions share an underlying logic.

It is worth emphasizing that none of this is to say that the decisions of members in formulating an immigration policy are beyond criticism or that the interests of outsiders bear no weight. Indeed, we specifically rejected both of these lines of argument in our discussion of statism (chapter 2). Instead, the point is that the mere non-consensual presence of an individual, their contribution to the relevant institutions, and the fact that their life will be shaped by those institutions do not mandate that full membership be granted to them.

Leaving illegal immigrants who make the decision to arrive in opposition to the requirements of the law without full status creates a non-ideal situation in that it leaves individuals living under the demands of laws that they have no role in creating, it violates the country's commitment to "no taxation without representation," and leaves undocumented workers in a precarious social and economic position. I have argued, however, that these facts are not sufficient to justify an integrationist position so long as the individuals in question come willingly and do not qualify for refugee status. Again, to grant all such individuals full membership in the political community would be to override the current citizenry's control over their association and ownership of the institutions they have built.

The balance of considerations shifts, however, when considering the children of illegal immigrants rather than illegal immigrants themselves. Because such individuals do not come willingly and are often without a meaningful connection to any other polity, their situation more strongly mirrors that of political refugees than it does their parents' position.

In such cases, there is no choice but to grant the children of illegal immigrants full and automatic membership. Such individuals are subjected – through no choice of their own – to the laws of the political community. To force such individuals to take on the uncertain status of their parents is to condemn them to statelessness as a result of circumstances in which they were placed by their parents. While granting such individuals full membership indeed limits the ability of citizens to collectively determine their future political lives, there is ultimately no alternative consistent with recognizing the equality and humanity of the children of illegal immigrants. Thus, the claims of the children of illegal immigrants, like the claims of refugees, limit the senses in which citizens may rightfully control the future of the association (despite their legitimate claims of ownership over it). Here, again, associative ownership departs from statism.

Indeed, it is important to recognize that allowing that children of many permanently settled illegal immigrants have legitimate claims to full citizenship status is not a deviation from the associative ownership position.

Instead, once again, this line of argument establishes only that citizens have an entitlement claim to the state they have built. It does not purport to show, with statists, that this claim outweighs *any* claim made by a foreigner. Instead, ownership claims are regularly outweighed by other, more basic, considerations.

One such consideration is the need for children of illegal immigrants to have the protection of, and status within, the state under whose dominion they simply find themselves. All individuals have very basic interests – in terms of bodily protection, the social bases of self-respect, and the possibility of being a part of a political community – that require membership in *some* state. Just as the interests of those who show up at the border seeking asylum have interests that trump the ownership claims of citizens, children of permanently settled illegal immigrants have claims to citizenship that simply outweigh the claims of citizens. Rather than a move away from the associative ownership position, the recognition of the claims of such individuals, and the limits on ownership claims, are integral features of the associative ownership position.

B The pragmatic case against restrictionism

In great contrast to the integrationist hope, especially in the public debate regarding illegal immigration, there is widespread support for further militarization of the US–Mexico border. Indeed, doing so is often seen as a pressing moral emergency. For example, Daniel James describes illegal immigration as posing a fundamental threat to the future of the United States:

> The rapid expansion of illegal immigration into the United States is a threat to the integrity of its legal system in general. By its very nature, illegal immigration constitutes a violation of US immigration legislation, and contributes to a growing sub-culture of lawlessness in which a host of federal, state, and local laws and ordinances are regularly violated. (James 1991, 30)

> The long-term danger is that illegals ... may come to believe that, in general, violating the law is the way to get ahead in the United States. If that became the universal trend among illegals, it could eat away at the very foundations of American society. (James 1991, 36)

This type of concern, according to which the future of civilized American society depends on establishing control of the US–Mexico border, is prevalent in arguments about immigration. Those who voice such concern typically advocate a militarized closing of the border. For example, in a subsection entitled "ILLEGAL IMMIGRATION: END IT," Peter Brimelow insists that the border "should be *sealed* (at long last) with a fence, a ditch and whatever other contrivances" are required (Brimelow 1995, 259, italics added).

In this section, I shall grant, with restrictionists, that the political community has the right – should it democratically decide to do so – to construct a border fence. To deny this (with advocates of open borders) is to fail to recognize the legitimate ownership claims of the citizenry. This much follows from the arguments of the previous chapters. However, although it is within the right of the state to construct a fence for these purposes, I argue against doing so. Thus, the case I present against a fence does not deny – as advocates of open borders would – the state's *right* to do so.

According to current estimates, there are roughly 12 million illegal immigrants residing in the United States (Camarota 2007, 31). This population accounts for roughly 5 percent of the country's workforce. Although significant resources are spent controlling the border (well over $3 billion from 1994 to 1998 [Andreas 2000, 90]), these efforts have been largely ineffective. Evidence suggests that migrants "unlucky enough to get caught and returned to Mexico ... simply [try] again until they get in" (Massey *et al.* 2002, 45). Likewise, Thomas Espenshade explains that:

> Practically all Mexican migrants who manage to reach the US–Mexican border are able to enter the United States, if not on their first attempt, then on a second or third. Moreover, once an unauthorized alien moves into the interior of the country, the chances of subsequently being apprehended by the INS Investigations Unit are about 1–2 percent every year.[8] (Espenshade 1994, 886)

In the words of the Border Patrol's San Diego chief: "When they run, we grab as many as we can. We take them back to the border and they try again. Eventually, most of them get through" (quoted in Andreas 2000, 108). Survey evidence corroborates this testimony by suggesting that 92 percent of those apprehended "attempted the crossing again on the same trip to the border, succeeding in entering on the second or third try" (Fuentes *et al.* 2007, 65).

Indeed, that current funds (the 2008 federal budget set aside slightly under $2 billion for border control) are inadequate to accomplish their alleged purpose is demonstrated by the fence periodically separating the countries:

[8] Although enforcement within the country remains a symbolic effort, it has been significantly ratcheted up in recent years: arrests of illegal immigrants inside the country increased by sevenfold between 2002 and 2006 (Center for American Progress 2007, 6).

> The oldest section of the existing border fence begins at the Pacific Ocean and continues inland for 42 miles . . . This "primary fence" averages only 10 feet high, and is made of corrugated steel panels about 20 inches wide and 12 feet long, welded onto upright posts. But because the corrugations run horizontally, they form a kind of ladder that makes scaling the fence easy for young and old. And because there is no continuous concrete footing, this fence is easy to dig under . . . Border Patrol agents report that individuals routinely manage to scramble over both the primary and secondary fences in less than one minute. (Skerry 2006)

As a result, scholars suggest that "effective border regulations have long been more myth than reality, a political construct providing an appearance of control" (Andreas 2000, 22). On this view, although Border Patrol may play a "symbolic purpose by signaling that the nation [is] being defended, it [does] not really deter Mexicans from attempting an undocumented border crossing" (Massey *et al.* 2002, 45; also see Cornelius 1997).

The pragmatic case against a border fence consists of four main points: (1) the construction of such a fence promises to be extremely expensive; (2) it is – despite this cost – unlikely to be efficacious; (3) the benefits it promises – even if effective – are ambiguous; and even if it managed to provide some benefits (4) its pursuit would conflict with other kinds of important goals. In the following, I briefly elaborate each of these points.

First, the amount of money that would need to be spent to effectively control cross-border traffic rather than just "symbolically reaffirming the state's territorial authority" far exceeds what is now being spent (Andreas 2000, x).[9] To give an idea, the estimated cost of the second layer of fencing for a mere fourteen-mile stretch south of San Diego was $25 million (Andreas 2000, 91), and a 2008 estimate suggested that the cost of the new fence was closer to $4 million per mile (Allen 2008). And, again, this is the cost for a fence that is regularly, easily, and quickly breached or avoided. Moreover, the required costs will predictably and continuously spiral upwards as smugglers find new ways to circumvent Border Patrol. For instance, recent investigations have suggested that a large number of Border Patrol officers are employed by smuggling operations, making it particularly easy to illegally cross the border (Archibold and Becker 2008).

Indeed, analysts suggest that enhanced border control's most sizable effect is channeling migrants "to less visible locations along the two-thousand-mile

[9] This discrepancy between political rhetoric regarding territorial control and the reality of largely ineffective policy is not unique to the United States; far from it, "the gap between the *goals* of national immigration policy (laws, regulations, executive actions, etc.) and the actual results of policies in this area (policy *outcomes*) is wide and growing wider in all major industrialized democracies" (Cornelius *et al.* 1994, 3).

border" (Massey *et al.* 2002, 94). Survey evidence suggests that relatively few migrants think of increased border control as an important reason not to migrate (Cornelius 1997, 11). Rather than crossing in San Diego or El Paso, migrants cross in less developed and more dangerous areas. If this is correct, it is likely that halting illegal crossings will require a much more intensive effort, and one that extends across the entire border. It is thus important to note that while public debate regarding immigration typically proceeds as if effective border control is but a small increase in cost and effort away, it seems extremely unlikely that this is true.

Second, there are two important reasons to think that even a more expansive and expensive fencing system would be ineffective. First, because there is strong evidence that those who are caught simply continue try to cross the border until they succeed, a successful effort likely requires deterring potential border-crossers by jailing, for substantial stretches, those who are caught. Otherwise, a fence only increases the number of attempts made by border-crossers. Such a policy significantly adds to the costs of border control, and has costs in humanitarian terms. Indeed, the further militarization of the border carries with it the inevitable risk of unauthorized humanitarian costs. For example, in the fall of 2005 six individuals attempting to cross from Africa into Spain were lethally shot by Moroccan border control agents (Morris 2005). Second, approximately half of illegal immigrants enter the country legally, only to overstay their visas (Congressional Budget Office 2007, 4). As a result, even a perfectly effective fence is incapable of eliminating illegal immigration. Likewise, these reasons for thinking that a fence will be of limited effectiveness in restricting illegal immigration also cast doubt on its putative national security benefits. Such benefits are overstated since such a fence would be easily breached and, anyway, there are alternative and easy ways to gain access to the country (via Canada, entry for travel, etc.).

Third, the supposed benefits of keeping out illegal immigrants are highly uncertain. This is especially so because illegal immigrants contribute to economic life by working jobs, providing a variety of important services to citizens, and paying taxes. Indeed, the consequences of increased immigration are far more ambiguous than typically supposed in the public debate. Rather than trying to review the large literature on the effects of immigration, I merely point out that "there is substantial disagreement among the experts on the nature and size of those impacts" (Calavita 1996, 291) and that there is a "substantial gap between the speculative and contradictory nature of these findings and the unwavering convictions of most Americans" that immigration is harmful (Calavita 1996, 291). Gregory

Huber and Thomas Espenshade note that "despite a widely shared view among the American public that immigrants take jobs away from US workers, increase unemployment and depress wages, most research has failed to provide strong support for these beliefs' (Huber and Espenshade 1997, 1031–1032).[10]

Likewise, although the received public view suggests that illegal immigrants – through their use of social services – constitute a significant drain on public resources, available evidence does not bear out that claim. The vast majority of social service programs are not available to, and are not collected by, illegal immigrants. For example, of illegal immigrants making trips after 1993, only 2.6 percent receive unemployment, 2.9 percent obtain food stamps, and 4 percent receive welfare (Massey *et al.* 2002, 135). No public policy is perfectly executed and without waste, but these numbers hardly suggest a mortal threat to the public coffers. Thus, the evidence does not support the claim, so common in the public debate, that illegal immigrants impose excessive costs on the citizenry.

Finally, the construction of a fence and substantial tightening of border security promises to interfere with other important goals. For example, it is not clear that one can consistently support *both* the free trade of goods and the construction of a fence. NAFTA requires relatively unconstrained flow of goods across borders, but it is impossible to achieve this while at the same time stopping all human traffic across the border. In particular, border control agents will have to be able to distinguish between legitimate border-crossers and illegitimate ones quickly enough to keep trade moving between countries. However, accomplishing this goal makes it difficult, if not impossible, to accurately control human traffic across the border. As Stephen Castles and Mark Miller note:

> In the international debates on mass migration there has been growing agreement that entry restrictions could have only limited success. The amount of control and surveillance needed to make borders impenetrable is inconsistent with the trend towards increased interchange and communication ... The disparities between economic and social conditions in the South and the North are such that illegal migration is likely to grow whatever the barriers. (Castles and Miller 1998, 100)

Those who promise free trade *and* a border secure from illicit crossing promise more than can be delivered.

While this is – of course – only a sketch of the case against the militarization of the border, it at least shows how that argument ought to proceed. In particular, and contrary to proponents of open borders, the best way to

[10] For a good and wide-ranging review of the literature, also see Kapur and McHale 2006.

oppose restrictionists is to insist that a pragmatic analysis weighs strongly against further militarization of the border. So far this chapter has argued that it is a mistake to either (a) insist that all long-term illegal immigrants are entitled to citizenship; or (b) militarize the border in the hope of ending illegal immigration. If we eliminate these possibilities, it might seem that we are left countenancing a large population of illegal immigrants. Against this view, I will argue in the next section that the best way to handle the pressures that lead to the current levels of illegal immigration – without succumbing to the extremes advocated by restrictionists or integrationists – is to adopt a certain type of guest-worker program.

II THE GUEST-WORKER ALTERNATIVE

It is important to recognize that it is often not membership that migrants seek, but access to the economic opportunities provided by working in a given territory.

> *Migrants who enter a developed country for the first time generally do not intend to settle there permanently* ... Rather than moving abroad permanently to maximize earnings, they seek to leave *temporarily* to generate earnings that can be repatriated to diversify risks, accumulate capital, and circumvent a lack of credit. These motivations imply that, initially at least, most migrants *expect to return*. (Massey *et al.* 2002, 145, emphases in original)

Long-term estimates suggest that approximately 30 percent of migrants to the United States eventually return to their home countries (Kapur and McHale 2005, 170) and the "overwhelming majority of Mexican migrants plan to return, seeking to work in the United States for short periods" in order to overcome failures in Mexican insurance or credit markets (Durand and Massey 2004, 6). Indeed, the Census Bureau estimates that about 280,000 immigrants (legal and illegal) depart annually (Camarota 2007).

Moreover, the tendency toward return migration is much stronger among certain groups, especially those who participate in a long-established cyclical or seasonal labor migration between the United States and Mexico. Evidence suggests that most Mexican immigrants neither stay nor intend to stay permanently in the United States; instead, approximately 55 percent of undocumented Mexican male immigrants stay for under one year, 70 percent for under two years, and 80 percent under three years (Reyes 2001, 1193). The rate of return is even higher for those employed in the agricultural industry, as a result of its seasonal needs. Moreover, survey evidence suggests that single migrants are likely to be temporary workers in the US labor market. They view their jobs as temporary and are likely to return to Mexico after a brief stay in the United States. They maintain strong social and economic relationships to their place of origin. In contrast, undocumented immigrants living with their families in the US are likely to view their jobs as relatively secure and desire to continue residing in the United States. (Chavez 1988, 95)

Large numbers of immigrants, especially undocumented workers coming from Mexico, exhibit little interest in permanent residence and membership claims.

A Reasons to consider a guest-worker program

Given the interest of so many Mexican immigrants in temporary access to the US labor market, it is worth saying that there are at least two kinds of normative reasons to take seriously the possibility of a substantial guest-worker program. First, no matter what policy we select, we are bound – because of the difficulty of policing the border and the great pull of the accumulated wealth of the US labor market – to attract a large number of Mexican workers. Providing legal status to such workers in the right way (more on which below) promises to render them less exploitable.

Second, the fact that the border was established (as most are) through a history of injustice that continues to play an important role in defining the life chances of those left on either side of it seems to provide at least some reason to prioritize the needs and interests of those who continue to be worse off than they otherwise might be as a result of the shape of the political regime that won out (as against foreigners whom the imposition of the boundaries of the political community did not directly affect).

B The Bracero Program and its aftermath

Because the United States – like other developed countries[11] – has an earlier experience with guest-worker programs, it is important to be aware of the shortcomings of that experience. World War II brought significant demand for Mexican labor, and in response the United States undertook its most extensive experiment with guest workers. The Bracero Program, initiated in 1942 as a way to supplement labor shortages, ultimately lasted until 1964. It became a substantial program, through which over 400,000 people a year

[11] All of Western Europe's highly developed countries initiated guest-worker programs between 1945 and 1973 (Castles and Miller 1998, 68).

entered the country in the 1950s. Indeed, during the 1950s, remittances from Braceros constituted the third-largest industry in Mexico (Ngai 2004, 142).

The major US advocates of the program were large-scale farming outfits that wanted access to cheap labor: "Growers wanted not only seasonal workers. They also wanted a labor *surplus* so they could obtain workers on demand, at low wages, and in plentiful supply to pick their crops early and quickly" (Ngai 2004, 135). So, for "over two decades, the US government recruited, distributed, and controlled a massive foreign labor force for agriculture" (Calavita 1992, 18). Indeed, "from 1948 to 1964, the United States imported, on average, 200,000 braceros a year" (Ngai 2004, 139). Notice that, nevertheless, Braceros constituted only 2 percent of the US agricultural labor force (Ngai 2004, 139). While some reports suggest that Braceros "typically earned ten to fifteen times what they could earn in Mexico" (Stout 2008, 2), such claims are not highly reliable because of administrative irregularities.

Those imported under the Bracero Program unfortunately worked under particularly vulnerable conditions. While the program promised a minimum wage, a form of pension, decent working and living conditions, and round-trip transportation, employers regularly violated such rules – often failing to provide the required working conditions and labor standards. In practice, guest workers were unable to negotiate the terms of their employment, were only allowed to work for a single employer (thus hindering their bargaining leverage), and were deported for efforts at collective bargaining (Calavita 1992, 144). The "contract laborer was not free to bargain over wages or working conditions, either individually or collectively. He did not have the right to choose his employer or quit" (Ngai 2004, 138). Important criticisms of the program included "wholesale corruption [especially with regard to the recruitment process in Mexico], ramshackle and overcrowded housing, unsafe working conditions, wage cheating, unsafe transportation, nonexistent health protections, and few opportunities for recreation" (Gonzalez 2006, 57).

Even today, the H-2A Program provides temporary access to agricultural workers, but it is of very limited scope (approximately 32,000 participants in 2005). As in the Bracero Program, participants do not have the right to change employers, are inadequately protected from dangerous working conditions, often cheated out of wages, and face a constant threat of deportation and abuse. Likewise, in recent years almost 90,000 non-agricultural workers have been admitted – with even less in the way of legal protection – under the H-2B Program. People continue to participate in such programs because wages for unskilled laborers are approximately ten times higher in the United States than in Mexico and similar countries. Additionally, the dangers and drawbacks of such programs are often unclear to those in sending countries.

However, the program advocated here is importantly distinct from the H-2A Program and its predecessors in that it allows participants the opportunity to work for a wide range of employers. By increasing their exit power, such a program will facilitate more humane treatment of workers. Workers would be granted a seasonal working permit with (a) no promise of future access to citizenship; (b) no access to membership services (such as social security);[12] and (c) no access for their families. The rationale for the program's seasonal and non-family-based nature is to provide incentive for migration between the two countries to be largely cyclical (and avoid, as far as possible, the permanent settling of families via the guest-worker program).

C Designing a better program

Three basic points about the program I envision are worth making. First, it is of crucial importance that those granted the right to work in the US economy do not – as in past programs – have their right to do so tied to a single employer. Instead, those granted access to the labor market must be allowed to work for a wide array of employers. Tying guest workers to a single employer renders workers highly vulnerable to workplace exploitation (including harassment, underpayment, unsafe working conditions, and threat of deportation). Much of the standard criticism of guest-worker programs hinges on the unfairness of tying workers to particular employers, but such unfairness is a feature of particular guest-worker programs rather than an inherent feature of all such programs. No guest-worker program that fails to give workers a substantial range of options in regard to employers ought to be accepted. The right to change employers is the linchpin of an acceptable program because this helps secure and enforce basic workplace rights.

Second, it is imperative that the basic interests of guest workers be assiduously protected. This includes protecting their civil liberties (notably free speech, assembly, and religion) and basic workplace rights. It is important to note that taxes should be collected from the workers themselves to contribute to funding such protections. This should present no great

[12] Obviously, if the political community chose to exclude guest workers from social security benefits, they could not legitimately collect taxes from them for the purpose of funding the program.

obstacle, as taxes are already collected from illegal immigrants and this type of program would only render such taxation easier and more transparent. If the money is largely collected at the federal level, ways of distributing it to the localities heavily trafficked by guest workers should be devised (already programs exist to help distribute additional funds to localities where large numbers of illegal immigrants settle [Huber and Espenshade 1997, 1044–1046]).

Third, the acceptability of the program depends on the establishment of a transparent and humane recruitment process. Some of the worst abuses of the Bracero Program's recruitment mechanism can be overcome by providing the required documents at the homes of applicants rather than asking all potential participants to come to particular meeting places, to which many individuals would travel great distances at significant expense only to be turned away (Gonzalez 2006, chapter 2). The most obvious way to circumvent such problems is to set the number of available temporary visas at a high enough number to cover, or largely cover, demand. Precisely how many this would require is unclear, but estimates suggest numbers between 400,000 and 1,000,000 (Cornelius 1981; Massey *et al.* 2002; Portes 2007).

There is evidence that the basic types of protections that I am advocating for guest workers may render such programs far less exploitative. While both Hong Kong and Singapore have significant guest-worker programs, those in Hong Kong are much better protected than their counterparts in Singapore. One important reason for the differences in treatment is that those in Hong Kong are granted short periods of time between employers whereas workers in Singapore are expelled from the country if they change employers (Bell 2006, 285). Once again: a right of exit helps deter exploitative employers. Because guest workers in Singapore are forced to leave the country if they leave their employer, employers are more likely to act in unacceptable ways. Alternatively, workers in Hong Kong are afforded basic political rights; they are, for example, "free to organize self-help groups and public protests to secure their interests" (Bell 2006, 285). This political leverage has been used to lobby for permission for longer periods of time between employers as a way of enhancing the leverage of workers' right to exit. As Daniel Bell notes, it is unlikely that foreign workers would prefer a system that promised full legal rights, but accepted very few (thus ushering many into illegal immigration) to a relatively humane guest-worker program that allowed entry for enough to satiate labor demand (Bell 2006, 300n59).

D Objections to guest-worker programs

Having put forward the general line of argument meant to support the claim that there is reason to think that the difficulties growing out of the existing regime of tolerating illegal immigration can be better handled through the development of an appropriately designed guest-worker program, I now want to resist several worries commonly expressed about such programs.[13]

First, guest-worker programs are often criticized because it is assumed that it is inevitably the case that participants in such programs will stay permanently in the host country. Most often, the German experience with Turkish guest workers is cited as evidence of this claim (see, for example, Walzer 1983, 56–61). Although nobody ought to pretend that a guest-worker program can be designed that will ensure that 100 percent of participants return, the case of US–Mexico migration is significantly different from that of German–Turkish migration.

The disanalogies between the cases provide ample reason not to generalize from the German experience. Most importantly: because the United States and Mexico share a substantial land border, return migration is far simpler in this case than in the case of Germany and Turkey, which are separated by – among others – Austria, Slovakia, Hungary, and Serbia. Connectedly, there is already – largely as a result of the Bracero Program – a long history of circular seasonal migration between the United States and Mexico. It is not true, then, as Walzer claims in his denouncement of guest-worker programs, that "departure is only a formal option" (Walzer 1983, 59). Instead, for Mexican workers in the United States, departure is a substantive and, as we have seen, oft-exercised possibility. Hence, in the United States (quite unlike in Germany) a guest-worker program would bring out of the shadows what is already occurring. There is little reason to think that guest workers will be as prone to stay in the country after participation as were Turkish participants in Germany and, more importantly, there is little reason to think that participants in a properly designed guest-worker program are less likely to return to Mexico than are illegal immigrants under the current regime.

[13] For a thoughtful argument against guest-worker programs, see Martin and Teitelbaum 2001. In my opinion, their case against such programs hinges on a too-optimistic view of our ability to control illegal immigration. As a result, it compares guest-worker programs to an irrelevant alternative (that in which there is no illicit movement across the border) instead of the alternative of a regime that implicitly tolerates illegal immigration.

Prominent scholars have argued that increased border security makes undocumented immigrants – unwilling or unable to again face the costs and dangers of crossing the border – less likely to return:

> Hardening the border through repressive police actions only undermines the inclination to return, ultimately reducing the flow of people and migradollars back to sending regions to choke off their development. A smarter strategy would be to cultivate the natural inclination of migrants to remain abroad temporarily by facilitating return migration and the repatriation of funds. (Massey *et al.* 2002, 157)

There is, thus, reason to believe that a properly designed guest-worker program may do a *better* job of promoting return migration than does the existing regime (for example, a system of tolerated illegal immigration).

Indeed, there are a number of ways for a well-designed program to facilitate return migration (though, of course, no program is capable of eliminating the settling of illegal immigrants). First, one way to increase the proportion of guest workers who return home is to create pension funds, in cooperation with the Mexican government, that workers do not have access to until their return is confirmed. Second, the program may be designed to focus on those individuals most likely to participate in cyclical migration on their own accord. Third, and more conjecturally, it seems likely that there are ways in which a community's access to the program can be conditioned on the return of previous community members, thus creating social incentives – à la the Grameen Bank – for cooperation with the program.

The second common objection to guest-worker programs that I would like to respond to here is concern that such programs illegitimately treat participants as inferiors (Barbieri 1998; Walzer 1983). Although not directly addressing the possibility of a guest-worker program, Charles Taylor worries about any public policy that fails to see all individuals as sharing an equal status:

> Our identity is partly shaped by recognition or its absence, often by the *mis*recognition of others, and so a person or group of people can suffer real damage, real distortion, if the people or society around them mirror back to them a confining or demeaning or contemptible picture of themselves. Nonrecognition or misrecognition can inflict harm, can be a form of oppression, imprisoning some in a false, distorted, and reduced mode of being. (Taylor 1994, 25)

Thus, Taylor argues that a society harms individuals by failing to see them as equals. Indeed, he goes on to suggest that "the principle of equal citizenship has come to be universally accepted" such that "what is to be avoided at all costs is the existence of 'first-class' and 'second-class' citizens" (Taylor 1994, 37–38). Without denying the importance of such recognition and the legitimacy, in general, of worries regarding multiple classes of citizenship, two points are important to make in response.

First, it is imperative to keep in mind that participation in such a program would, of course, be entirely voluntary. By presenting non-members with an option not currently present (access to the labor market of the developed world), a new option is added. Those who see such an option as demeaning are free not to participate and continue on just as before. Objecting to a guest-worker program on the grounds that it creates a second-class status paternalistically suggests that, for their own protection, foreigners must not even be given the option to participate in guest-worker programs.

Second, the recognition-based criticism does not, anyway, apply to the position on offer, for this position *already* sees all individuals as equal sources of moral claims. Those who would claim that such a scheme is an affront to political equality wrongly assume that a commitment to the equality of individuals provides a "direct constraint on the structure of democratic processes themselves" (Beitz 1989, 17). Instead, a commitment to equality "is mainly constraining in its effects on the *reasons* that may be given to explain why we should accept one rather than another conception of fair terms of participation" (Beitz 1989, 18, emphasis added).

There is no reason to interpret a denial of citizenship as a "form of oppression" manifested through a "false, distorted, and reduced" image of non-members. Instead, it reflects the judgment that non-members did not participate in the creation of associational goods in the relevant way or have membership passed to them by those who did. Likewise, when members of a congregation do not admit outsiders (whether because of their beliefs or limitations on capacity), they do not refuse to recognize the humanity or basic equality of these people. Instead, they elect not to share the benefits of their collective accomplishments, and they do not act wrongly in the process (so long as the goods in question are not ones to which all individuals are entitled on account of their humanity). Alternatively, if – in the process of exclusion – they demean and ridicule outsiders, treating them as beasts and refusing to acknowledge them as individuals, they act wrongly. They do so, however, not by excluding outsiders from their accomplishments, but by refusing them the basic treatment owed to others *qua* equals. Although the two courses of action both reflect unequal conceptions of what is owed to people, only the latter comes to this conclusion by denying the equal status of the individuals in question.

Finally, to the extent that the egalitarian commitment is valued because sharing in a political community as an equal is itself an important and value-generating activity, one must recognize that guest workers will retain access to membership claims in their home community. Indeed, retaining citizenship can be an important source of status even while workers are in foreign countries because home governments may work (and, historically, have often worked) to protect those citizens who choose to find work abroad. As Mexican president Felipe Calderòn recently insisted:

> Mexico does not stop at its border ... wherever there is a Mexican, there is Mexico ... and, for this reason, the government action on behalf of our countrymen is guided by principles, for the defense and protection of their rights. (Quoted in McKinley 2007)

As a result, guest workers are rightly seen as members of a different political community, rather than *non*-members or individuals of inferior status.

In this chapter, I argued against two popular approaches to illegal immigration. First, I argued that the integrationist demand that political communities give full citizenship to all longstanding illegal immigrants ignores important facts about the non-consensual arrival of some such individuals and the citizenry's ownership over the relevant institutions. Second, I argued that the insistence that illegal immigration be eradicated through the construction of a secure and militarized border ignores the cost and difficulty of such an approach even while exaggerating its benefits and disregarding the important goals with which such a quest will conflict. Finally, I have argued that a properly designed guest-worker program can respond to the concerns of integrationists regarding the exploitative nature of the current regime without following restrictionists into the costly and ineffective game of trying to create and enforce a hard border between political communities that share not just an expansive land border, but also a long history of economic interaction and cyclical migration.

III CONCLUSION

Having now applied the associative ownership framework to a range of policy issues, I want to restate the two major claims that I have been trying to advance throughout. We have seen that much of the existing literature on the ethics of immigration policy falls into three broad camps: statism; open borders; and views based on the importance of shared identity (including liberal nationalism).

My first goal in advancing the associative ownership view has been to suggest that there is a way of justifying claims of self-determination and some restrictions on immigration that does not hinge either on the significance of a shared national identity or on the claim that justice cannot extend beyond state borders. What I have hoped to show is that there is a way of making sense of the idea of "society as a fair system of cooperation over time, from one generation to the next" that does not depend on seeing that system as either a natural fact about sovereignty or a reflection of a shared national identity (Rawls 1993, 15). Instead, I have tried to suggest that there are good reasons to see political communities as ongoing collective projects that can gain entitlements to the institutions and resources that they construct. Thus, the first important point that I have tried to advance is that missing from the considerations of statists, liberal nationalists, and advocates of open borders is the recognition of the connection between the political institutions to which potential migrants seek access and the political community that brought them into existence.

The second important point that I have tried to make is that there is some truth in each approach to thinking about the ethics of immigration policy. Advocates of open borders are right to insist that border restrictions are often an affront to our alleged commitment to the equal moral status of all individuals. Liberal nationalists are correct that a cultural context in constant and rapid flux is a challenge to the autonomy of citizens trying to construct their lives within it. Statists are correct that citizens stand in a relationship with compatriots that raises moral issues distinct from the relationship we share with one another as a result of our humanity. However, extreme versions of each of these views wrongly elevate one particular consideration at the expense of the complexity of the moral issues involved.

Accordingly, by considering the arguments of advocates of each of these positions as well as a range of important policy questions, I have tried to show that – properly interpreted – the associative ownership view can make sense of (and incorporate) the strengths of other views. For example, I have tried to emphasize that recognizing that the political community has a special connection to the institutions that it brings forth does not suggest that it may restrict access to such institutions however it likes. Instead, as with other claims of ownership, the particular form it takes depends on the social circumstances and a range of competing concerns that may arise. In a world haunted by severe poverty, one cannot reasonably doubt that these restrictions run deep. Accordingly: the associative ownership view aims to ensure an appropriate fit between concerns related to distributive justice, rights of movement, political self-determination, and the special importance of the relationship shared by compatriots. It holds that membership in a political association may at least sometimes justify differences in treatment on the grounds that compatriots are engaged in a cooperative enterprise that brings valuable resources (including political institutions) into being. Accordingly, they stand in a relationship with one another that must meet distinct normative standards.

I have tried to show that differences in treatment thus justified need not violate the equal status of outsiders. Instead, through their contributions and efforts, citizens come to own the political association and its institutions and, as a result, have a special claim to those institutions and permission to design a (not unlimited) range of procedures for passing that membership to future citizens. It is in this way that we have arrived at a view that defends the right of a political community to chart its own course through history, even while accepting that the needs and interests of outsiders set important constraints on that project.

My hope is that the associative ownership framework helps to assess the range of issues relevant to arguments about the ethics of immigration policy in clearer and less dogmatic ways (both by helping to uncover the bases for such concerns and by explaining how such apparently conflicting bases can be made coherent). Hopefully it also illustrates the shape of the constraints justice imposes on immigration policy. In other words, the hope is that the position – unlike its more extreme competitors (such as statism, open borders, and certain forms of liberal nationalism) – has the benefit of explaining how apparently disparate convictions can fit "together into one coherent view," thus aligning principles and responses to particular cases into a consistent position (Rawls 1999b, 19). On questions of justice, achieving this kind of coherence is likely the best for which we can hope.

Bibliography

Abizadeh, Arash (2002). "Does Liberal Democracy Presuppose a Cultural Nation? Four Arguments" *American Political Science Review* vol. 96, no. 3, 495–509.

(2007). "Cooperation, Pervasive Impact, and Coercion: On the Scope (not Site) of Distributive Justice" *Philosophy and Public Affairs* vol. 35, no. 4, 318–358.

Ackerman, Bruce (1980). *Social Justice in the Liberal State* (New Haven: Yale University Press).

Adams, Richard H. Jr. (2006). "Remittances, Poverty, and Investment in Guatemala" *International Migration, Remittances and the Brain Drain* ed. Caglar Ozden and Maurice Schiff (Washington DC and New York: The World Bank and Palgrave Macmillan).

Alba, Richard N. and Victor Nee (2003). *Remaking the American Mainstream* (Cambridge, MA: Harvard University Press).

Alesina, A., R. Baquir, and W. Easterly (1999). "Public Goods and Ethnic Divisions" *Quarterly Journal of Economics* vol. 114, 1243–1284.

Allen, JoAnne (2008). "US Border 'Virtual Fence' to be Delayed: Report" Reuters, accessed at http://www.reuters.com/article/technologyNews/idUSN28510162200802229?feedType=RSS&feedName=technologyNews&pageNumber=2&virtualBrandChannel=10112&sp=true, March 7, 2008.

Anderson, Benedict (1991). *Imagined Communities* (New York: Verso).

Anderson, Elizabeth (1999). "What is the Point of Equality" *Ethics* vol. 109, no. 2, 287–337.

Andreas, Peter (2000). *Border Games: Policing the US–Mexico Divide* (Ithaca: Cornell University Press).

Archibold, Randal C. and Andrew Becker (2008). "Border Agents, Lured by the Other Side" *The New York Times* (May 27) US section.

Barbieri, William A. Jr. (1998). *Ethics of Citizenship* (Durham, NC: Duke University Press).

Barr, Nicholas (2001). *The Welfare State as Piggy Bank* (Oxford: Oxford University Press).

Barry, Brian (1983). "Self-Government Revisited" *The Nature of Political Theory* ed. David Miller and Larry Siedentop (Oxford: Clarendon Press).

(1989). *A Treatise on Social Justice: vol. 1: Theories of Justice* (Berkeley: University of California Press).

Bartels, Larry (2008). *Unequal Democracy* (Princeton: Princeton University Press).

Becker, Lawrence C. (1977). *Property Rights* (Boston: Routledge & Kegan Paul).
Beitz, Charles (1979). *Political Theory and International Relations* (Princeton: Princeton University Press).
(1989). *Political Equality* (Princeton: Princeton University Press).
Bell, Daniel A. (2006). *Beyond Liberal Democracy* (Princeton: Princeton University Press).
Blake, Michael (2001). "Distributive Justice, State Coercion and Autonomy" *Philosophy and Public Affairs* vol. 30, no. 3, 257–297.
Bloch, Marc (1961). *Feudal Society: Volume 1: The Growth of Ties of Dependence* Translated by L. A. Manyon (Chicago: University of Chicago Press).
Borjas, George J. (1999). *Heaven's Door* (Princeton: Princeton University Press).
Brimelow, Peter (1995). *Alien Nation* (New York: Random House).
Buchanan, Allen (1991). "Towards a Theory of Secession" *Ethics* vol. 101, no. 2, 322–342.
(2004). *Justice, Legitimacy, and Self-Determination* (Oxford: Oxford University Press).
Buchanan, Pat (2006). *State of Emergency* (New York: St. Martin's Press).
Cafaro, Philip and Winthrop Staples III (2008). "The Environmental Argument for Reducing Immigration into the United States" *Environmental Ethics* vol. 31, no. 1, 5–30.
Calavita, Kitty (1992). *Inside the State* (New York: Routledge).
(1996). "The New Politics of Immigration: 'Balanced-Budget Conservatism' and the Symbolism of Proposition 187" *Social Problems* vol. 43, no. 3, 284–305.
(2000). "The Paradox of Race, Class, Identity, and 'Passing': Enforcing the Chinese Exclusion Acts, 1882–1910" *Law and Social Inquiry* vol. 25, no. 1, 1–40.
Camarota, Steven A. (2007). "Immigrants in the United States, 2007" Center for Immigration Studies, Washington, DC, accessed at http://www.cis.org/articles/2007/back1007.html, February 5, 2008.
Card, David (2001). "Immigrant Inflows, Native Outflows, and the Local Market Impacts of Higher Immigration" *Journal of Labor Economics*, vol. 19, no. 1, 22–64.
Carens, Joseph H. (1987). "Aliens and Citizens: The Case for Open Borders" *The Review of Politics* vol. 49, no. 2, 251–273.
(1988). "Nationalism and the Exclusion of Immigrants" *Open Borders? Closed Societies?* ed. Mark Gibney (Westport: Greenwood Press).
(1992). "Migration and Morality" *Free Movement* ed. Brian Barry and Robert E. Goodin (University Park: Pennsylvania State University Press).
(1999). "A Reply to Meilaender: Reconsidering Open Borders" *International Migration Review* vol. 33, no. 4, 1082–1097.
(2005). "The Integration of Immigrants" *Journal of Moral Philosophy* vol. 2, no. 1, 29–46.
(2008). "The Rights of Irregular Migrants" *Ethics and International Affairs* vol. 22, no. 2, 163–186.

(2009). "The Case for Amnesty" *Boston Review*, May/June, accessed at http://bostonreview.net/BR34.3/carens.php, November 20, 2009.

Castles, Stephen and Mark J. Miller (1998). *The Age of Migration* 2nd edn. (New York: The Guilford Press).

Cavallero, Eric (2006). "An Immigration-Pressure Model of Global Distributive Justice" *Politics, Philosophy and Economics* vol. 5, no. 1, 97–127.

Center for American Progress (2007). *Principles for Immigration Reform*. Available at http://www.americanprogress.org/issues/2007/11/immigration_report.html.

Chang, Howard F. (2008). "The Economics of International Labor Migration and the Case for Global Distributive Justice in Liberal Political Theory" *Cornell International Law Journal* vol. 41, 1–25.

Chavez, Leo R. (1988). "Settlers and Sojourners: The Case of Mexicans in the United States" *Human Organization* vol. 47, no. 2, 95–108.

Citrin, Jack, Amy Lerman, Michael Murakami, and Kathryn Pearson (2007). "Testing Huntington: Is Hispanic Immigration a Threat to American Identity?" *Perspectives on Politics* vol. 5, no. 1, 31–48.

Cohen, G. A. (1991). "Incentives, Inequality, and Community" *Tanner Lectures*, accessed at www.tannerlectures.utah.edu/lectures/documents/cohen92.pdf, June 17, 2010.

Cohen, Joshua (1986). "An Epistemic Conception of Democracy" *Ethics* vol. 97, no. 1, 26–38.

(1989). "Deliberation and Democratic Legitimacy" *The Good Polity: Normative Analysis of the State* ed. Alan Hamlin and Phillip Petit (New York: Blackwell).

(2002). "Taking People as They Are?" *Philosophy and Public Affairs* vol. 4, no. 30, 363–386.

(2003). "For a Democratic Society" *The Cambridge Companion to Rawls* ed. Samuel Freeman (Cambridge: Cambridge University Press).

Cole, Phillip (2000). *Philosophies of Exclusion* (Edinburgh: University of Edinburgh Press).

Coleman, Jules L. and Sarah K. Harding (1995). "Citizenship, the Demands of Justice, and the Moral Relevance of Political Borders" *Justice in Immigration* ed. Warren F. Schwartz (Cambridge: Cambridge University Press).

Collier, Paul (1998). "The Political Economy of Ethnicity" World Bank Conference on Development Economics, April 20–21, 1998, Washington, DC.

(2007). *The Bottom Billion* (Oxford: Oxford University Press).

Congressional Budget Office (2007). "The Impact of Unauthorized Immigrants on the Budgets of State and Local Governments" (Washington DC: The Congress of the United States).

Cook, Karen S. and Robin M. Cooper (2003). "Experimental Studies of Cooperation, Trust, and Social Exchange" *Trust and Reciprocity* ed. Elinor Ostrom (New York: Russell Sage Foundation).

Copp, David (1997). "Democracy and Communal Self-Determination" *The Morality of Nationalism* ed. Robert McKim and Jeff McMahan (Oxford: Oxford University Press).

(1999). "The Idea of a Legitimate State" *Philosophy and Public Affairs* vol. 28, no. 1 (Winter), 3–45.

Cornelius, Wayne A. (1981). *Legalizing the Flow of Temporary Migrant Workers from Mexico: A Policy Proposal* (La Jolla, CA: Working Papers in US–Mexican Studies).

(1997) "Introduction: Does Border Enforcement Deter Unauthorized Immigration" *Impacts of Border Enforcement on Mexican Migration* ed. Wayne A. Cornelius and Jessa M. Lewis (La Jolla, CA: Center for Comparative Immigration Studies UCSD).

Cornelius, Wayne A., Philip L. Martin, and James F. Hollifield (1994). *Controlling Immigration: A Global Perspective* (Stanford: Stanford University Press).

Cornelius, Wayne A. and Marc R. Rosenblum (2005). "Immigration and Politics" *Annual Review of Political Science* vol. 8, 99–119.

Daniels, Norman (1979). "Wide Reflective Equilibrium and Theory Acceptance in Ethics" *The Journal of Philosophy* vol. 76, no. 5, 256–282.

Daniels, Roger (2004). *Guarding the Golden Door* (New York: Hill & Wang).

Docquier, F. and A. Marfouk (2004). "Measuring the International Mobility of Skilled Workers (1990–2000)," Policy Research Working Paper no. 3381 (Washington DC: The World Bank).

Dow, Mark (2004). *American Gulag* (Berkeley: University of California Press).

Dreben, Burton (2003). "On Rawls and Political Liberalism" *Cambridge Companion to Rawls* ed. Samuel Freeman (Cambridge: Cambridge University Press).

Dummett, Michael (2001). *On Immigration and Refugees* (New York: Routledge).

Durand, Jorge and Douglas S. Massey (eds.) (2004). *Crossing the Border: Research from the Mexican Migration Project* (New York: Russell Sage Foundation).

Dworkin, Ronald (1977). *Taking Rights Seriously* (Cambridge, MA: Harvard University Press).

(1986). *Law's Empire* (Cambridge, MA: Belknap Press).

(2000). *Sovereign Virtue* (Cambridge, MA: Harvard University Press).

Easterly, William (2006). *The White Man's Burden* (New York: The Penguin Press).

Easterly, William and Ross Levine (1997). "Africa's Growth Tragedy: Policies and Ethnic Divisions" *Quarterly Journal of Economics* vol. 4, no. 112, 1203–1250.

Espenshade, Thomas J. (1994). "Does the Threat of Border Apprehension Deter Undocumented US Immigration?" *Population and Development Review* vol. 20, no. 4, 871–892.

Estlund, David (1998). "Liberalism, Equality and Fraternity in Cohen's Critique of Rawls" *The Journal of Political Philosophy* vol. 6, no. 1, 99–112.

Faini, Riccardo (2005). "Migration Remittances and Growth" *Poverty, International Migration and Asylum* ed. G. Borjas and J. Crisp (New York: Macmillan).

(2006) "Remittances and the Brain Drain," Institute for the Study of Labor, Discussion Paper 2155. Available at http://ftp.iza.org/dp2155.pdf.

Fichte, Johann Gottlieb (1968 [1806]) "Thirteenth Address" *Addresses to the German Nation* ed. George A. Kelly (New York: Harper Torch Books).

Fine, Sarah (2010). "Freedom of Association is Not the Answer" *Ethics* vol. 120, no. 2, 338–356.

Finnis, John (1980). *Natural Law and Natural Rights* (Oxford: Oxford University Press).

Fix, Michael and Jeffrey S. Passel (1994). *Immigration and Immigrants: Setting the Record Straight* (Washington DC: The Urban Institute).

Frankfurt, Harry (1987). "Equality as a Moral Ideal" *Ethics* vol. 98, no. 1, 21–43.

Freeman, Samuel (2007). *Rawls* (New York: Routledge).

Fuentes, Jezmin, Henry L'Esperance, Raul Perez, and Caitlin White (2007). "Impacts of U.S. Immigration Policies on Migration Behavior" *Impacts of Border Enforcement on Mexican Migration* ed. Wayne A. Cornelius and Jessa M. Lewis (La Jolla, CA: Center for Comparative Immigration Studies UCSD).

Fuller, Lon L. (1964). *The Morality of Law* (New Haven: Yale University Press).

Galbraith, James K., Pedro Conceicao, and Pedro Ferreira (1999). "Inequality and Unemployment in Europe: The American Cure" *New Left Review* vol. 1, no. 237 (September–October), 28–51.

Geddes, Andrew (2003). *The Politics of Migration and Immigration in Europe* (Thousand Oaks, CA: Sage Publications).

Gellner, Ernest (1983). *Nations and Nationalism* (Ithaca: Cornell University Press).

Gibney, Matthew J. (1999). "Liberal Democratic States and Responsibilities to Refugees" *The American Political Science Review* vol. 93, no. 1, 169–181.

(2004). *The Ethics and Politics of Asylum* (Cambridge: Cambridge University Press).

Gilens, Martin (2005). "Inequality and Democratic Responsiveness" *Public Opinion Quarterly* vol. 69, no. 5, 778–796.

Gonzalez, Gilbert G. (2006). *Guest Workers or Colonized Labor?* (Boulder: Paradigm).

Goodin, Robert E. (1988). *Reasons for Welfare: The Political Theory of the Welfare State* (Princeton: Princeton University Press).

(2007). "Enfranchising All Affected Interests, and Its Alternatives" *Philosophy and Public Affairs* vol. 35, no. 1, 41–68.

Gould, Carol C. (2004). *Globalizing Democracy and Human Rights* (Cambridge: Cambridge University Press).

Graham, Otis L. Jr. (2004). *Unguarded Gates* (New York: Rowman & Littlefield Publishers, Inc.).

Gruber, L. (2001). "Power Politics and the Free Trade Bandwagon" *Comparative Political Studies* vol. 34, no. 7, 703–741.

Habermas, Jurgen (1995). "Citizenship and National Identity" *Theorizing Citizenship* ed. R. Beiner (Albany: SUNY Press).

Habyarimana, James, Macartan Humphreys, Daniel N. Posner, and Jeremy Weinstein (2006). "Why Does Ethnic Diversity Undermine Public Goods Provision? An Experimental Approach" IZA Discussion Papers.

Hadfield, Gillian K. (1995). "Just Borders: Normative Economics and Immigration Law" *Justice in Immigration* ed. Warren F. Schwartz Cambridge Studies in Philosophy and Law (Cambridge: Cambridge University Press).

Hainmueller, Jens and Michael J. Hiscox (2006). "Learning to Love Globalization: Education and Individual Attitudes Toward International Trade" *International Organization* vol. 60, no. 2, 469–498.

Hamilton, Robert and John Whalley (1984). "Efficiency and Distributional Implications of Global Restrictions on Labor Mobility" *Journal of Developmental Economics* vol. 14, 61–75.

Hampton, Jean (1995). "Immigration, Identity, and Justice" *Justice in Immigration* ed. Warren F. Schwartz Cambridge Studies in Philosophy and Law (Cambridge: Cambridge University Press).

Hardin, Russell (1995). *One for All* (Princeton: Princeton University Press).

Hart, H. L. A. (1961). *The Concept of Law* (Oxford: Oxford University Press).

(1963). *Law, Liberty and Morality* (Stanford: Stanford University Press).

Hartogh, Govert Den (1999). "The Architectonic of Michael Walzer's Theory of Justice" *Political Theory* vol. 27, no. 4, 491–522.

Haslett, D. W. (1986). "Is Inheritance Justified" *Philosophy and Public Affairs* vol. 15, no. 2, 122–155.

Hobbes, Thomas (1985 [1651]). *Leviathan* ed. C. B. MacPherson (New York: Penguin Classics).

Hobsbawm, E. J. (1990). *Nations and Nationalism Since 1780* (Cambridge: Cambridge University Press).

Holmes, Stephen and Cass Sunstein (1999). *The Cost of Rights: Why Liberty Depends on Taxes* (New York: W. W. Norton).

Huber, Gregory A. and Thomas J. Espenshade (1997). "Neo-Isolationism, Balanced-Budget Conservatism, and the Fiscal Impacts of Immigrants" *International Migration Review* vol. 31, no. 4, 1031–1054.

Hume, David (1985 [1739]). *A Treatise of Human Nature* (London: Penguin Classics).

Huntington, Samuel P. (2004). *Who Are We?* (New York: Simon & Schuster).

INS (2001). *Statistical Yearbook of the Immigration and Naturalization Service, 2001* (Washington DC: US Government Printing Office).

James, Daniel (1991). *Illegal Immigration: An Unfolding Crisis* (Washington DC: Mexico-United States Institute).

Jasso, Guillermina, Douglas S. Massey, Mark R. Rosenzweig, and James P. Smith (2000). "The New Immigrant Survey Pilot (NIS-P): Overview and New Findings about US Legal Immigrants at Admission" *Demography* vol. 37, no. 1, 127–138.

Johnson, James (2000). "Why Respect Culture?" *American Journal of Political Science* vol. 44, no. 3, 405–418.

Kapur, Devesh and John McHale (2005). *Give us Your Best and Brightest* (Washington DC: Center for Global Development).

(2006). "What is Wrong with Plan B? International Migration as an Alternative to Development Assistance" Brookings Trade Forum, accessed at http://www.brookings.edu/press/Journals/2006/brookingstradeforum2006.aspx, February 15, 2010.

King, Desmond (2000). *Making Americans* (Cambridge, MA: Harvard University Press).

Kitching, Gavin (2001). *Seeking Social Justice through Globalization* (University Park: Pennsylvania State University Press).

Klosko, George (2000). *Democratic Procedures and Liberal Consensus* (Oxford: Oxford University Press).

Knack, Stephen (2001). "Aid Dependence and Quality of Governance: Cross-Country Empirical Tests" *Southern Economic Journal* vol. 68, no. 2, 310–329.

Kolers, Avery (2009). *Land, Conflict, and Justice* (Cambridge: Cambridge University Press).

Kumlin, Staffan and Bo Rothstein (2007). "Minorities and Mistrust: The Cushioning Impact of Informal Social Contacts and Political-Institutional Fairness" paper presented at the European Consortium for Political Research Joint Session of Workshops, Helsinki, May 2007.

Kymlicka, Will (1989). *Liberalism, Community, and Culture* (Oxford: Clarendon Press).

(1995). *Multicultural Citizenship* (Oxford: Oxford University Press).

(2001). *Politics in the Vernacular* (Oxford: Oxford University Press).

Lee, Kenneth K. (1998). *Huddled Masses, Muddled Laws* (Westport: Praeger).

Lepoer, Barbara Leitch (ed.) (1989). *Singapore: A Country Study* (Washington: GPO for the Library of Congress).

Lincoln, Abraham (1863). *The Gettysburg Address*. Available at the Library of Congress website http://www.loc.gov/exhibits/gadd/images/Gettysburg-2.jpg.

Locke, John (1988). *Two Treatises of Government* ed. Peter Laslett Cambridge Studies in the History of Political Thought (Cambridge: Cambridge University Press).

Lomasky, Loren (2001). "Toward a Liberal Theory of National Boundaries" *Boundaries and Justice* ed. David Miller and Sohail H. Hashmi (Princeton: Princeton University Press).

Macedo, Stephen (2007). "The Moral Dilemma of US Immigration Policy: Open Borders vs. Social Justice?" *Debating Immigration* ed. Carol Swain (Cambridge: Cambridge University Press).

Maddison, Angus (2003). *The World Economy: Historical Statistics* (Paris: OECD).

Margalit, Avishai and Joseph Raz (1990). "National Self-Determination" *The Journal of Philosophy* vol. 87, no. 9, 439–461.

Martin, Philip (2004). "Migration" *Global Crises, Global Solutions* ed. Bjorn Lomborg (Cambridge: Cambridge University Press).

Martin, Philip and Michael S. Teitelbaum (2001). "The Mirage of Mexican Guest Workers" *Foreign Affairs* vol. 80, no. 6, 117–130.

Marx, Karl (1978). *The Marx–Engels Reader* 2nd edn., ed. Robert C. Tucker (New York: Norton).

Mason, Andrew (2000). *Community, Solidarity and Belonging* (Cambridge: Cambridge University Press).

Massey, Douglas S., Jorge Durand, and Nolan J. Malone (2002). *Beyond Smoke and Mirrors* (New York: Russell Sage Foundation).

Mayer, Robert (2005). "Guest Workers and Exploitation" *The Review of Politics* vol. 67, no. 2, 311–334.

McKinley, James C. (2007). "Mexican President Assails US Measures on Migrants" *The New York Times* (September 3).

Mearsheimer, John (2001). *The Tragedy of Great Power Politics* (New York: W. W. Norton & Company).

Migrants Resource Centre (2006). "Seeking Asylum: A Report on the Living Conditions of Asylum Seekers in London." Available at www.migrantsresource centre.org.uk.

Mill, John Stuart (1976). *Principles of Political Economy* ed. William J. Ashley (London: Longmans, Green & Co.).

Miller, David (1995). *On Nationality* (Oxford: Oxford University Press).

(2005). "Immigration: The Case for Limits" *Contemporary Debates in Applied Ethics* ed. Andrew I. Cohen and Christopher Heath Wellman (Oxford: Blackwell).

(2007). *National Responsibility and Global Justice* (Oxford: Oxford University Press).

(2009a). "Democracy's Domain" *Philosophy and Public Affairs* vol. 37, no. 3, 201–228.

(2009b). "Justice and Boundaries" *Politics, Philosophy, and Economics* vol. 8, no. 3, 291–309.

Miller, Richard (1998). "Cosmopolitan Respect and Patriotic Concern" *Philosophy and Public Affairs* vol. 27, no. 3, 202–224.

Moellendorf, Darrel (2002). *Cosmopolitan Justice* (Boulder: Westview Press).

Moorehead, Caroline (2006). *Human Cargo* (New York: Henry Holt).

Morris, Chris (2005). "Dying to Get to the Promised Land" BBC News, accessed at http://news.bbc.co.uk/2/hi/programmes/from_our_own_correspondent/4322026.stm, March 7, 2008.

Murphy, Liam (2000). *Moral Demands in Nonideal Theory* (Oxford: Oxford University Press).

Murphy, Liam and Thomas Nagel (2002). *The Myth of Ownership: Taxes and Justice* (Oxford: Oxford University Press).

Nagel, Thomas (2005). "The Problem of Global Justice" *Philosophy and Public Affairs* vol. 33, no. 2, 113–147.

Nannestad, Peter and Gert Tinggaard Svendsen (2005). "Institutions, Culture, and Trust," accessed at http://www.qog.pol.gu.se/conferences/november2005/papers/Nannestad.pdf, 22 June 2007.

Nathanson, Stephen (1989). "In Defense of Moderate Patriotism" *Ethics* vol. 99, no. 3, 535–552.

Neher, Clark D. (2000). *Southeast Asia: Crossroads of the World* (DeKalb, IL: Center for Southeast Asian Studies).

Nett, Roger (1971). "The Civil Right We Are Not Ready For: The Right of Free Movement of People on the Face of the Earth" *Ethics* vol. 81, no. 3, 212–227.

Ngai, Mae M. (2004). *Impossible Subjects* (Princeton: Princeton University Press).

Nickel, James W. (2007). *Making Sense of Human Rights* 2nd edn. (Oxford: Blackwell).

Nozick, Robert (1974). *Anarchy, State and Utopia* (New York: Basic Books).

(1997) "Coercion" *Socratic Puzzles* (Cambridge, MA: Harvard University Press).

O'Neill, Onora (2000). *Bounds of Justice* (Cambridge: Cambridge University Press).

Ozden, Caglar and Maurice Schiff (eds.) (2006). *International Migration, Remittances, and the Brain Drain* (New York: The World Bank and Palgrave Macmillan).

Perry, Stephen R. (1995). "Immigration, Justice, and Culture" *Justice in Immigration* ed. Warren F. Schwartz (Cambridge: Cambridge University Press).

Pevnick, Ryan (2008). "Political Coercion and the Scope of Distributive Justice" *Political Studies* vol. 56, no. 2, 399–413.

Philpott, Daniel (1995). "In Defense of Self-Determination" *Ethics* vol. 105, no. 2, 352–385.

Pogge, Thomas (1997). "Migration and Poverty" *Citizenship and Exclusion* ed. Veit Bader (New York: St. Martin's Press).

(2002). *World Poverty and Human Rights* (Malden, MA: Polity).

Portes, Alejandro (2007). "The Fence to Nowhere" *American Prospect* October 25–29.

Price, Matthew E. (2009). *Rethinking Asylum: History, Purpose, and Limits* (Cambridge: Cambridge University Press).

Pritchett, Lant (2006). *Let their People Come* (Washington DC: Center for Global Development).

Przeworski, Adam (1999). "Minimalist Conceptions of Democracy: A Defense" *Democracy's Value* ed. Ian Shapiro and Casiano Hacker-Cordon (Cambridge: Cambridge University Press, 1999).

Putnam, Robert (2007). "*E Pluribus Unum*: Diversity and Community in the Twenty-first Century" *Scandinavian Political Studies* vol. 30, no. 2, 137–174.

Rawls, John (1951). "Outline of a Decision Procedure for Ethics" *The Philosophical Review* vol. 60, no. 2, 177–197.

(1993). *Political Liberalism* (New York: Columbia University Press).

(1999a). *The Law of Peoples* (Cambridge, MA: Harvard University Press).

(1999b [1971]). *A Theory of Justice* rev. edn. (Cambridge, MA: Harvard University Press).

(2001). *Justice as Fairness: A Restatement* ed. Erin Kelly (Cambridge, MA: Harvard University Press).

Raz, Joseph (1986). *The Morality of Freedom* (Oxford: Oxford University Press).

Reidy, David A. (2004). "Rawls on International Justice: A Defense" *Political Theory* vol. 32, no. 3, 291–319.

Reyes, Belinda I. (2001). "Immigrant Trip Duration: The Case of Immigrants from Western Mexico" *International Migration Review* vol. 35, no. 4, 1185–1204.

Rice, Tom and Jan L. Feldman (1997). "Civic Culture and Democracy from Europe to America" *The Journal of Politics* vol. 59, no. 4, 1143–1172.

Rothstein, Bo (1998). *Just Institutions Matter* (Cambridge: Cambridge University Press).

Rousseau, Jean-Jacques (1987). *On the Social Contract* Translated by Donald A. Cress (Indianapolis: Hackett Publishing Company).

Rubio-Marín, Ruth (2000). *Immigration as a Democratic Challenge* (Cambridge: Cambridge University Press).

Russell, Daniel (2004). "Locke on Land and Labor" *Philosophical Studies* vol. 117, 303–325.

Sangiovanni, Andrea (2007). "Global Justice, Reciprocity, and the State" *Philosophy and Public Affairs* vol. 35, no. 1, 3–39.

Scanlon, T. M. (2003). "Rawls on Justification" *Cambridge Companion to Rawls* ed. Samuel Freeman (Cambridge: Cambridge University Press).

Scheffler, Samuel (2003). "What is Egalitarianism?" *Philosophy and Public Affairs* vol. 31, no. 1, 5–39.

(2007). "Immigration and the Significance of Culture" *Philosophy and Public Affairs* vol. 35, no. 2, 93–125.

Schiff, Maurice (2006). "Brain Drain, Brain Gain, Brain Waste" *International Migration, Remittances, and the Brain Drain* ed. Caglar Ozden and Maurice Schiff (Washington DC and New York: The World Bank and Palgrave Macmillan).

Schmidtz, David (2006). *Elements of Justice* (Cambridge: Cambridge University Press).

Schuck, Peter (1998). *Citizens, Strangers, and In-Betweens* (Boulder: Westview Press).

Seglow, Jonathon (2005). "The Ethics of Immigration" *Political Studies Review* vol. 3, 317–334.

Sen, Amartya (1994). "Freedom and Needs" *The New Republic* January 10–17.

Shachar, Ayelet (2009). *The Birthright Lottery* (Cambridge, MA: Harvard University Press).

Shacknove, Andrew E. (1985). "Who Is a Refugee?" *Ethics* vol. 95, no. 2, 274–284.

Shaughnessy v. United States ex rel. Mezei 345 US 206 (1953).

Shayo, Moses (2009). "A Model of Social Identity with an Application to Political Economy: Nation, Class, and Redistribution" *American Political Science Review* vol. 103, no. 2, 147–174.

Shue, Henry (1980). *Basic Rights: Subsistence, Affluence, and US Foreign Policy* (Princeton: Princeton University Press).

Sidgwick, Henry (1908 [1891]). *The Elements of Politics* 3rd edn. (London: Macmillan & Company).

Simmons, A. John (1979). *Moral Principles and Political Obligations* (Princeton: Princeton University Press).

(1992). *The Lockean Theory of Rights* (Princeton: Princeton University Press).

(2001a). *Justification and Legitimacy* (Princeton: Princeton University Press).

(2001b). "On the Territorial Rights of States" *Philosophical Issues* vol. 11, 300–326.

Singer, Peter (1972). "Famine, Affluence and Morality" *Philosophy and Public Affairs* vol. 1, no. 3, 229–243.

(2002). *One World* (New Haven: Yale University Press).

Skerry, Peter (2006). "How Not to Build a Fence" *Foreign Policy* September–October.

Soroka, Stuart, Keith Banting, and Richard Johnson (2006). "Immigration and Redistribution in a Global Era" *Globalization and Egalitarian Redistribution* ed. Pranab Bardhan, Samuel Bowles, and Michael Wallerstein (Princeton and New York: Princeton University Press and Russell Sage Foundation).

Stana, Richard M. (2008). "Alien Detention Standards" GAO Report. Testimony before the Subcommittee on Immigration, Citizenship, Refugees, Border Security and International Law, Committee on the Judiciary, House of Representatives. Available at http://www.gao.gov/new.items/d08869t.pdf.

Stilz, Anna (2009). "Why do States have Territorial Rights?" *International Theory* vol. 1, no. 2, 185–213.

Stout, Robert Joe (2008). *Why Immigrants Come to America* (Westport: Praeger).

Svallfors, Stefan (1993). "Dimensions of Inequality: A Comparison of Attitudes in Sweden and Britain" *European Sociological Review* vol. 9, no. 3, 267–287.

(1997). "Worlds of Welfare and Attitudes of Redistribution: A Comparison of Eight Western Nations" *European Sociological Review* vol. 13, no. 3, 283–304.

Tamir, Yael (1993). *Liberal Nationalism* (Princeton: Princeton University Press).

Taylor, Charles (1994). "The Politics of Recognition" *Multiculturalism* ed. Amy Gutmann (Princeton: Princeton University Press).

(1995). "Irreducibly Social Goods" *Philosophical Arguments* (Cambridge, MA: Harvard University Press).

Tichenor, Daniel J. (2002). *Dividing Lines: The Politics of Immigration Control in America* (Princeton: Princeton University Press).

United Nations (1948). *Universal Declaration of Human Rights*. Available at the United Nations website http://www.un.org/Overview/rights.html, accessed January 22, 2008.

(2006). "World Population Prospects: The 2006 Revision," accessed at http://esa.un.org.unpp/, February 27, 2008.

USCIRF (2005). "Report on Asylum Seekers in Expedited Removal." Available at www.uscirf.gov.

Uslaner, Eric (2008). "Where you Stand Depends Upon Where your Grandparents Sat" *Public Opinion Quarterly* vol. 72, no. 4, 725–740.

Waldron, Jeremy (1988). *The Right to Private Property* (Oxford: Clarendon Press).

(1992). "Superseding Historic Injustice" *Ethics* vol. 103, no. 1, 4–28.

(1995). "Minority Cultures and the Cosmopolitan Alternative" *The Rights of Minority Cultures* ed. Will Kymlicka (Oxford: Oxford University Press).

(2004). "Property" *Stanford Encyclopedia of Philosophy*. Available at plato.stanford.edu/entries/property, accessed September 16, 2009.

The Wall Street Journal (1984). "In Praise of Huddled Masses" July 3, p. 24.

Walzer, Michael (1983). *Spheres of Justice* (New York: Basic Books).

The Washington Post (2007). "A Self-Inflicted Wound" March 12, A12.

Wellman, Christopher Heath (2005). *A Theory of Secession: The Case for Political Self-Determination* (Cambridge: Cambridge University Press).

(2008). "Immigration and Freedom of Association" *Ethics* vol. 119, no. 1, 109–141.

Whelan, Frederick G. (1983). "Prologue: Democratic Theory and the Boundary Problem" *Liberal Democracy* ed. J. Roland Pennock and John W. Chapman NOMOS 25 (New York: New York University Press).

Woodward, James (1992). "Liberalism and Migration" *Free Movement* ed. Brian Barry and Robert E. Goodin (University Park: Pennsylvania State University Press).

World Bank (2009). World Development Indicators Database. Available at http://www.worldbank.org/.

Zolberg, Aristide (1981). "International Migrations in Political Perspective" *Global Trends in Migration* ed. Mary M. Kritz, Charles B. Keely, and Silvano M. Tomasi (New York: Center for Migration Studies).

Zucker, Norman L. and Naomi Flink Zucker (1987). *The Guarded Gate* (New York: Harcourt Brace Jovanovich).

Index

www.ingramcontent.com/pod-product-compliance
Lightning Source LLC
LaVergne TN
LVHW101502200926
848483LV00001B/199
* 9 7 8 0 5 2 1 7 6 8 9 8 6 *